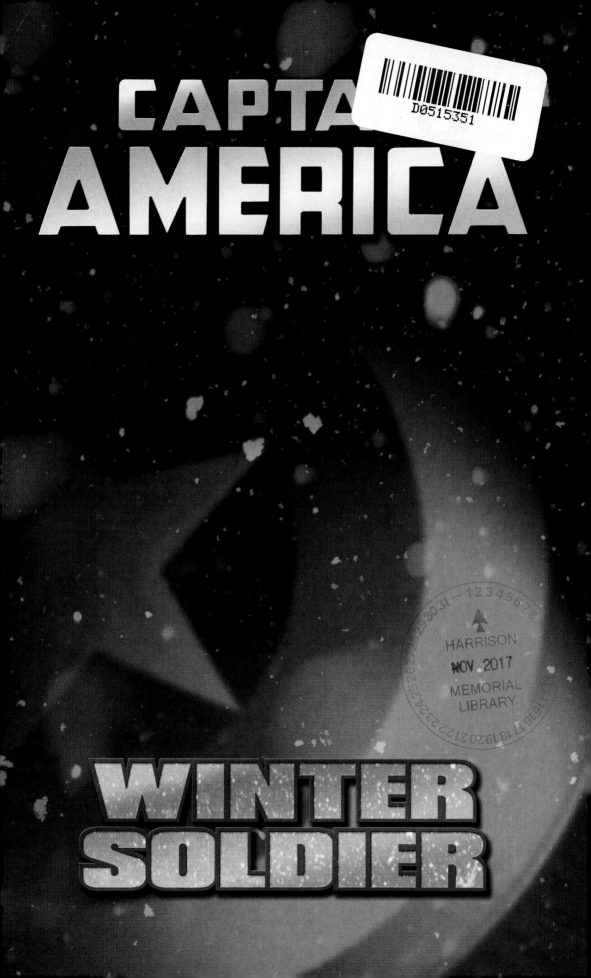

CAPTAIN AMERICA

WINTER SOLDIER

CAPTAIN AMERICA
WINTER SOLDIER

WRITER: Ed Brubaker
PENCILERS: Steve Epting
Michael Lark (Issue #9 and Issue #12 Flashback Art)
FINISHES: Steve Epting & Mike Perkins
Michael Lark (Issue #9 and Issue #12 Flashback Art)
COLORIST: Frank D'Armata
LETTERERS: Virtual Calligraphy's Chris Eliopoulos,
Randy Gentile & Joe Caramagna
COVERS: Steve Epting & Frank D'Armata
ASSISTANT EDITORS: Molly Lazer & Aubrey Sitterson
ASSOCIATE EDITOR: Andy Schmidt
EDITOR: Tom Brevoort

Captain America created by
Joe Simon & Jack Kirby

COLLECTION EDITOR: Jennifer Grünwald
ASSISTANT EDITOR: Michael Short
SENIOR EDITOR, SPECIAL PROJECTS: Jeff Youngquist
VICE PRESIDENT OF SALES: David Gabriel
PRODUCTION: Jerron Quality Color & Jerry Kalinowski
VICE PRESIDENT OF CREATIVE: Tom Marvelli

EDITOR IN CHIEF: Joe Quesada
PUBLISHER: Dan Buckley

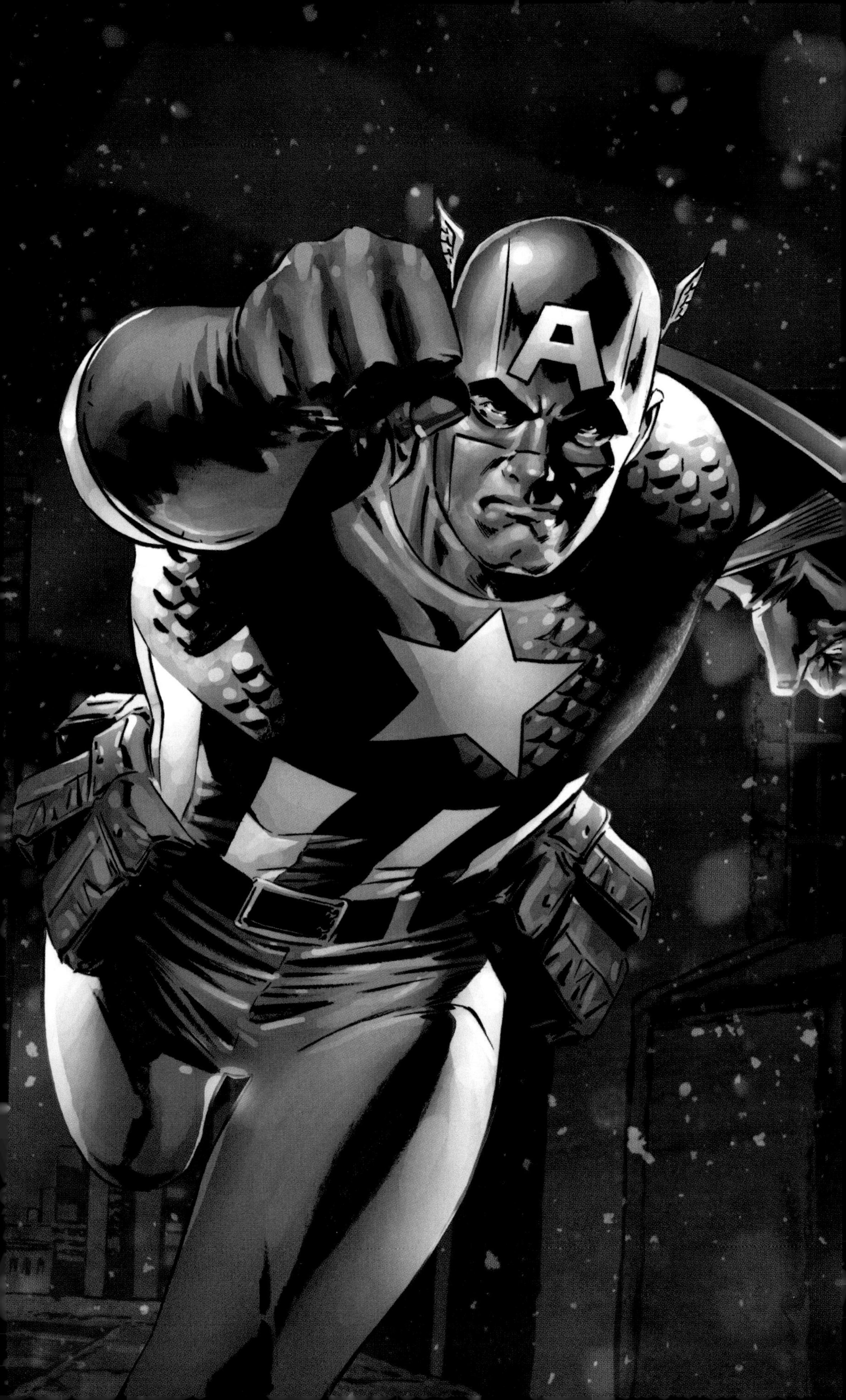

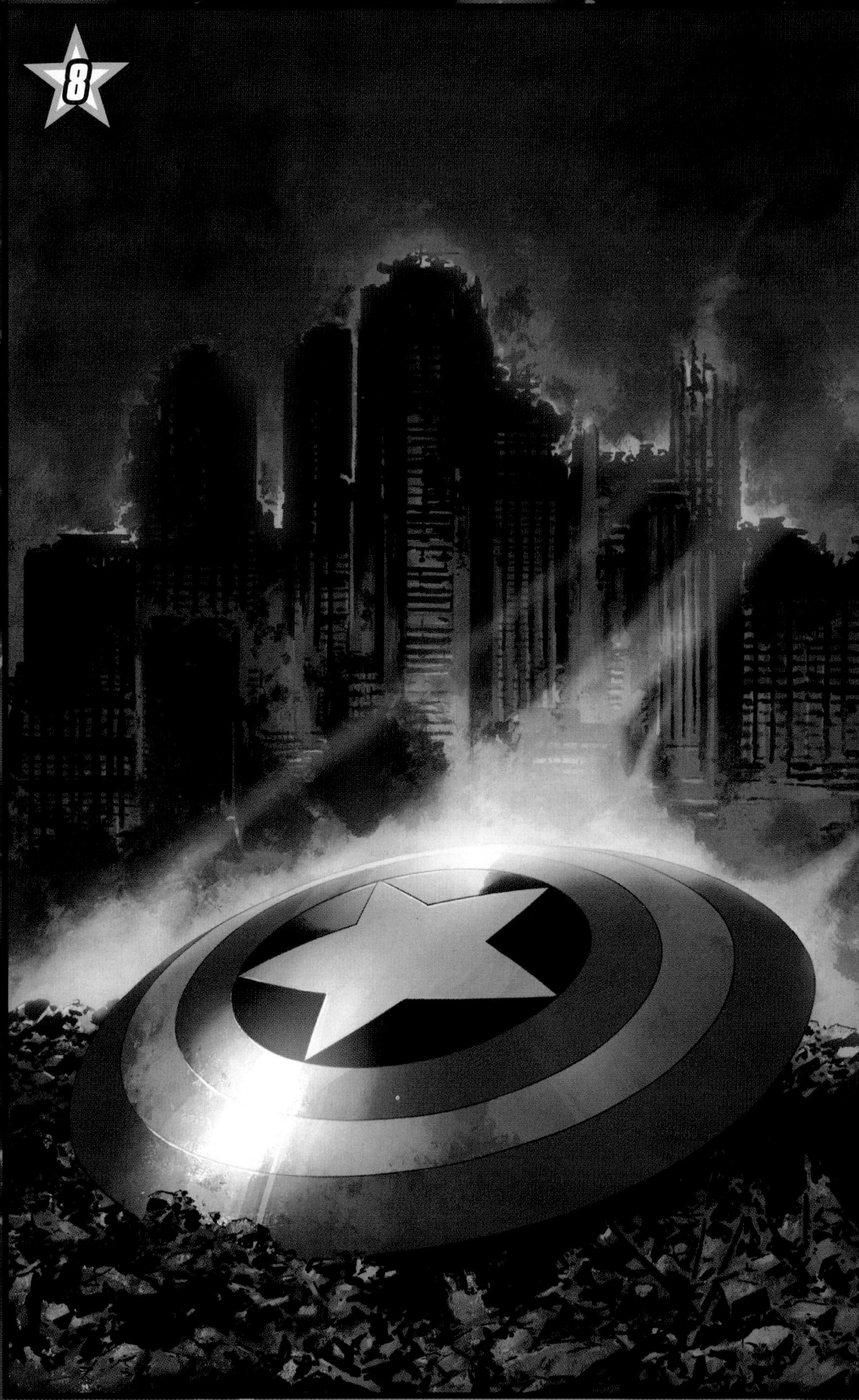
8

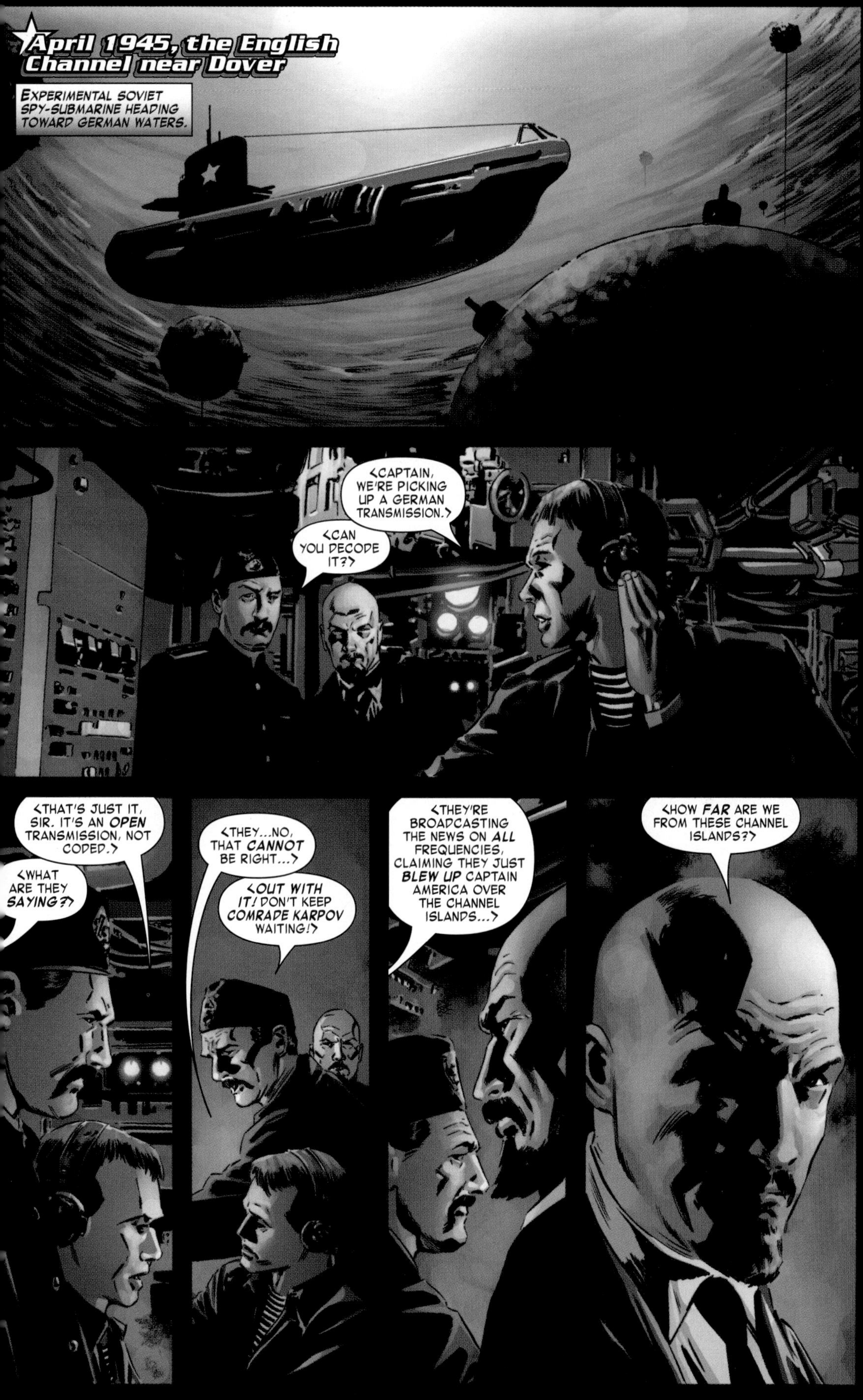
April 1945, the English Channel near Dover
EXPERIMENTAL SOVIET SPY-SUBMARINE HEADING TOWARD GERMAN WATERS.
<CAPTAIN, WE'RE PICKING UP A GERMAN TRANSMISSION.>
<CAN YOU DECODE IT?>
<THAT'S JUST IT, SIR. IT'S AN OPEN TRANSMISSION, NOT CODED.>
<WHAT ARE THEY SAYING?>
<THEY...NO, THAT CANNOT BE RIGHT...>
<OUT WITH IT! DON'T KEEP COMRADE KARPOV WAITING!>
<THEY'RE BROADCASTING THE NEWS ON ALL FREQUENCIES, CLAIMING THEY JUST BLEW UP CAPTAIN AMERICA OVER THE CHANNEL ISLANDS...>
<HOW FAR ARE WE FROM THESE CHANNEL ISLANDS?>

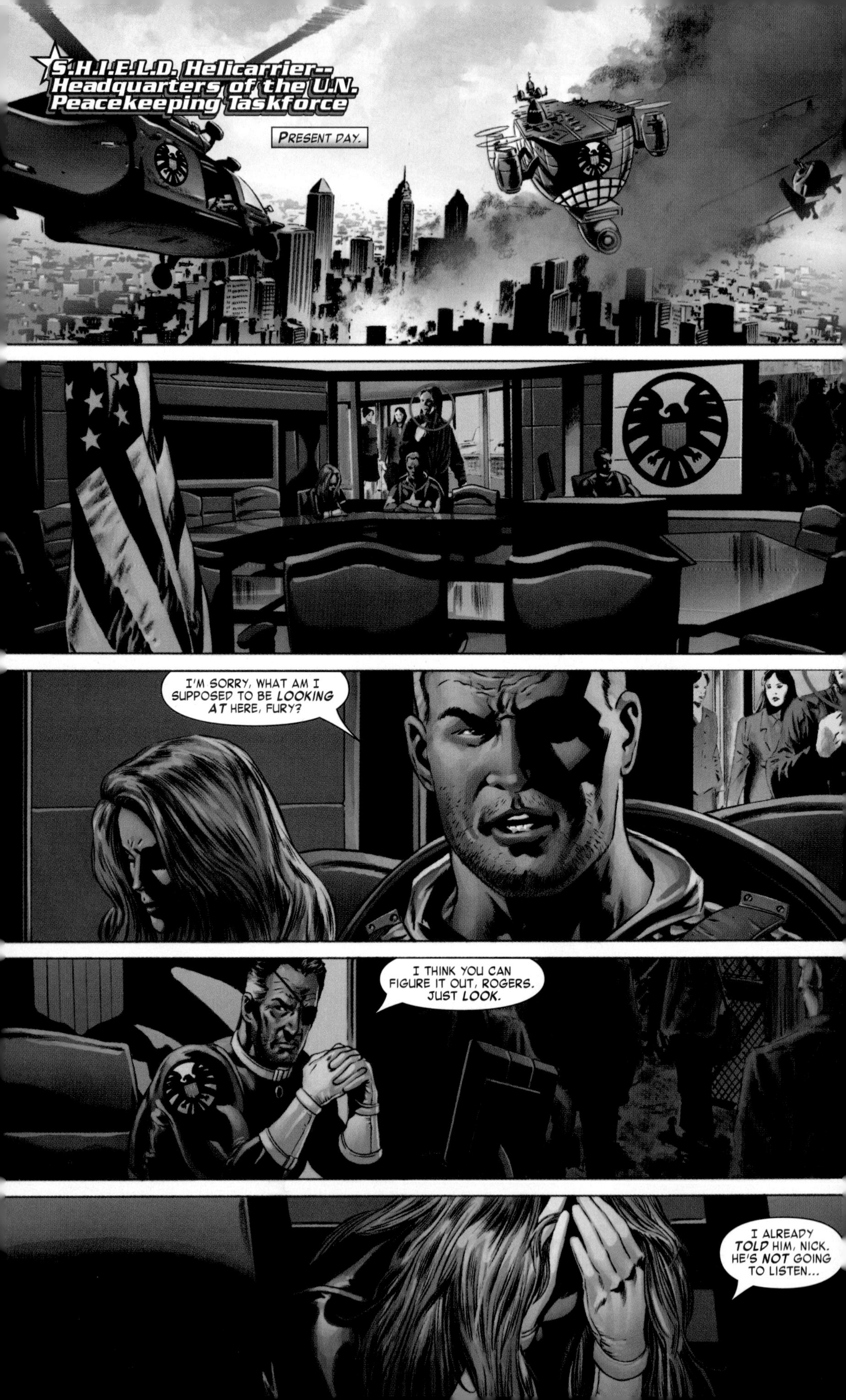
S.H.I.E.L.D. Helicarrier--
Headquarters of the U.N.
Peacekeeping Taskforce
PRESENT DAY.
I'M SORRY, WHAT AM I SUPPOSED TO BE LOOKING AT HERE, FURY?
I THINK YOU CAN FIGURE IT OUT, ROGERS. JUST LOOK.
I ALREADY TOLD HIM, NICK. HE'S NOT GOING TO LISTEN...

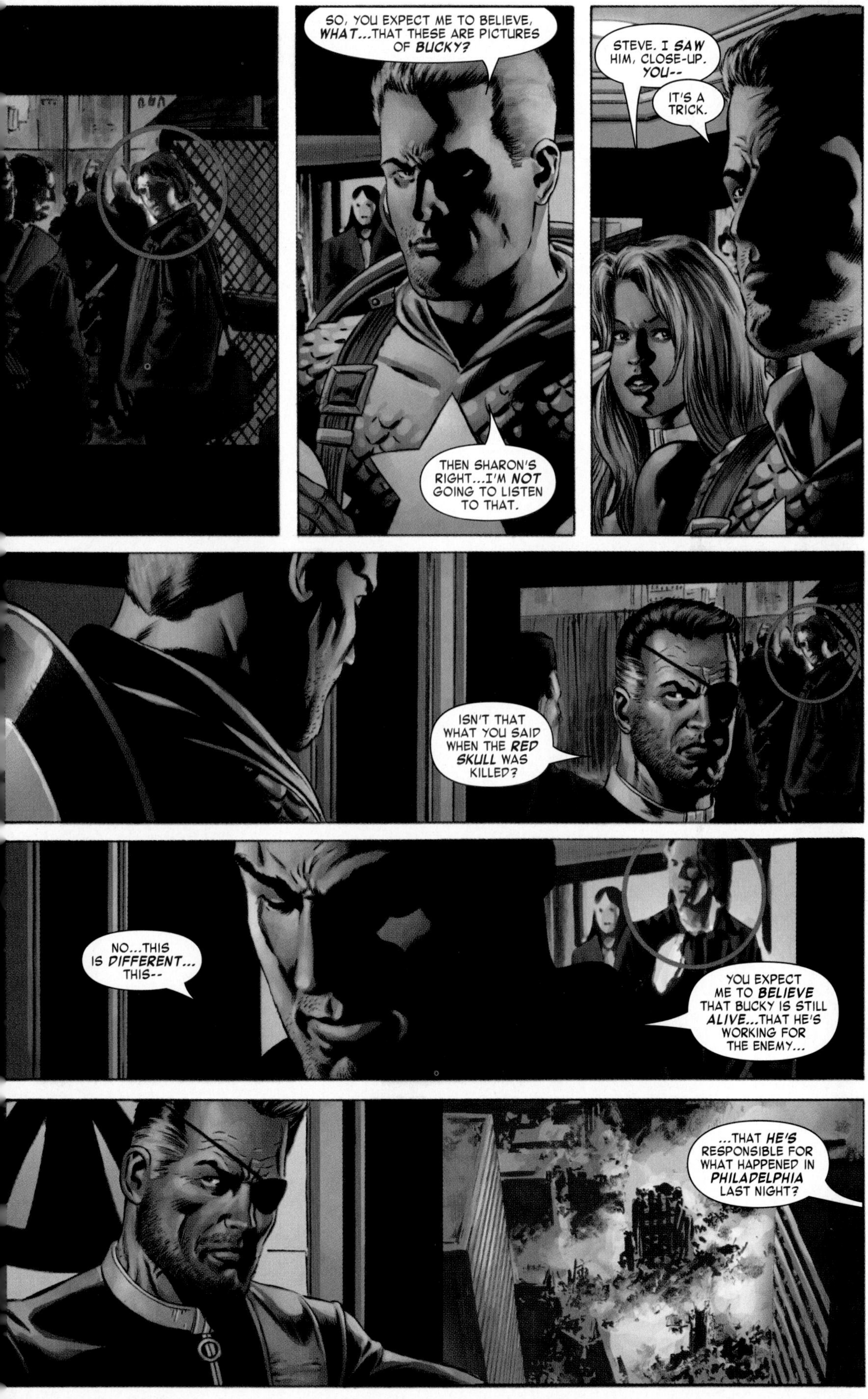

SO, YOU EXPECT ME TO BELIEVE, WHAT...THAT THESE ARE PICTURES OF BUCKY?
THEN SHARON'S RIGHT...I'M NOT GOING TO LISTEN TO THAT.
STEVE. I SAW HIM, CLOSE-UP. YOU--
IT'S A TRICK.
ISN'T THAT WHAT YOU SAID WHEN THE RED SKULL WAS KILLED?
NO...THIS IS DIFFERENT... THIS--
YOU EXPECT ME TO BELIEVE THAT BUCKY IS STILL ALIVE...THAT HE'S WORKING FOR THE ENEMY...
...THAT HE'S RESPONSIBLE FOR WHAT HAPPENED IN PHILADELPHIA LAST NIGHT?

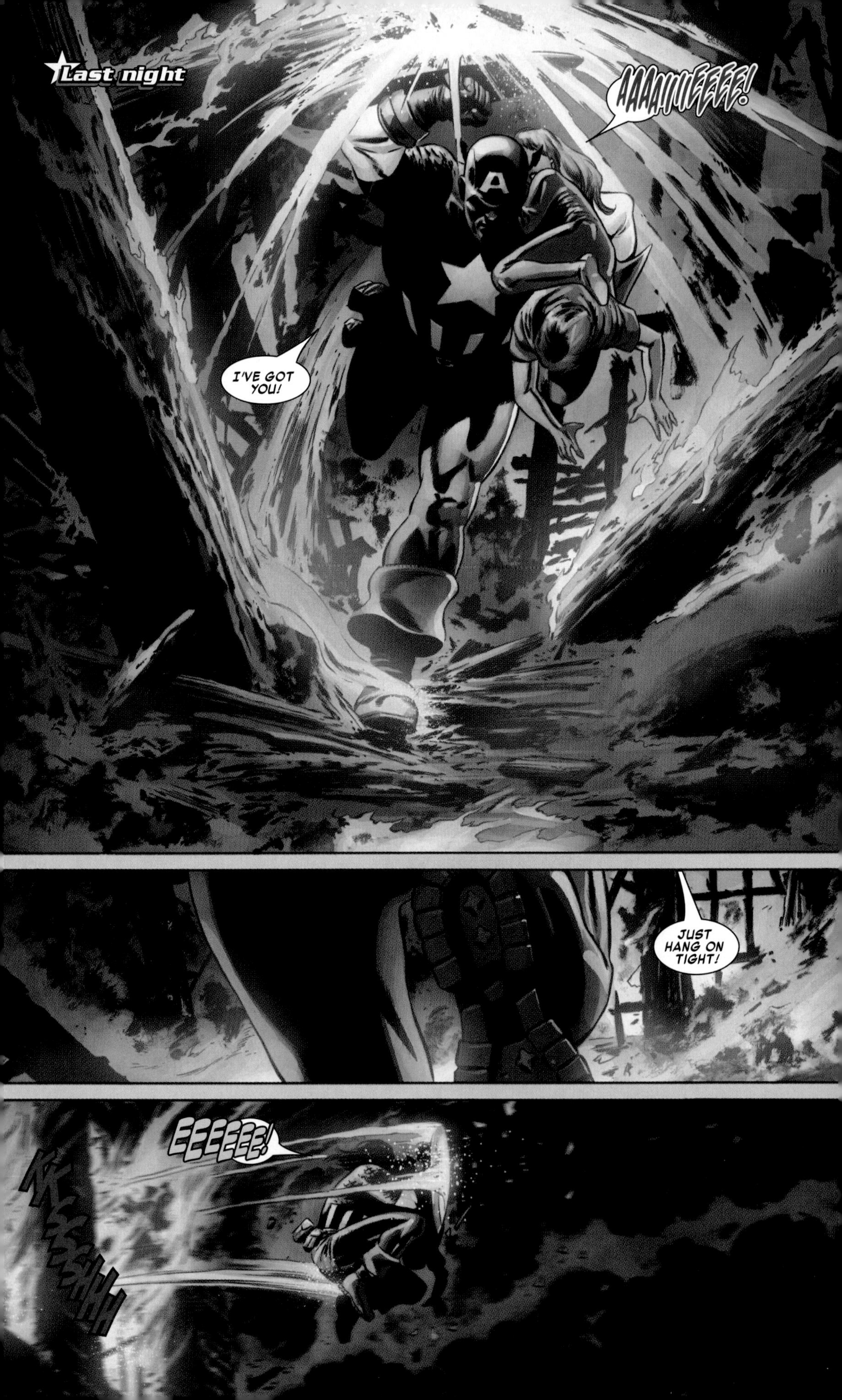
Last night
AAAAIIIIEEEE!
I'VE GOT YOU!
JUST HANG ON TIGHT!
EEEEEE!
KKSSHHH

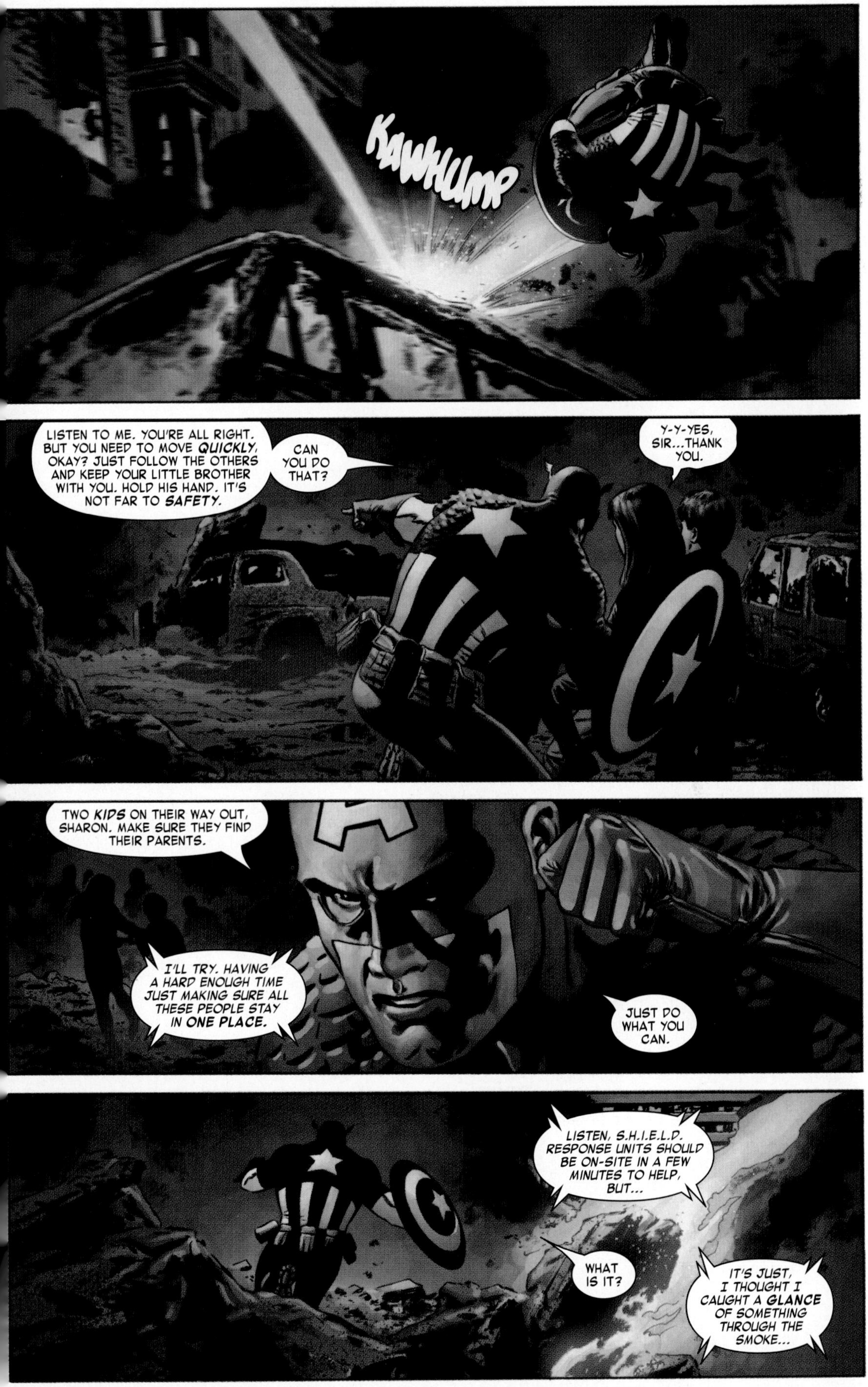
KAWHUMP
LISTEN TO ME. YOU'RE ALL RIGHT. BUT YOU NEED TO MOVE QUICKLY, OKAY? JUST FOLLOW THE OTHERS AND KEEP YOUR LITTLE BROTHER WITH YOU. HOLD HIS HAND. IT'S NOT FAR TO SAFETY.
CAN YOU DO THAT?
Y-Y-YES, SIR...THANK YOU.
TWO KIDS ON THEIR WAY OUT, SHARON. MAKE SURE THEY FIND THEIR PARENTS.
I'LL TRY. HAVING A HARD ENOUGH TIME JUST MAKING SURE ALL THESE PEOPLE STAY IN ONE PLACE.
JUST DO WHAT YOU CAN.
LISTEN, S.H.I.E.L.D. RESPONSE UNITS SHOULD BE ON-SITE IN A FEW MINUTES TO HELP, BUT...
WHAT IS IT?
IT'S JUST, I THOUGHT I CAUGHT A GLANCE OF SOMETHING THROUGH THE SMOKE...

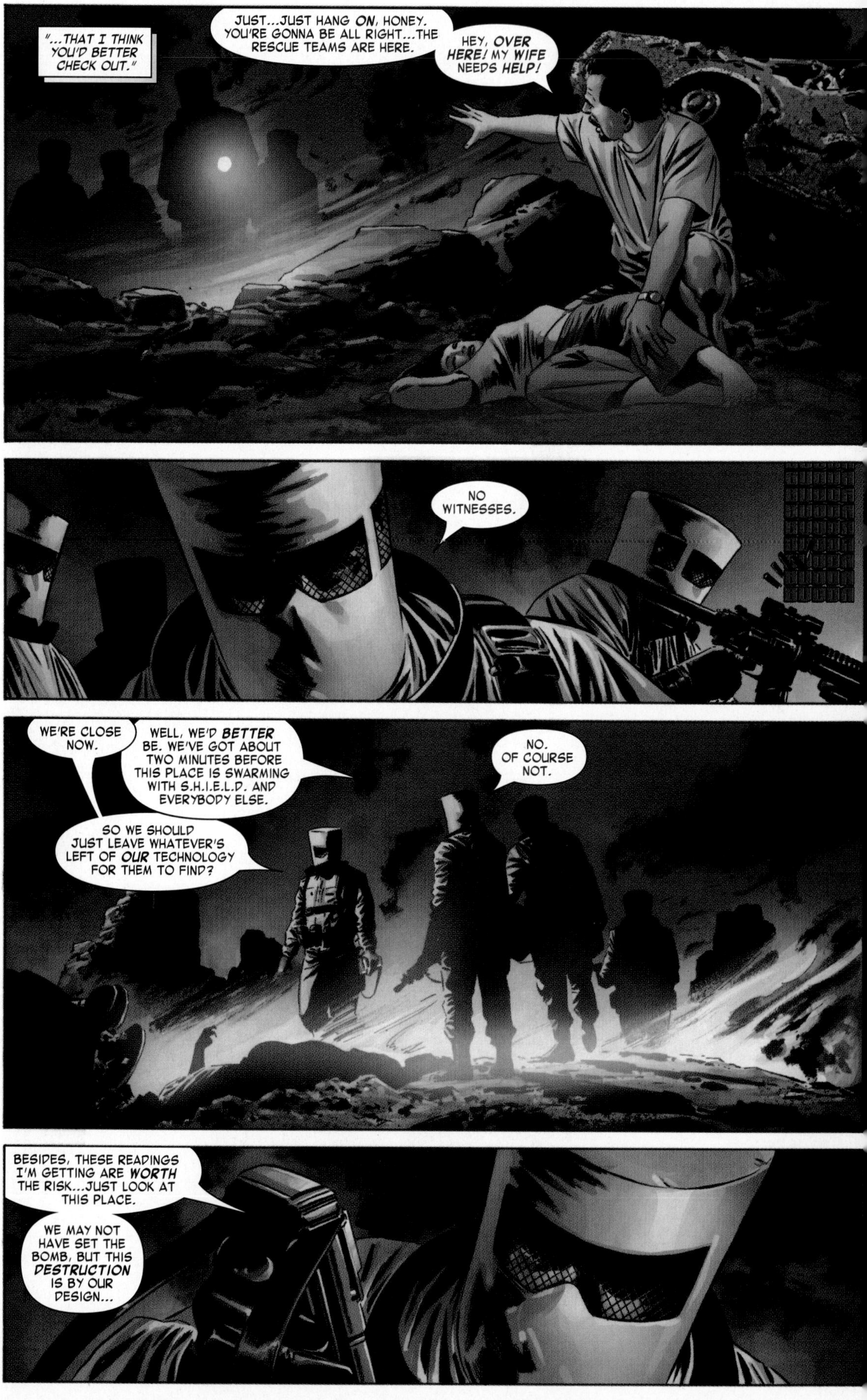
"...THAT I THINK YOU'D BETTER CHECK OUT."
JUST...JUST HANG ON, HONEY. YOU'RE GONNA BE ALL RIGHT...THE RESCUE TEAMS ARE HERE.
HEY, OVER HERE! MY WIFE NEEDS HELP!
NO WITNESSES.
WE'RE CLOSE NOW.
WELL, WE'D BETTER BE. WE'VE GOT ABOUT TWO MINUTES BEFORE THIS PLACE IS SWARMING WITH S.H.I.E.L.D. AND EVERYBODY ELSE.
SO WE SHOULD JUST LEAVE WHATEVER'S LEFT OF OUR TECHNOLOGY FOR THEM TO FIND?
NO. OF COURSE NOT.
BESIDES, THESE READINGS I'M GETTING ARE WORTH THE RISK...JUST LOOK AT THIS PLACE.
WE MAY NOT HAVE SET THE BOMB, BUT THIS DESTRUCTION IS BY OUR DESIGN...

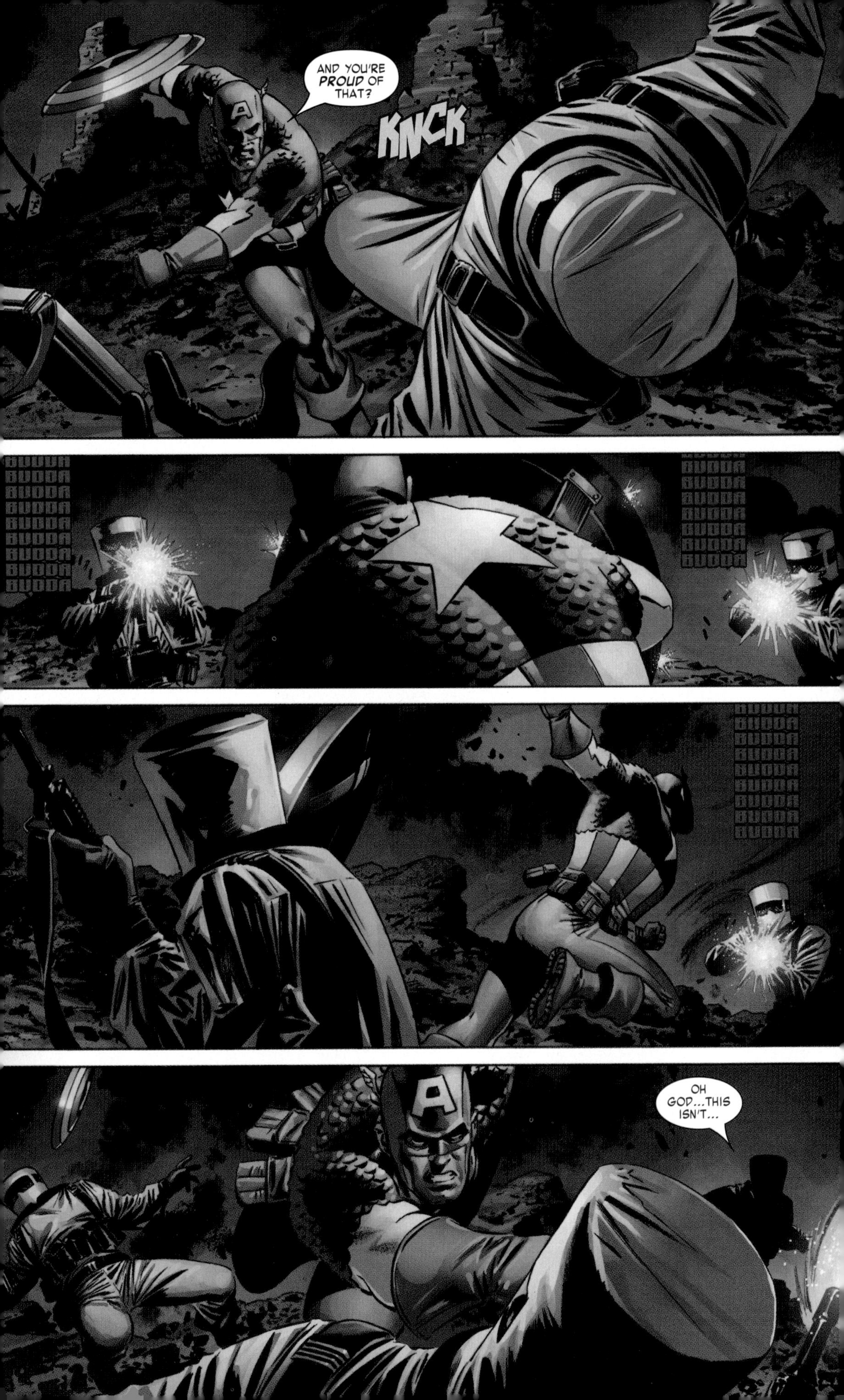
AND YOU'RE *PROUD* OF THAT?
KNCK
BUDDA BUDDA BUDDA BUDDA BUDDA BUDDA BUDDA BUDDA BUDDA
BUDDA BUDDA BUDDA BUDDA BUDDA BUDDA BUDDA
BUDDA BUDDA BUDDA BUDDA BUDDA BUDDA BUDDA BUDDA
OH GOD...THIS ISN'T...

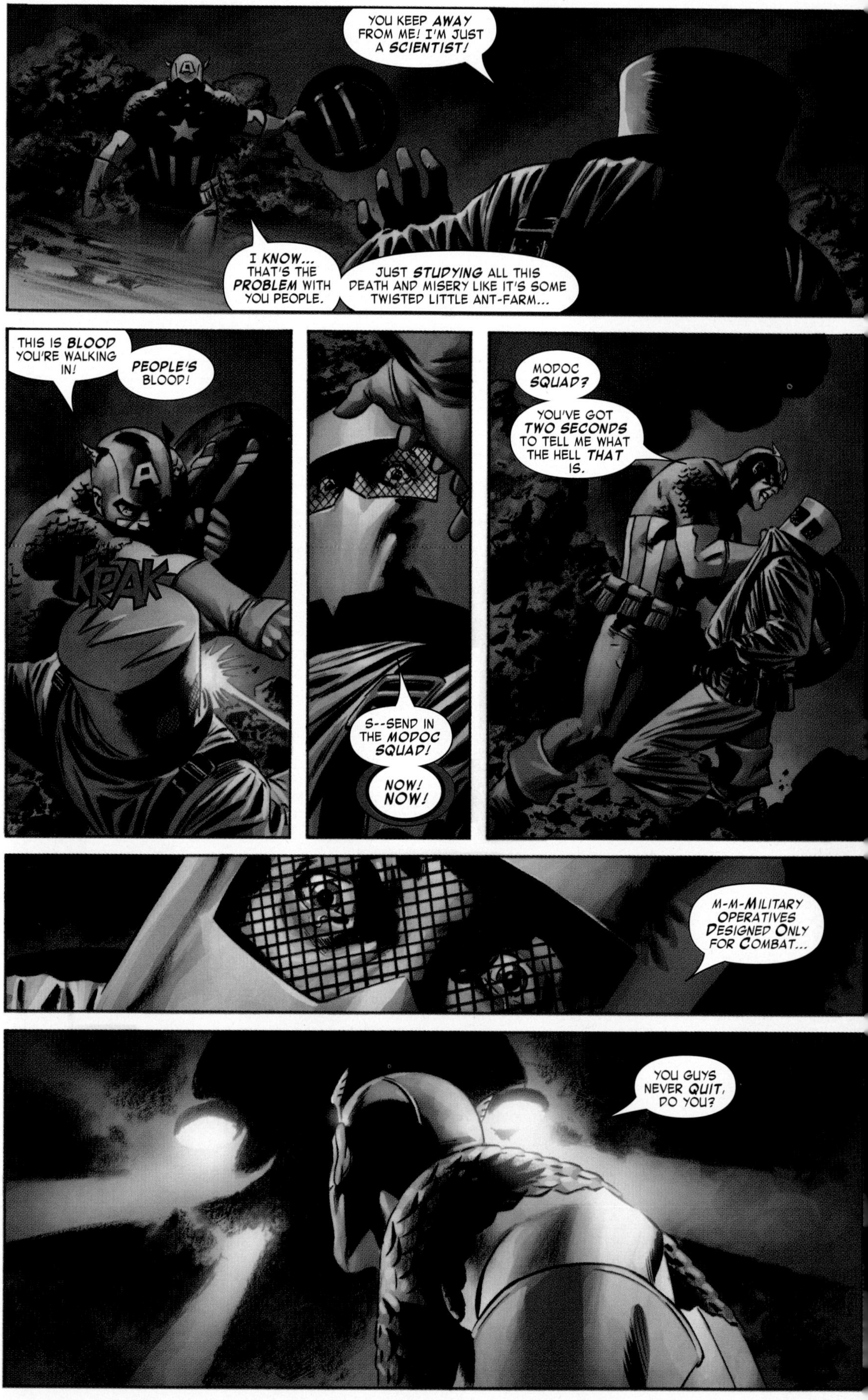

YOU KEEP AWAY FROM ME! I'M JUST A SCIENTIST!
I KNOW... THAT'S THE PROBLEM WITH YOU PEOPLE.
JUST STUDYING ALL THIS DEATH AND MISERY LIKE IT'S SOME TWISTED LITTLE ANT-FARM...
THIS IS BLOOD YOU'RE WALKING IN!
PEOPLE'S BLOOD!
KRAK
S--SEND IN THE MODOC SQUAD!
NOW! NOW!
MODOC SQUAD?
YOU'VE GOT TWO SECONDS TO TELL ME WHAT THE HELL THAT IS.
M-M-MILITARY OPERATIVES DESIGNED ONLY FOR COMBAT...
YOU GUYS NEVER QUIT, DO YOU?

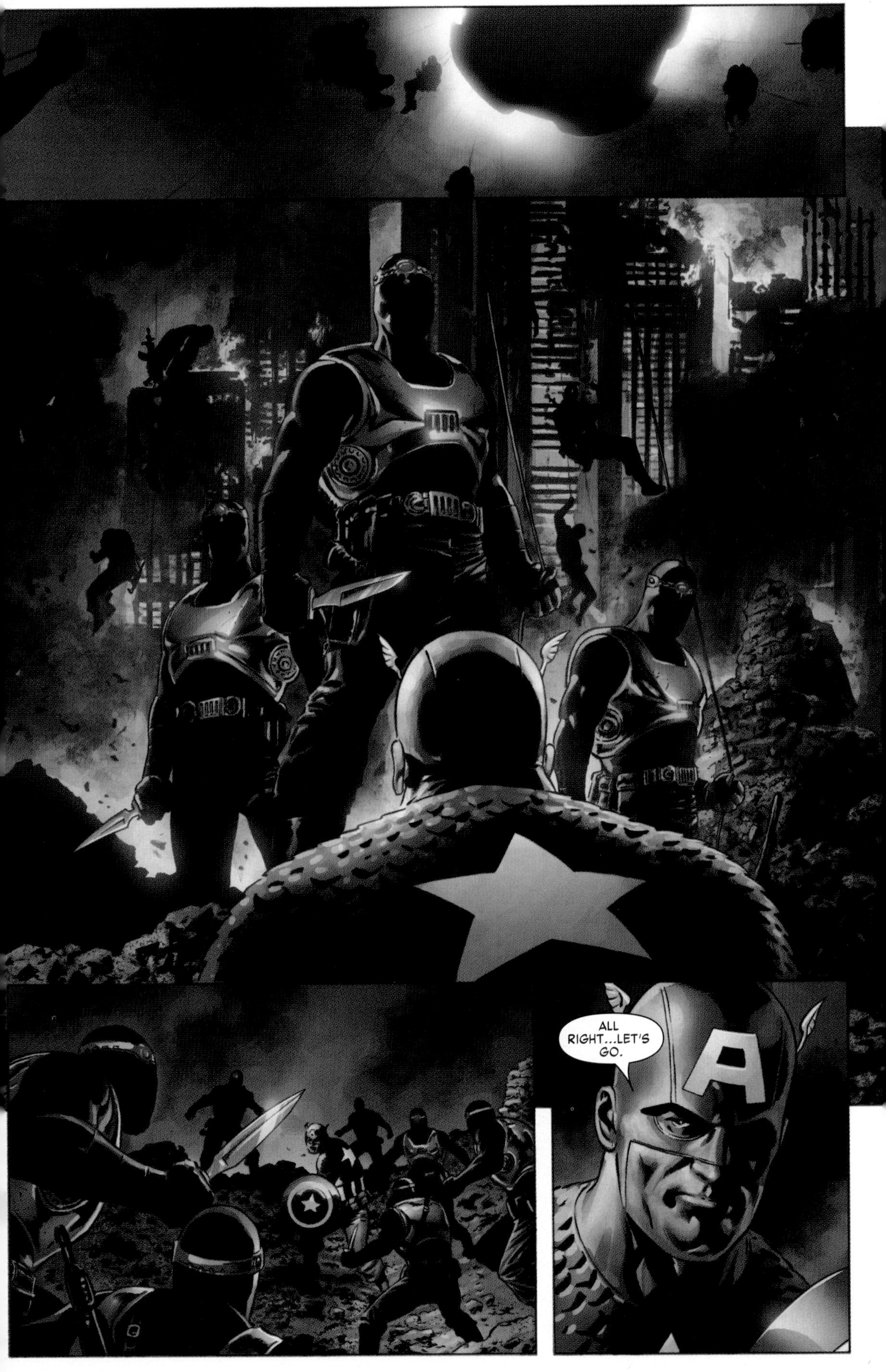
ALL RIGHT...LET'S GO.

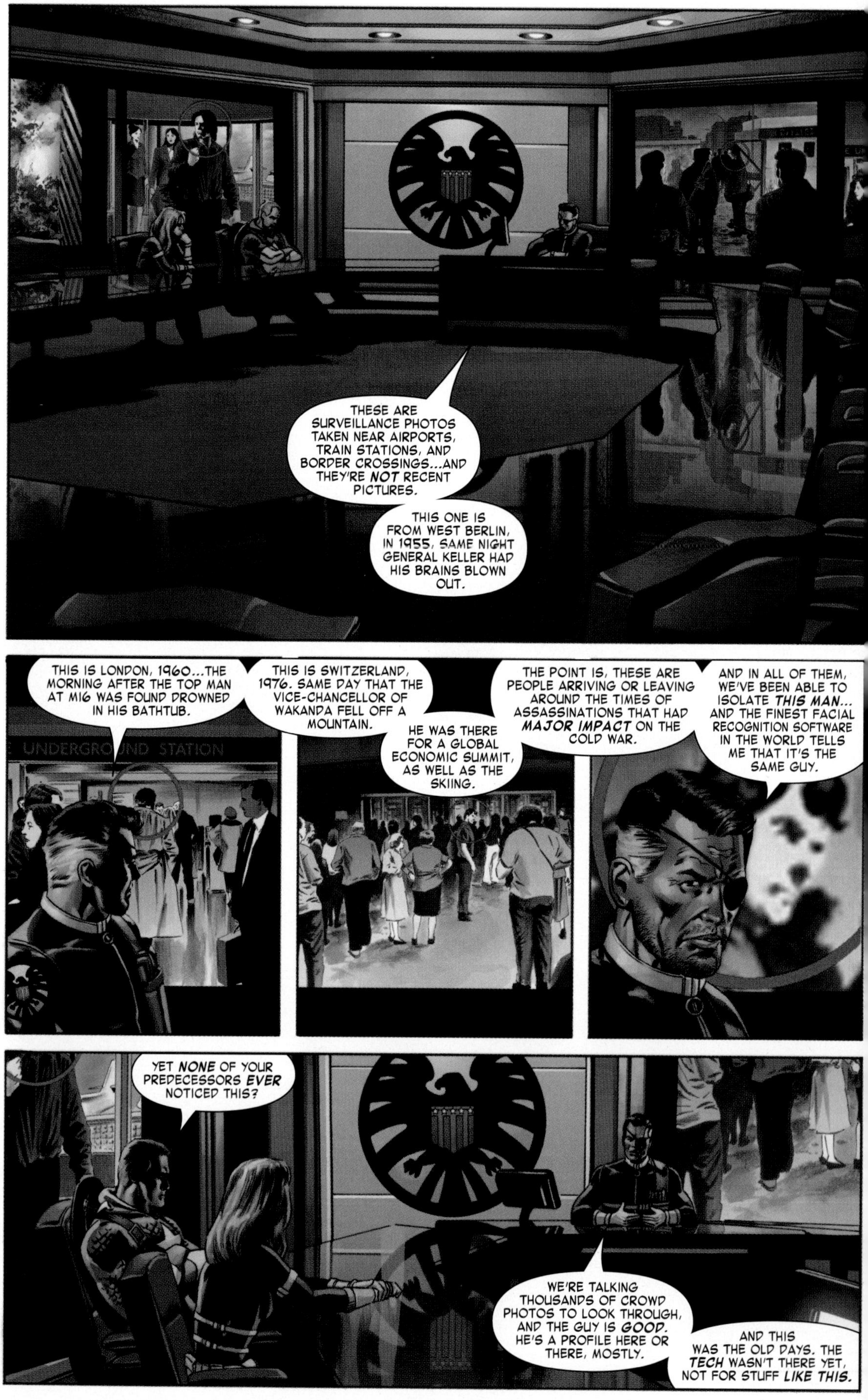
THESE ARE SURVEILLANCE PHOTOS TAKEN NEAR AIRPORTS, TRAIN STATIONS, AND BORDER CROSSINGS...AND THEY'RE **NOT** RECENT PICTURES.
THIS ONE IS FROM WEST BERLIN, IN 1955, SAME NIGHT GENERAL KELLER HAD HIS BRAINS BLOWN OUT.
THIS IS LONDON, 1960...THE MORNING AFTER THE TOP MAN AT MI6 WAS FOUND DROWNED IN HIS BATHTUB.
UNDERGROUND STATION
THIS IS SWITZERLAND, 1976. SAME DAY THAT THE VICE-CHANCELLOR OF WAKANDA FELL OFF A MOUNTAIN.
HE WAS THERE FOR A GLOBAL ECONOMIC SUMMIT, AS WELL AS THE SKIING.
THE POINT IS, THESE ARE PEOPLE ARRIVING OR LEAVING AROUND THE TIMES OF ASSASSINATIONS THAT HAD **MAJOR IMPACT** ON THE COLD WAR.
AND IN ALL OF THEM, WE'VE BEEN ABLE TO ISOLATE **THIS MAN...** AND THE FINEST FACIAL RECOGNITION SOFTWARE IN THE WORLD TELLS ME THAT IT'S THE SAME GUY.
YET **NONE** OF YOUR PREDECESSORS **EVER** NOTICED THIS?
WE'RE TALKING THOUSANDS OF CROWD PHOTOS TO LOOK THROUGH, AND THE GUY IS **GOOD**. HE'S A PROFILE HERE OR THERE, MOSTLY.
AND THIS WAS THE OLD DAYS. THE **TECH** WASN'T THERE YET, NOT FOR STUFF **LIKE THIS.**

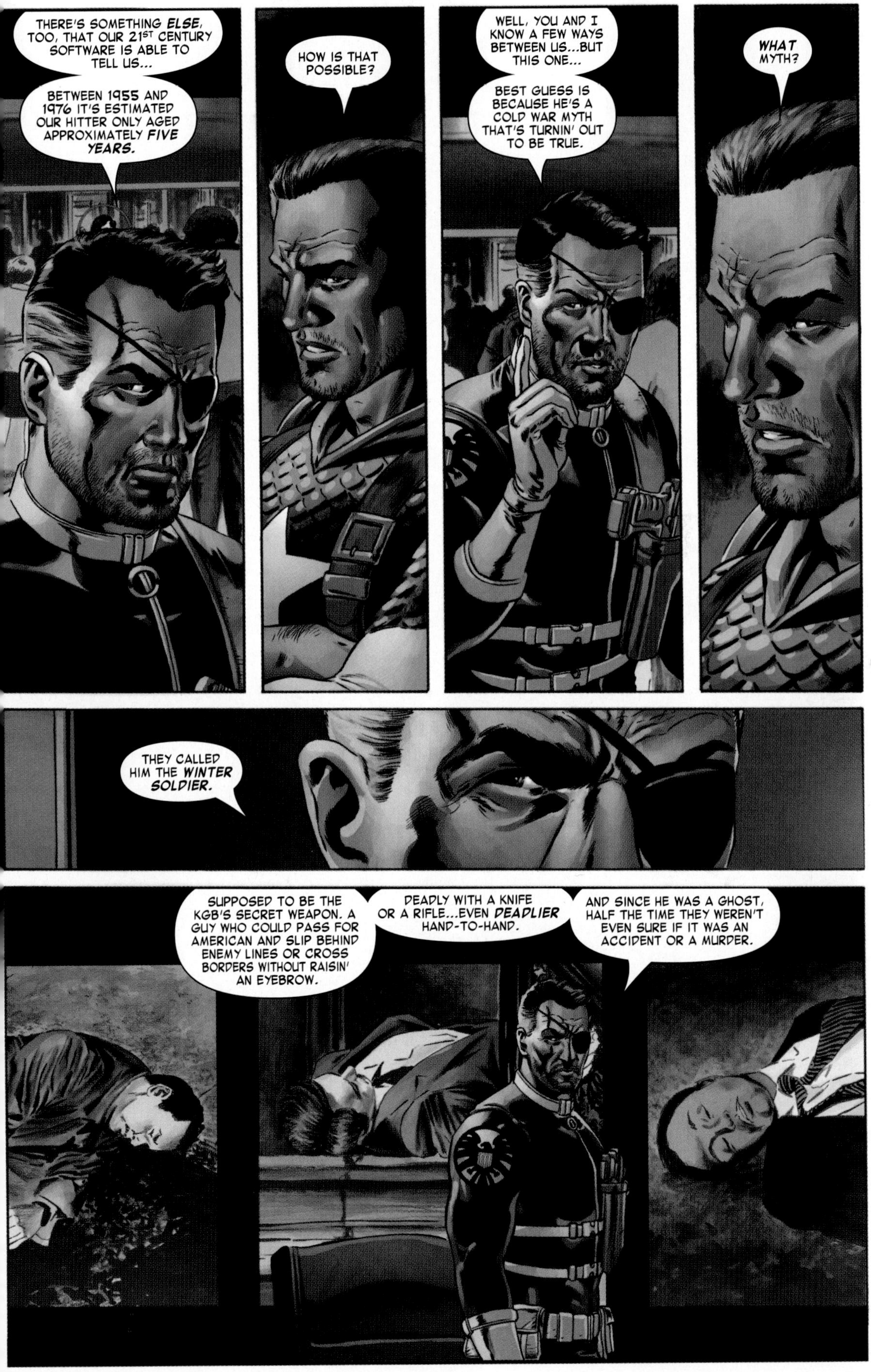
THERE'S SOMETHING ELSE, TOO, THAT OUR 21ST CENTURY SOFTWARE IS ABLE TO TELL US...
BETWEEN 1955 AND 1976 IT'S ESTIMATED OUR HITTER ONLY AGED APPROXIMATELY FIVE YEARS.
HOW IS THAT POSSIBLE?
WELL, YOU AND I KNOW A FEW WAYS BETWEEN US...BUT THIS ONE...
BEST GUESS IS BECAUSE HE'S A COLD WAR MYTH THAT'S TURNIN' OUT TO BE TRUE.
WHAT MYTH?
THEY CALLED HIM THE WINTER SOLDIER.
SUPPOSED TO BE THE KGB'S SECRET WEAPON. A GUY WHO COULD PASS FOR AMERICAN AND SLIP BEHIND ENEMY LINES OR CROSS BORDERS WITHOUT RAISIN' AN EYEBROW.
DEADLY WITH A KNIFE OR A RIFLE...EVEN DEADLIER HAND-TO-HAND.
AND SINCE HE WAS A GHOST, HALF THE TIME THEY WEREN'T EVEN SURE IF IT WAS AN ACCIDENT OR A MURDER.

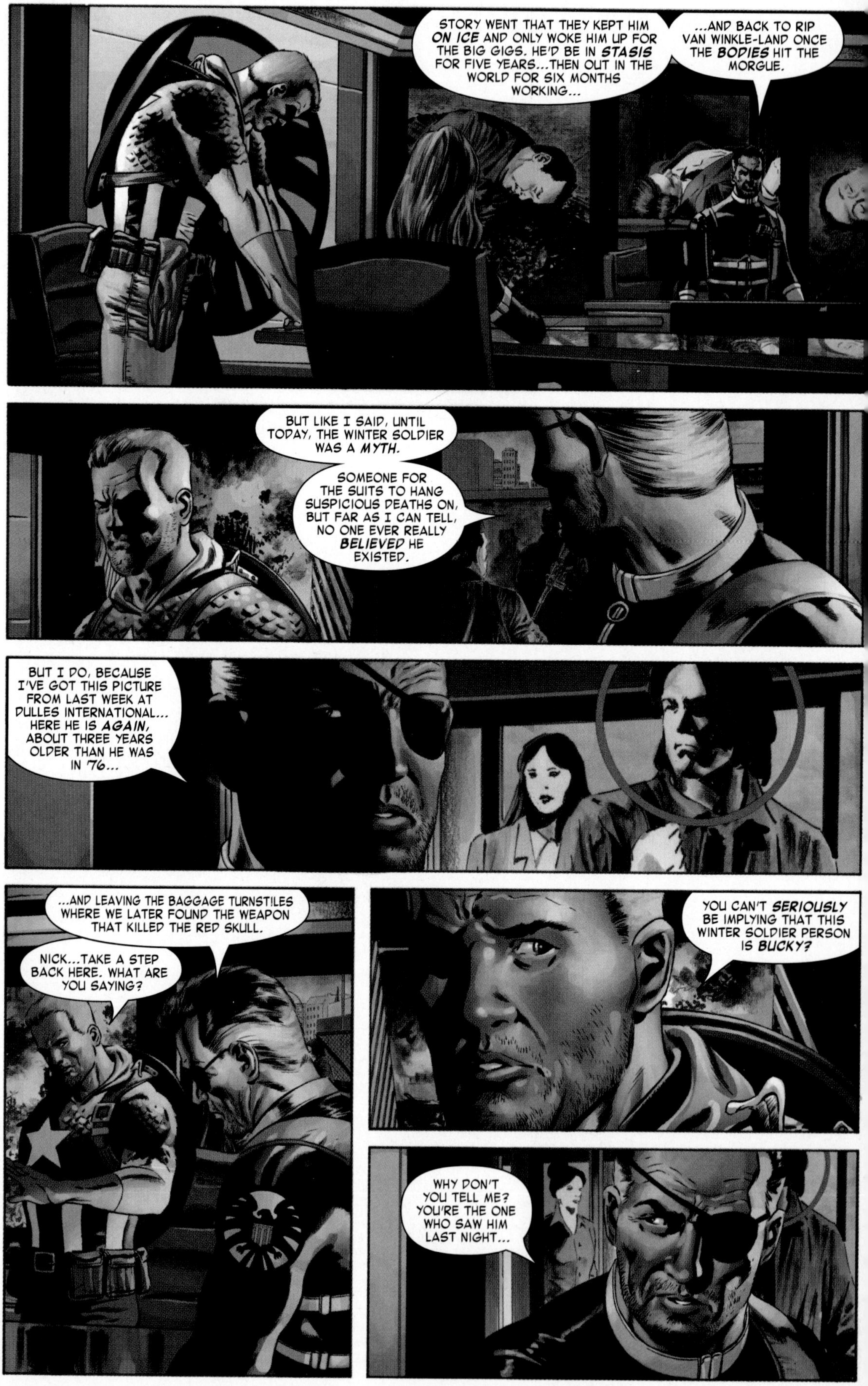
STORY WENT THAT THEY KEPT HIM ON ICE AND ONLY WOKE HIM UP FOR THE BIG GIGS. HE'D BE IN STASIS FOR FIVE YEARS...THEN OUT IN THE WORLD FOR SIX MONTHS WORKING...
...AND BACK TO RIP VAN WINKLE-LAND ONCE THE BODIES HIT THE MORGUE.
BUT LIKE I SAID, UNTIL TODAY, THE WINTER SOLDIER WAS A MYTH.
SOMEONE FOR THE SUITS TO HANG SUSPICIOUS DEATHS ON, BUT FAR AS I CAN TELL, NO ONE EVER REALLY BELIEVED HE EXISTED.
BUT I DO, BECAUSE I'VE GOT THIS PICTURE FROM LAST WEEK AT DULLES INTERNATIONAL... HERE HE IS AGAIN, ABOUT THREE YEARS OLDER THAN HE WAS IN '76...
...AND LEAVING THE BAGGAGE TURNSTILES WHERE WE LATER FOUND THE WEAPON THAT KILLED THE RED SKULL.
NICK...TAKE A STEP BACK HERE. WHAT ARE YOU SAYING?
YOU CAN'T SERIOUSLY BE IMPLYING THAT THIS WINTER SOLDIER PERSON IS BUCKY?
WHY DON'T YOU TELL ME? YOU'RE THE ONE WHO SAW HIM LAST NIGHT...

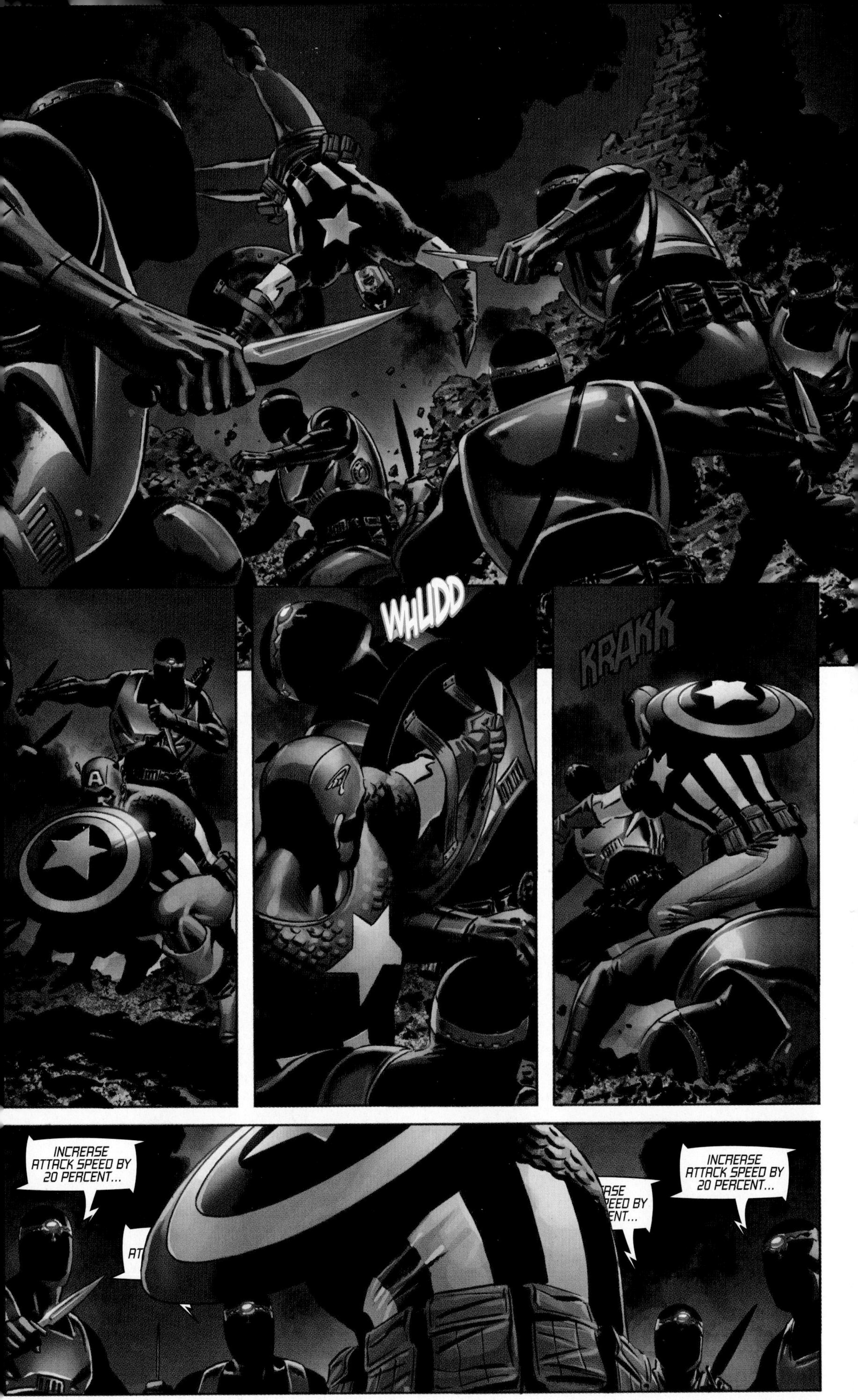
WHUDD
KRAKK
INCREASE ATTACK SPEED BY 20 PERCENT...
INCREASE ATTACK SPEED BY 20 PERCENT...

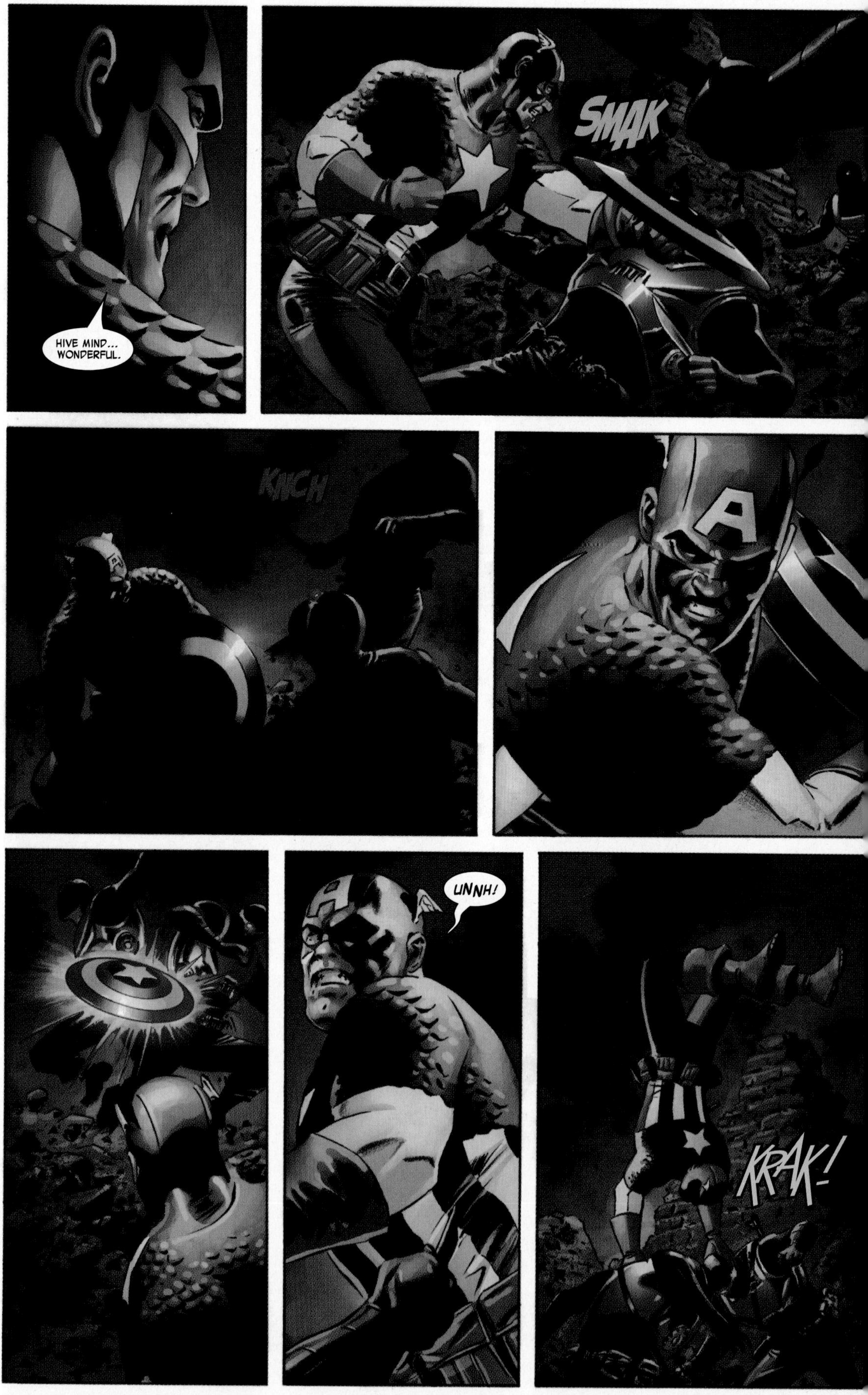
HIVE MIND...
WONDERFUL.
SMAK
KNCH
UNNH!
KRAK!

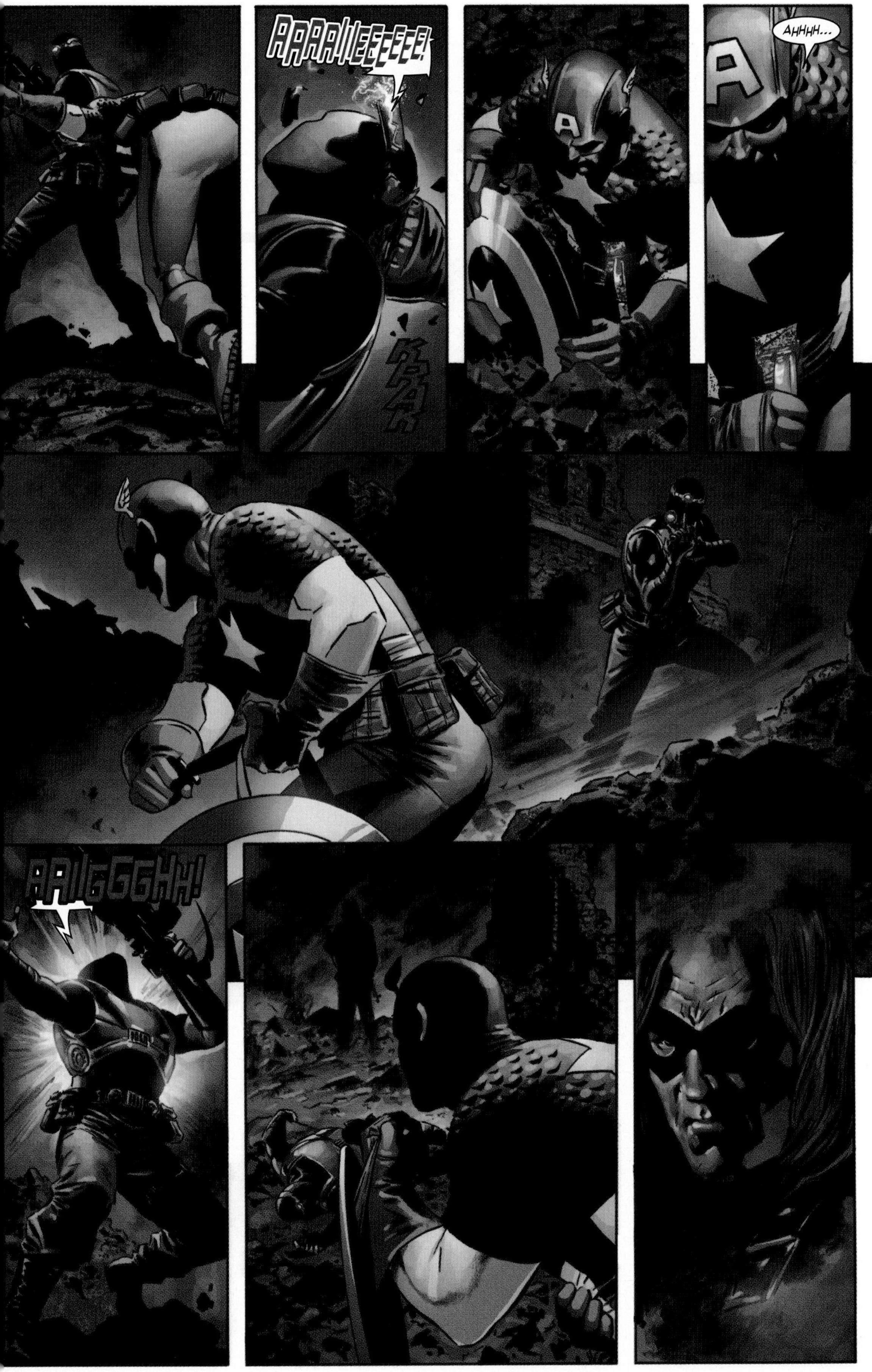
AAAAIIEEEEEEE!
AHHHH...
AAIIGGGHH!

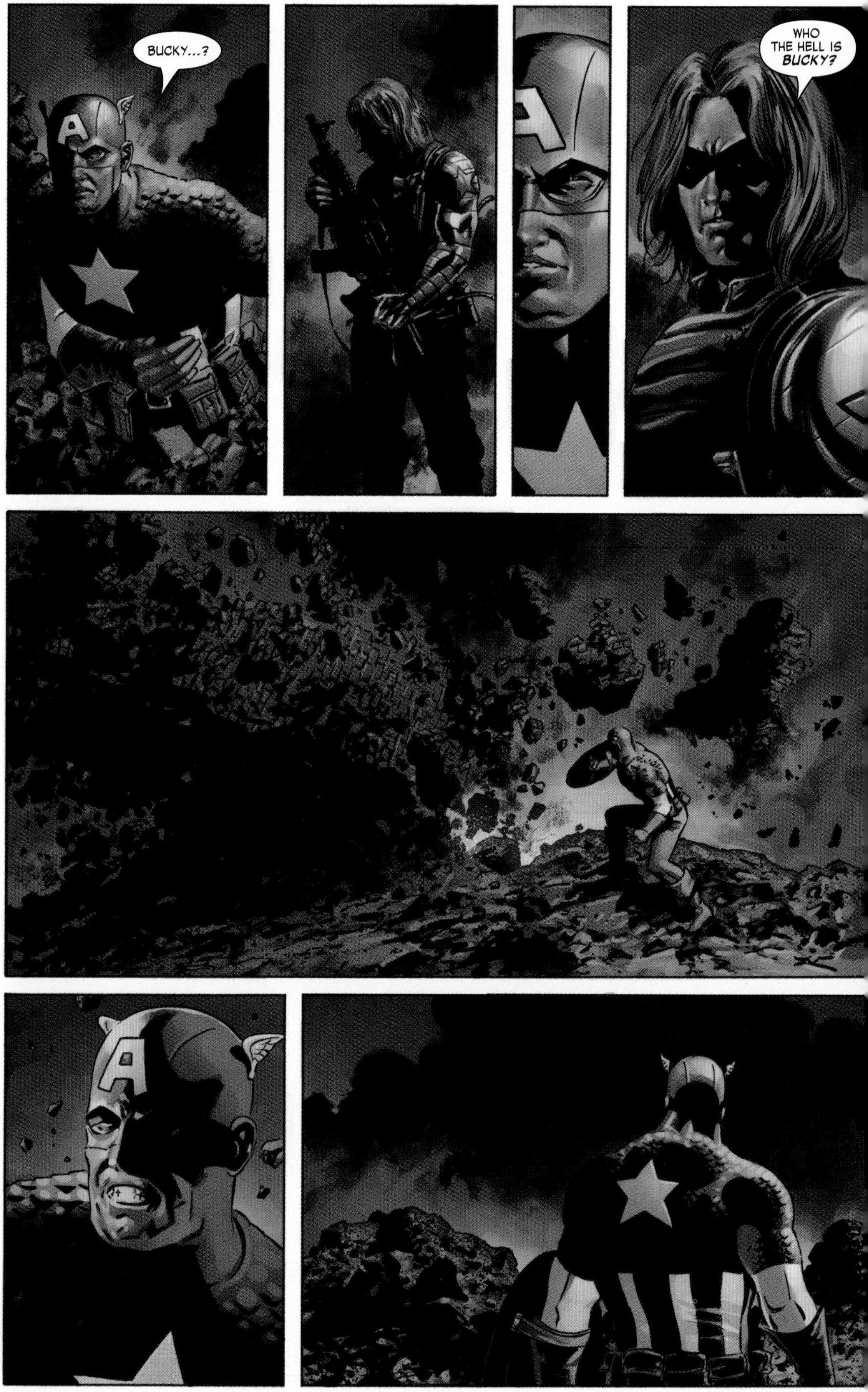
BUCKY...?
WHO THE HELL IS BUCKY?

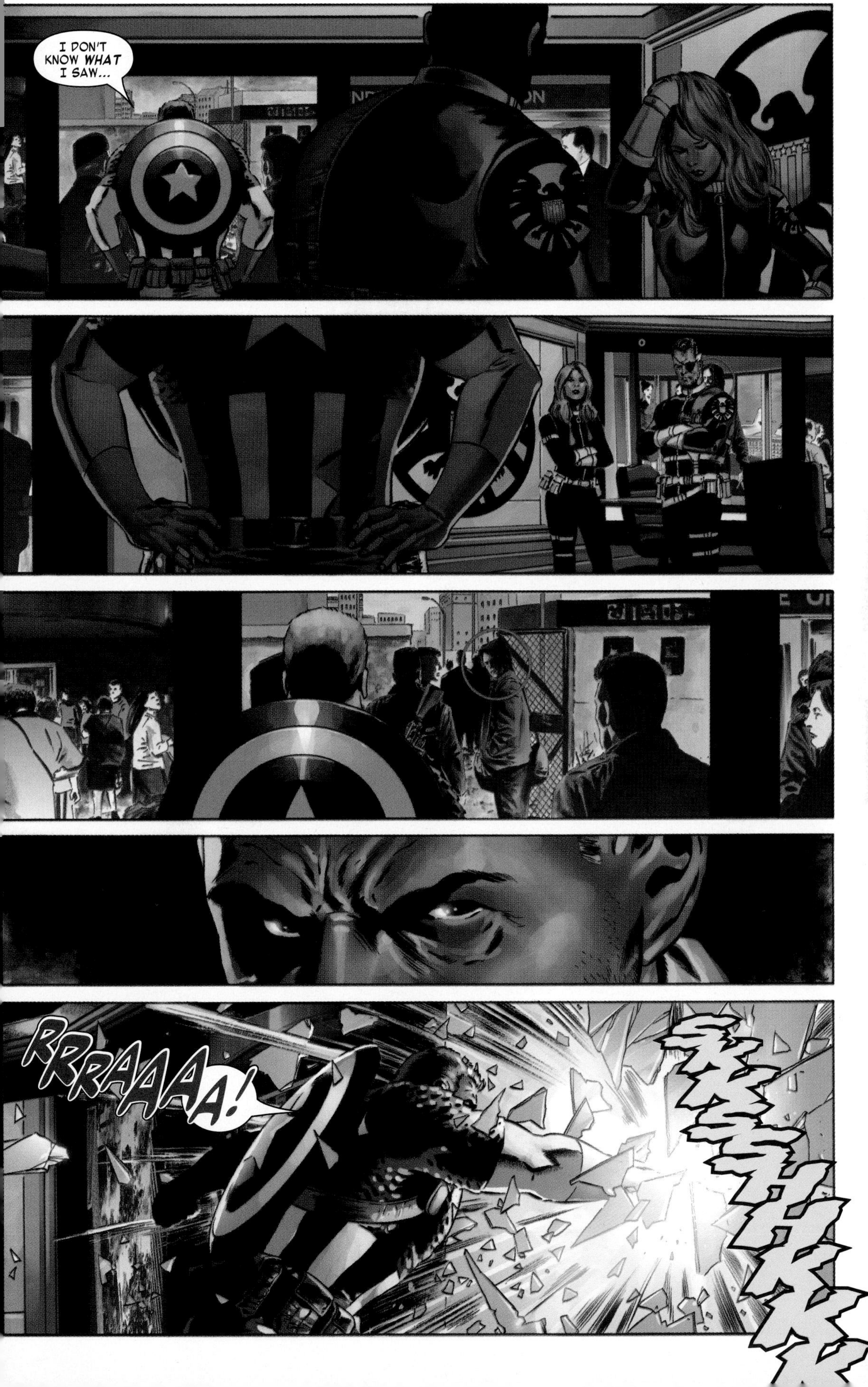

I DON'T KNOW WHAT I SAW...
RRRAAAAA!
SSSHKKK

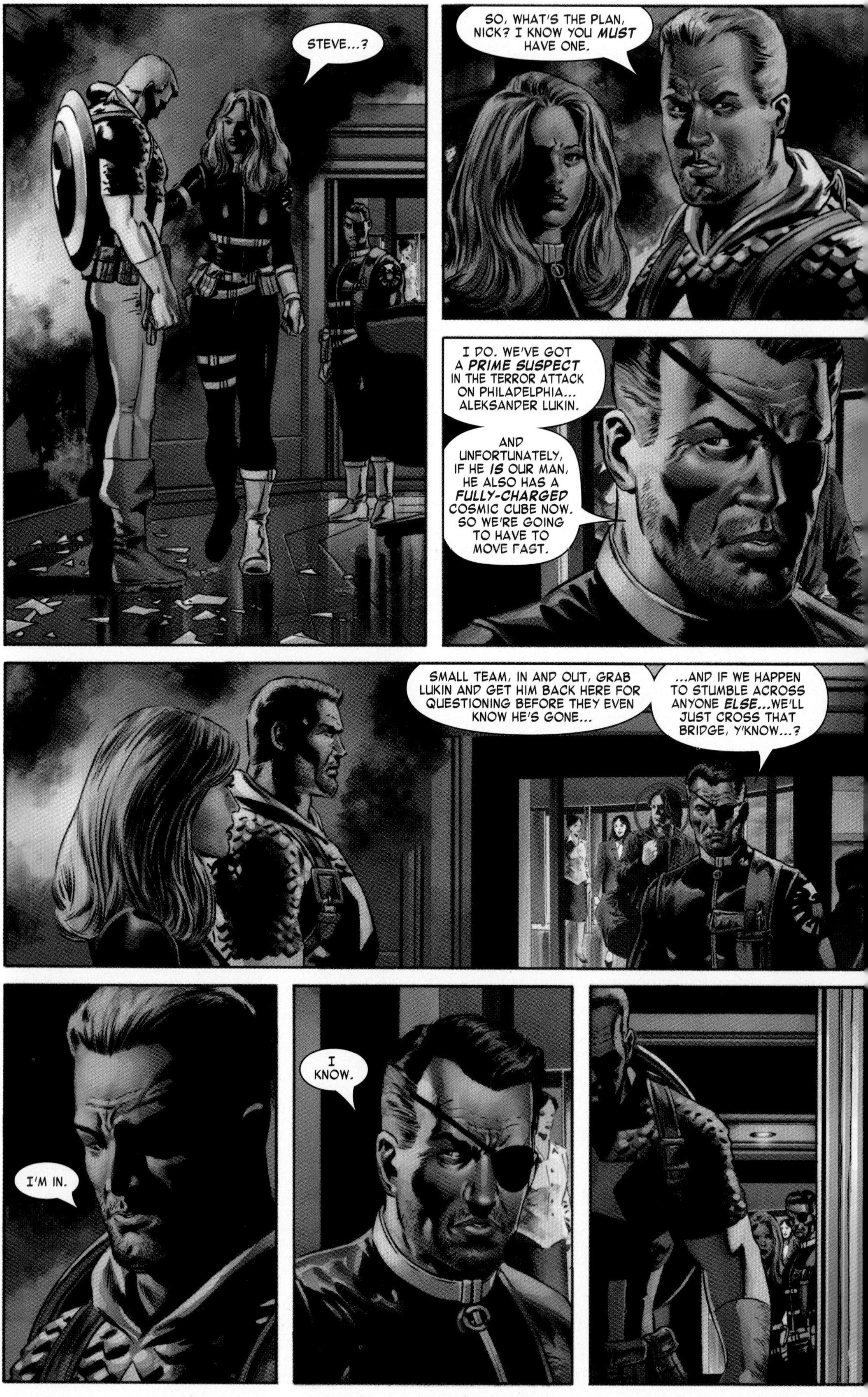
STEVE...?
SO, WHAT'S THE PLAN, NICK? I KNOW YOU MUST HAVE ONE.
I DO. WE'VE GOT A PRIME SUSPECT IN THE TERROR ATTACK ON PHILADELPHIA... ALEKSANDER LUKIN.
AND UNFORTUNATELY, IF HE IS OUR MAN, HE ALSO HAS A FULLY-CHARGED COSMIC CUBE NOW. SO WE'RE GOING TO HAVE TO MOVE FAST.
SMALL TEAM, IN AND OUT, GRAB LUKIN AND GET HIM BACK HERE FOR QUESTIONING BEFORE THEY EVEN KNOW HE'S GONE...
...AND IF WE HAPPEN TO STUMBLE ACROSS ANYONE ELSE...WE'LL JUST CROSS THAT BRIDGE, Y'KNOW...?
I'M IN.
I KNOW.

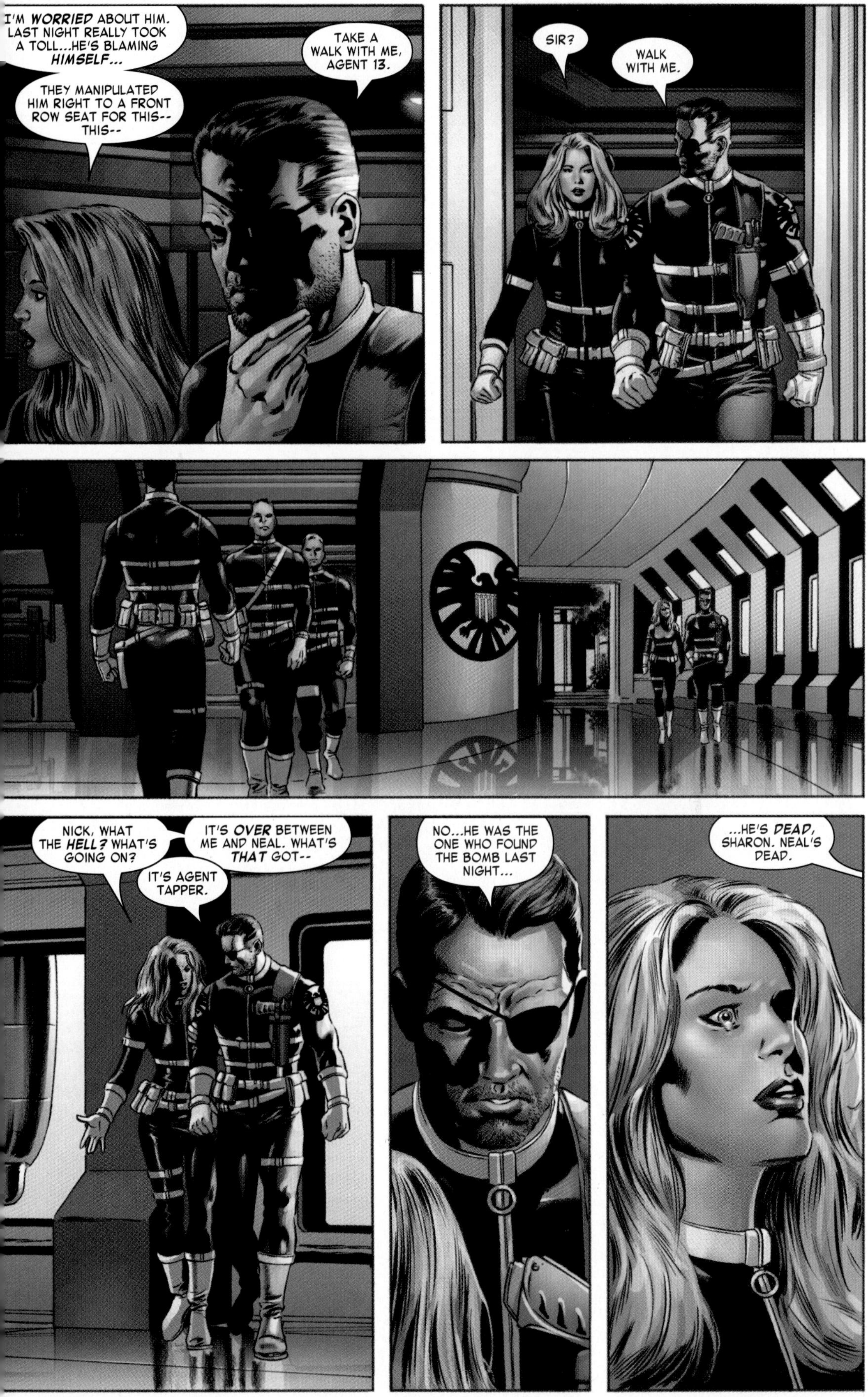
I'M WORRIED ABOUT HIM. LAST NIGHT REALLY TOOK A TOLL...HE'S BLAMING HIMSELF...
THEY MANIPULATED HIM RIGHT TO A FRONT ROW SEAT FOR THIS-- THIS--
TAKE A WALK WITH ME, AGENT 13.
SIR?
WALK WITH ME.
NICK, WHAT THE HELL? WHAT'S GOING ON?
IT'S OVER BETWEEN ME AND NEAL. WHAT'S THAT GOT--
IT'S AGENT TAPPER.
NO...HE WAS THE ONE WHO FOUND THE BOMB LAST NIGHT...
...HE'S DEAD, SHARON. NEAL'S DEAD.

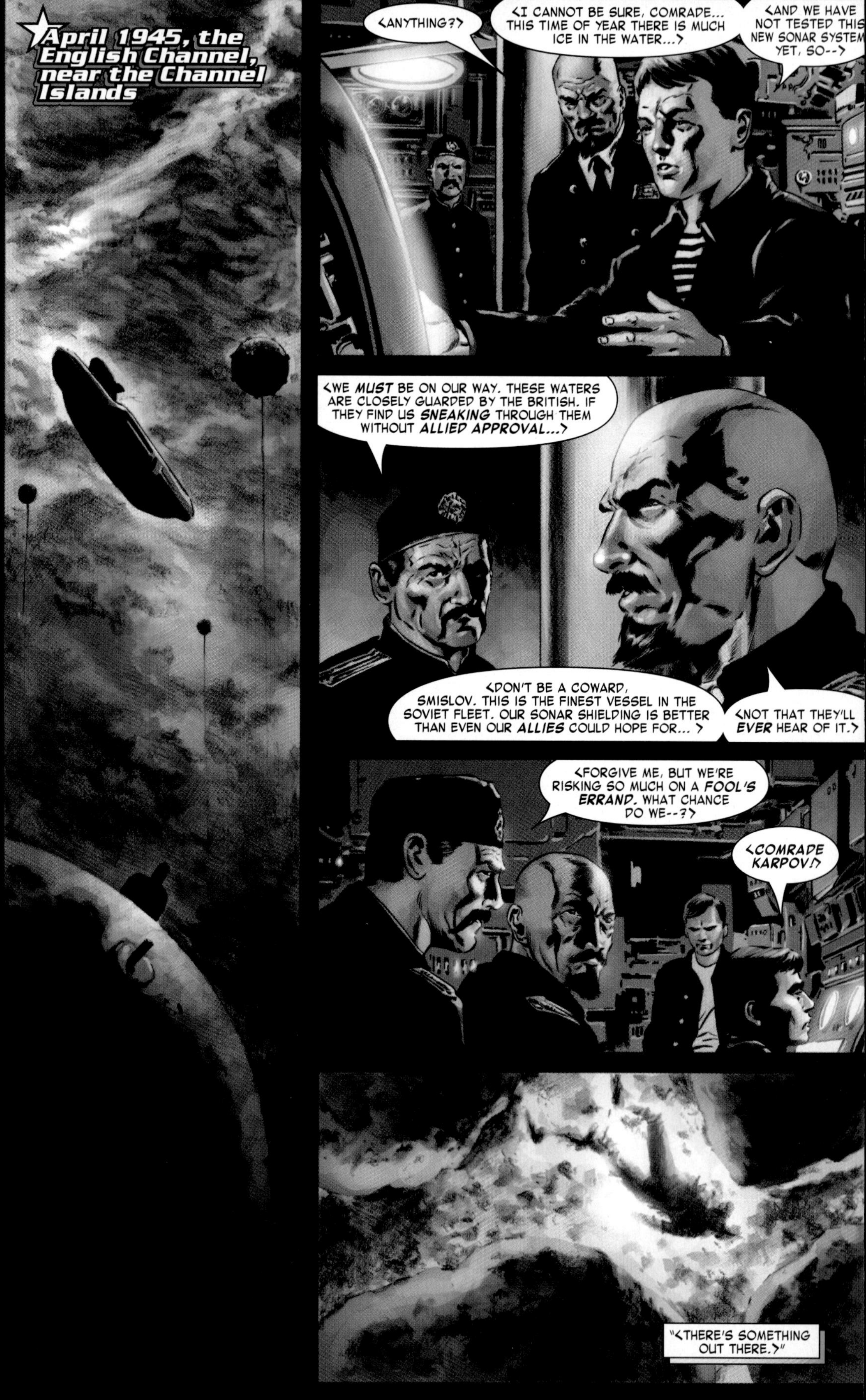
April 1945, the English Channel, near the Channel Islands
<ANYTHING?>
<I CANNOT BE SURE, COMRADE... THIS TIME OF YEAR THERE IS MUCH ICE IN THE WATER...>
<AND WE HAVE NOT TESTED THIS NEW SONAR SYSTEM YET, SO-->
<WE MUST BE ON OUR WAY. THESE WATERS ARE CLOSELY GUARDED BY THE BRITISH. IF THEY FIND US SNEAKING THROUGH THEM WITHOUT ALLIED APPROVAL...>
<DON'T BE A COWARD, SMISLOV. THIS IS THE FINEST VESSEL IN THE SOVIET FLEET. OUR SONAR SHIELDING IS BETTER THAN EVEN OUR ALLIES COULD HOPE FOR... >
<NOT THAT THEY'LL EVER HEAR OF IT.>
<FORGIVE ME, BUT WE'RE RISKING SO MUCH ON A FOOL'S ERRAND. WHAT CHANCE DO WE--?>
<COMRADE KARPOV!>
"<THERE'S SOMETHING OUT THERE.>"

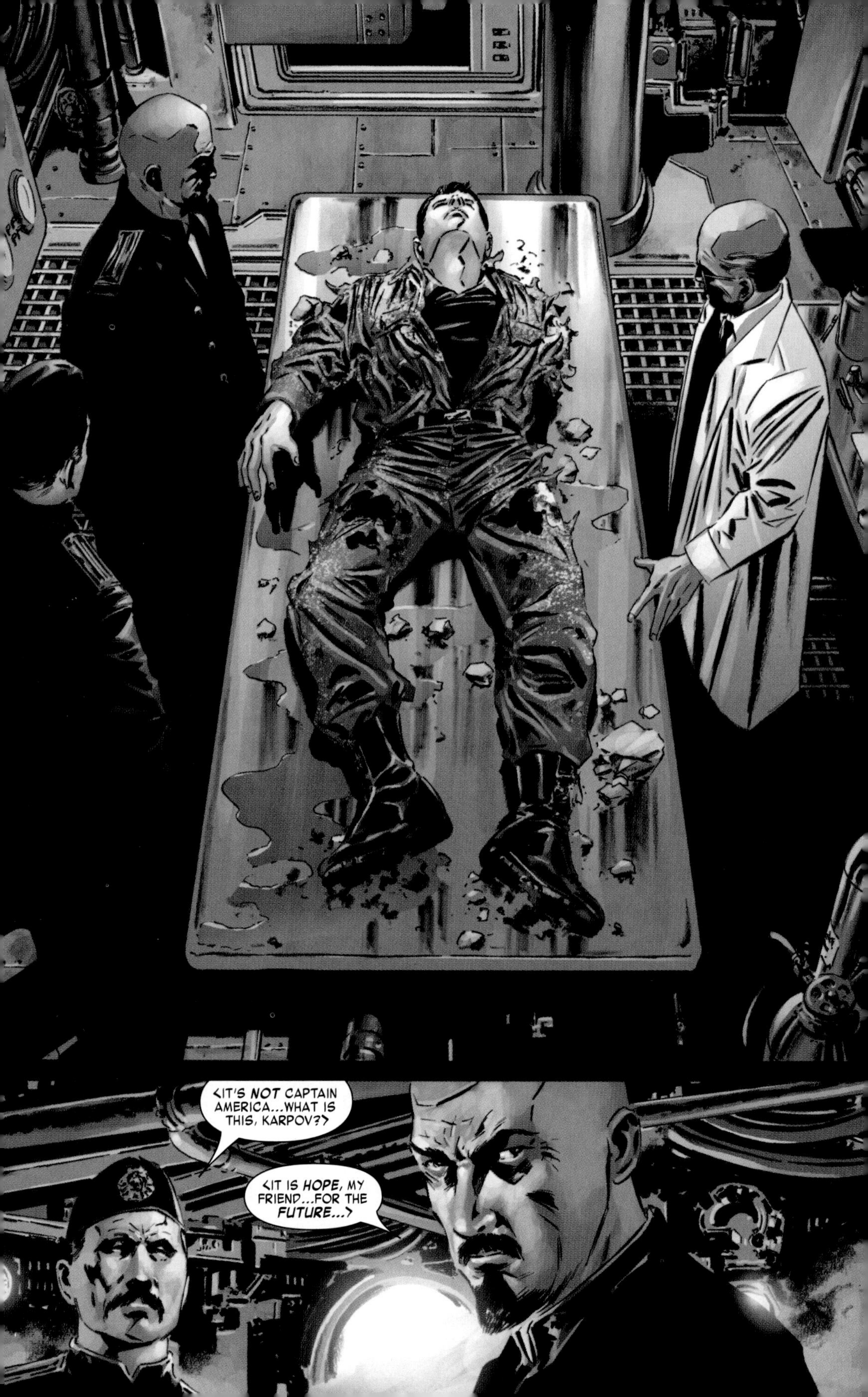
<IT'S NOT CAPTAIN AMERICA...WHAT IS THIS, KARPOV?>
<IT IS HOPE, MY FRIEND...FOR THE FUTURE...>

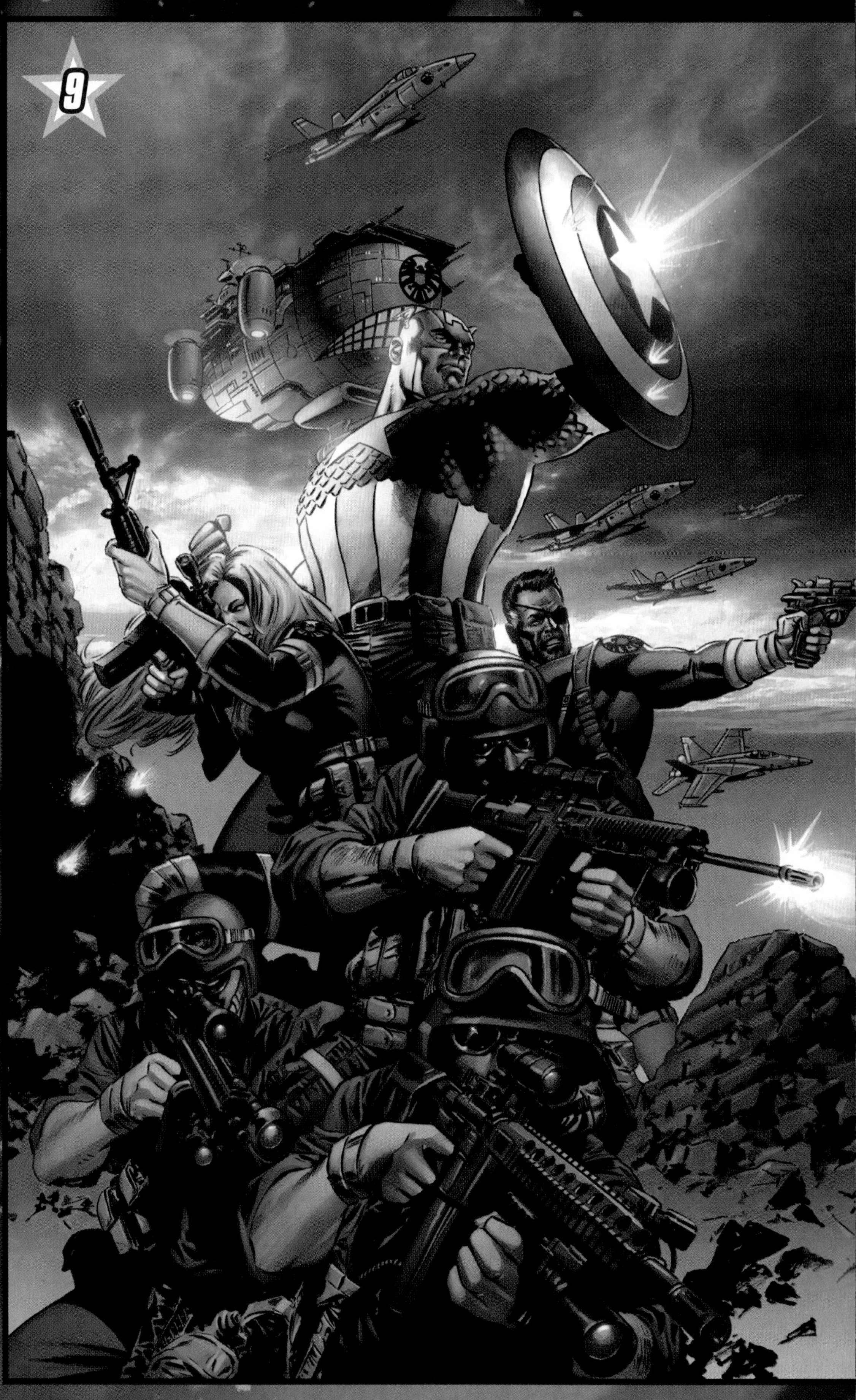
9

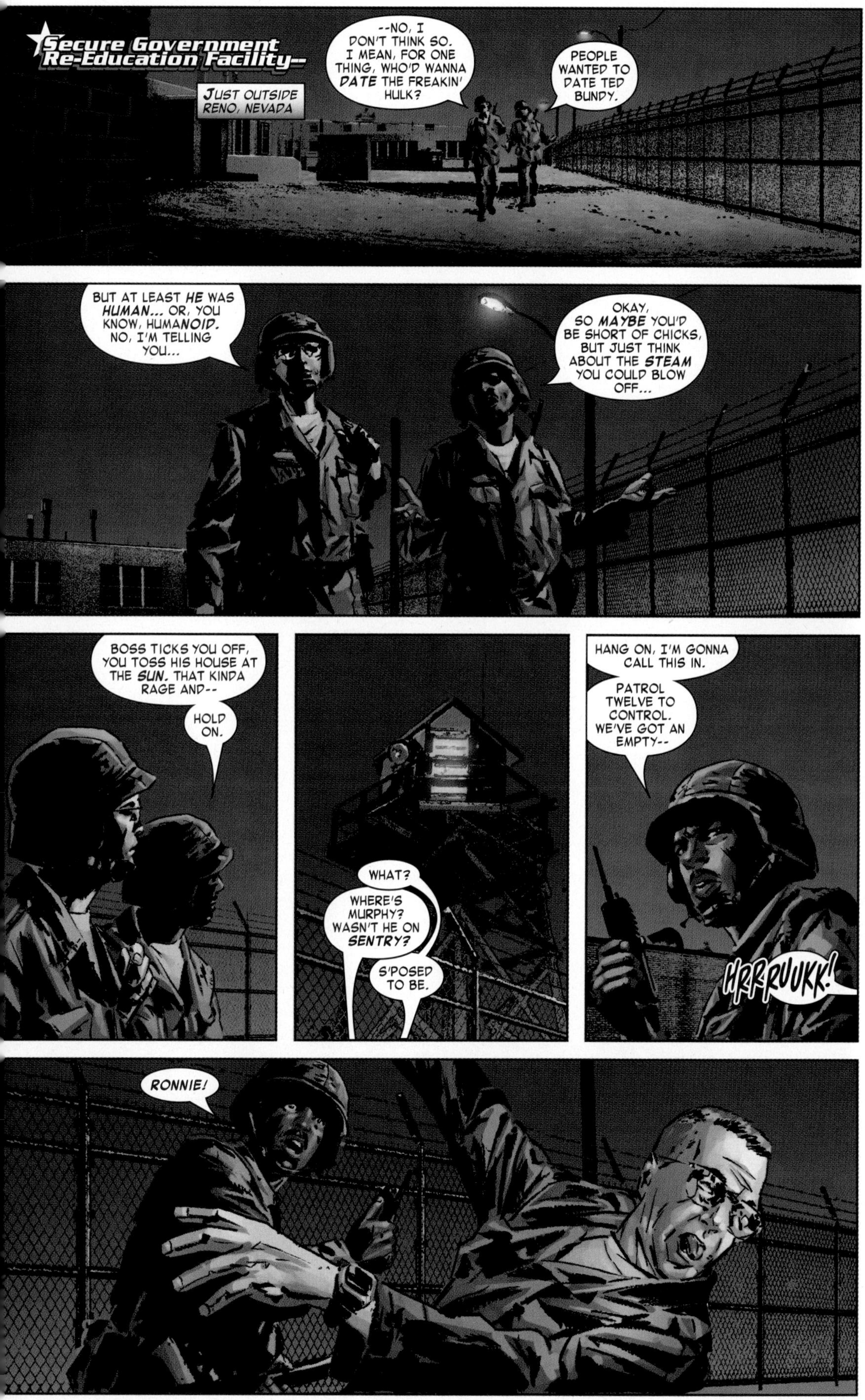

Secure Government Re-Education Facility--
JUST OUTSIDE RENO, NEVADA
--NO, I DON'T THINK SO. I MEAN, FOR ONE THING, WHO'D WANNA DATE THE FREAKIN' HULK?
PEOPLE WANTED TO DATE TED BUNDY.
BUT AT LEAST HE WAS HUMAN... OR, YOU KNOW, HUMANOID. NO, I'M TELLING YOU...
OKAY, SO MAYBE YOU'D BE SHORT OF CHICKS, BUT JUST THINK ABOUT THE STEAM YOU COULD BLOW OFF...
BOSS TICKS YOU OFF, YOU TOSS HIS HOUSE AT THE SUN. THAT KINDA RAGE AND--
HOLD ON.
WHAT?
WHERE'S MURPHY? WASN'T HE ON SENTRY?
S'POSED TO BE.
HANG ON, I'M GONNA CALL THIS IN.
PATROL TWELVE TO CONTROL. WE'VE GOT AN EMPTY--
HRRRUUKK!
RONNIE!

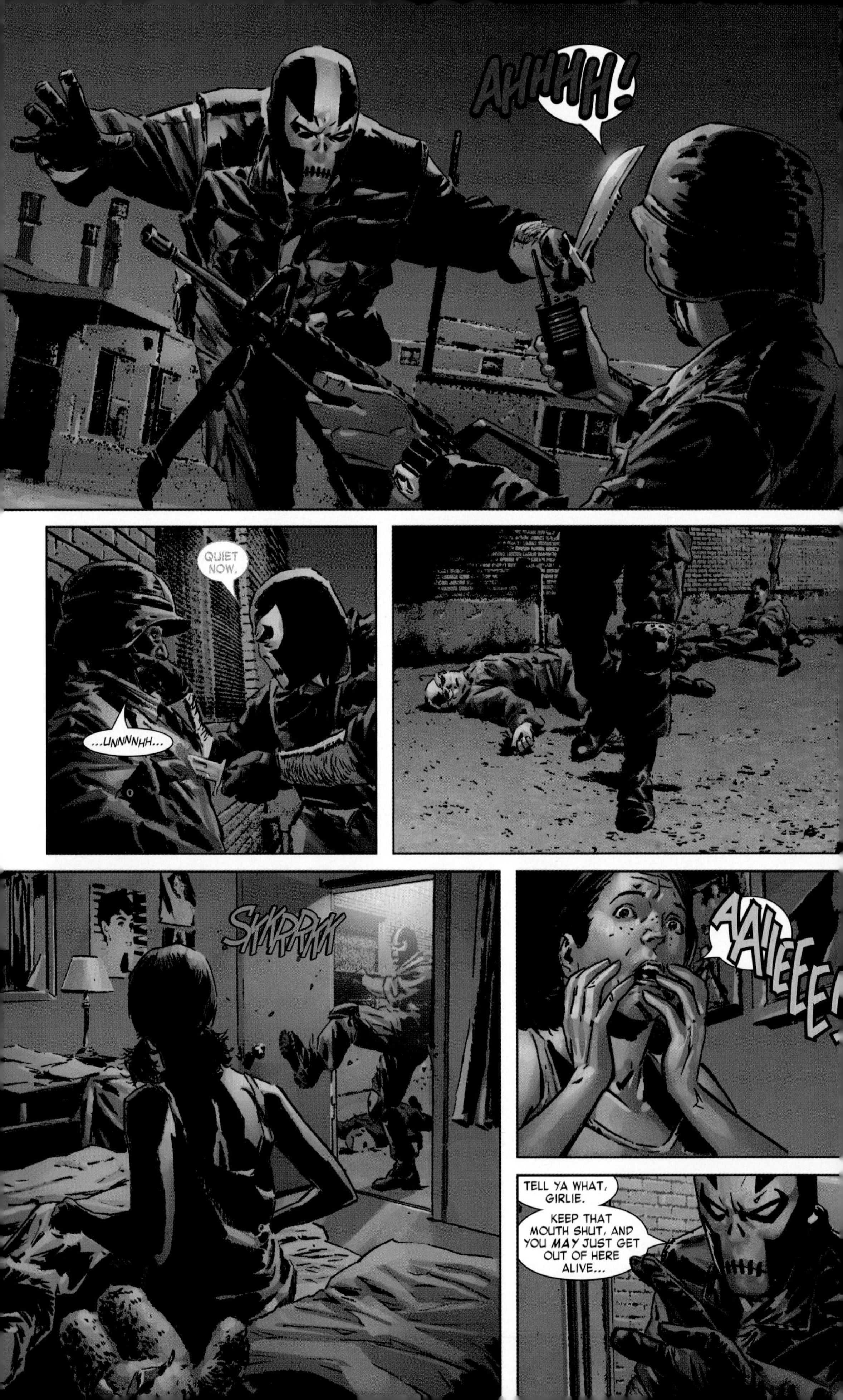
AHHHH!
QUIET NOW.
...UNNNNHH...
SKRRKK
AAIIEEEE!
TELL YA WHAT, GIRLIE.
KEEP THAT MOUTH SHUT, AND YOU MAY JUST GET OUT OF HERE ALIVE...

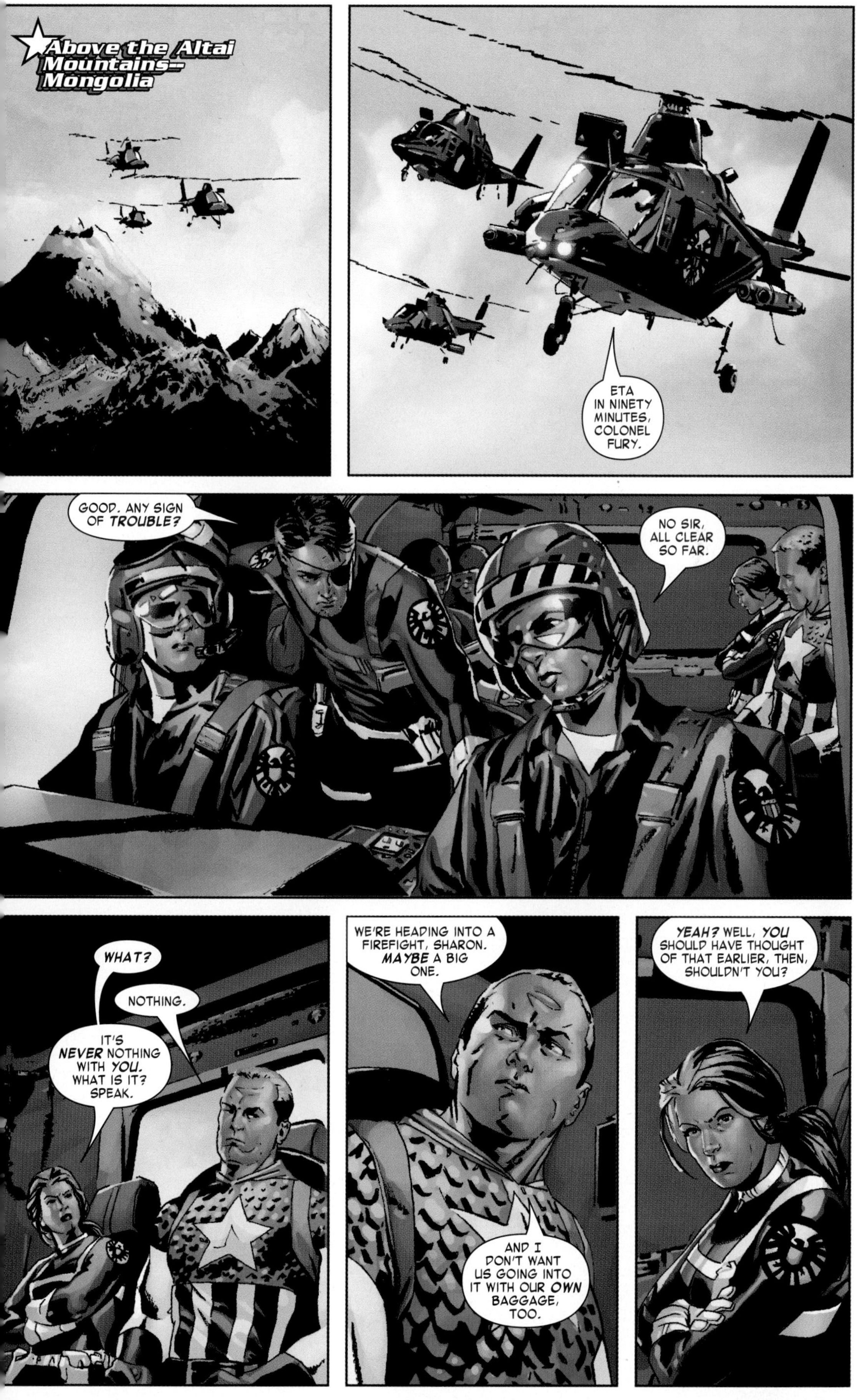
Above the Altai Mountains-- Mongolia
ETA IN NINETY MINUTES, COLONEL FURY.
GOOD. ANY SIGN OF TROUBLE?
NO SIR, ALL CLEAR SO FAR.
WHAT?
NOTHING.
IT'S NEVER NOTHING WITH YOU. WHAT IS IT? SPEAK.
WE'RE HEADING INTO A FIREFIGHT, SHARON. MAYBE A BIG ONE.
AND I DON'T WANT US GOING INTO IT WITH OUR OWN BAGGAGE, TOO.
YEAH? WELL, YOU SHOULD HAVE THOUGHT OF THAT EARLIER, THEN, SHOULDN'T YOU?

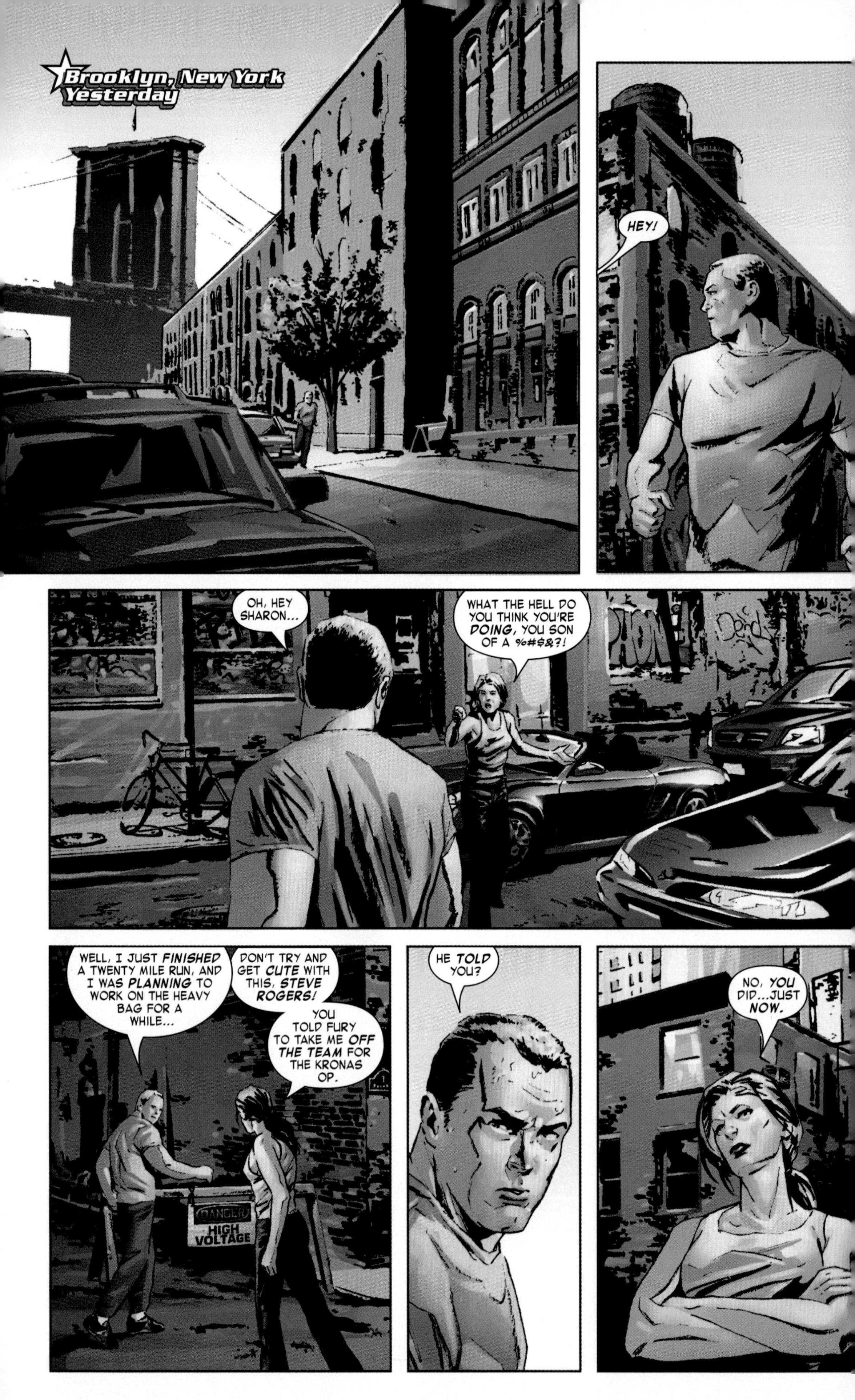
Brooklyn, New York
Yesterday
HEY!
OH, HEY SHARON...
WHAT THE HELL DO YOU THINK YOU'RE DOING, YOU SON OF A %#$&?!
WELL, I JUST FINISHED A TWENTY MILE RUN, AND I WAS PLANNING TO WORK ON THE HEAVY BAG FOR A WHILE...
DON'T TRY AND GET CUTE WITH THIS, STEVE ROGERS!
YOU TOLD FURY TO TAKE ME OFF THE TEAM FOR THE KRONAS OP.
DANGER
HIGH VOLTAGE
HE TOLD YOU?
NO, YOU DID...JUST NOW.

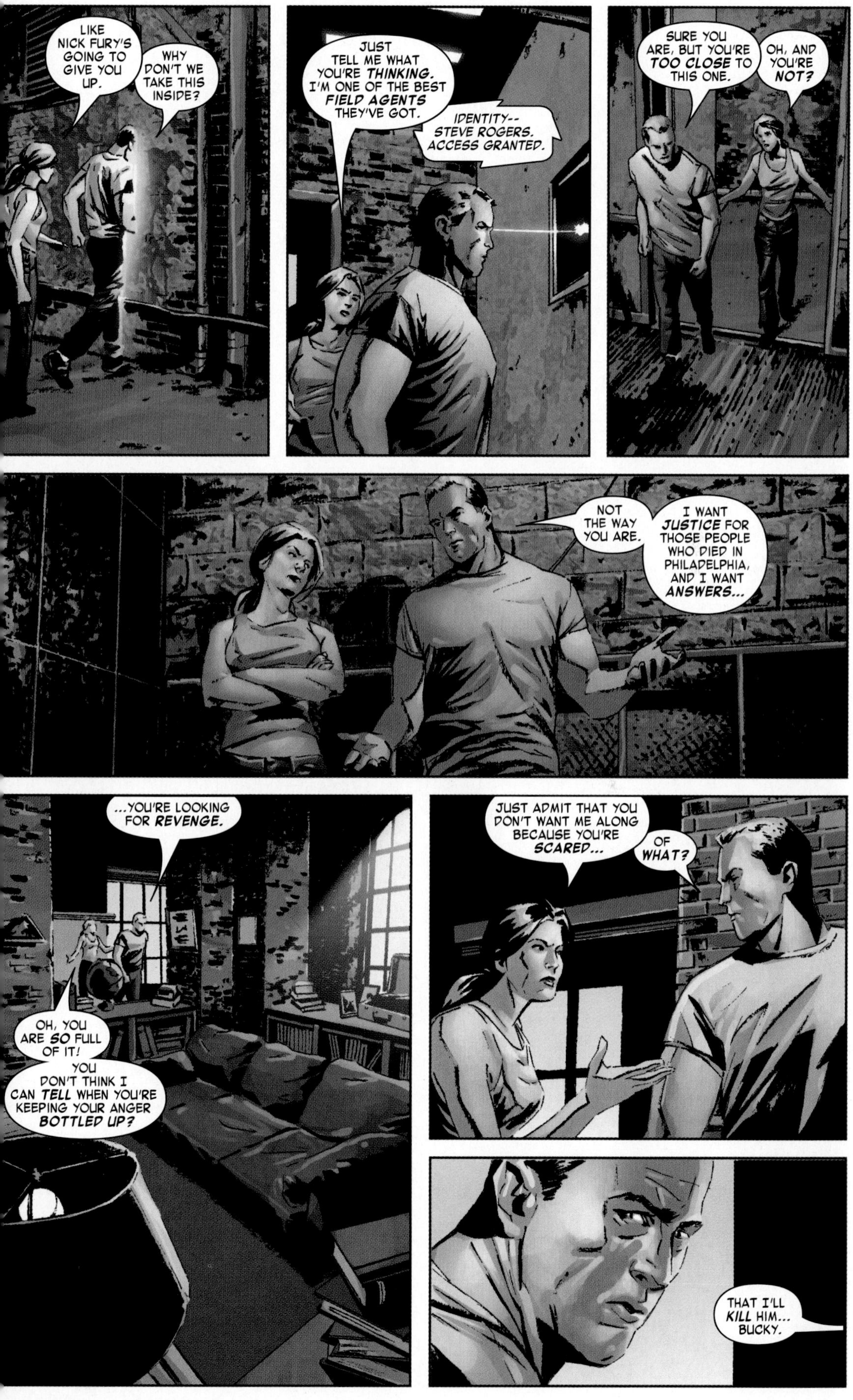
LIKE NICK FURY'S GOING TO GIVE YOU UP.
WHY DON'T WE TAKE THIS INSIDE?
JUST TELL ME WHAT YOU'RE THINKING. I'M ONE OF THE BEST FIELD AGENTS THEY'VE GOT.
IDENTITY-- STEVE ROGERS. ACCESS GRANTED.
SURE YOU ARE, BUT YOU'RE TOO CLOSE TO THIS ONE.
OH, AND YOU'RE NOT?
NOT THE WAY YOU ARE.
I WANT JUSTICE FOR THOSE PEOPLE WHO DIED IN PHILADELPHIA, AND I WANT ANSWERS...
...YOU'RE LOOKING FOR REVENGE.
OH, YOU ARE SO FULL OF IT!
YOU DON'T THINK I CAN TELL WHEN YOU'RE KEEPING YOUR ANGER BOTTLED UP?
JUST ADMIT THAT YOU DON'T WANT ME ALONG BECAUSE YOU'RE SCARED...
OF WHAT?
THAT I'LL KILL HIM... BUCKY.

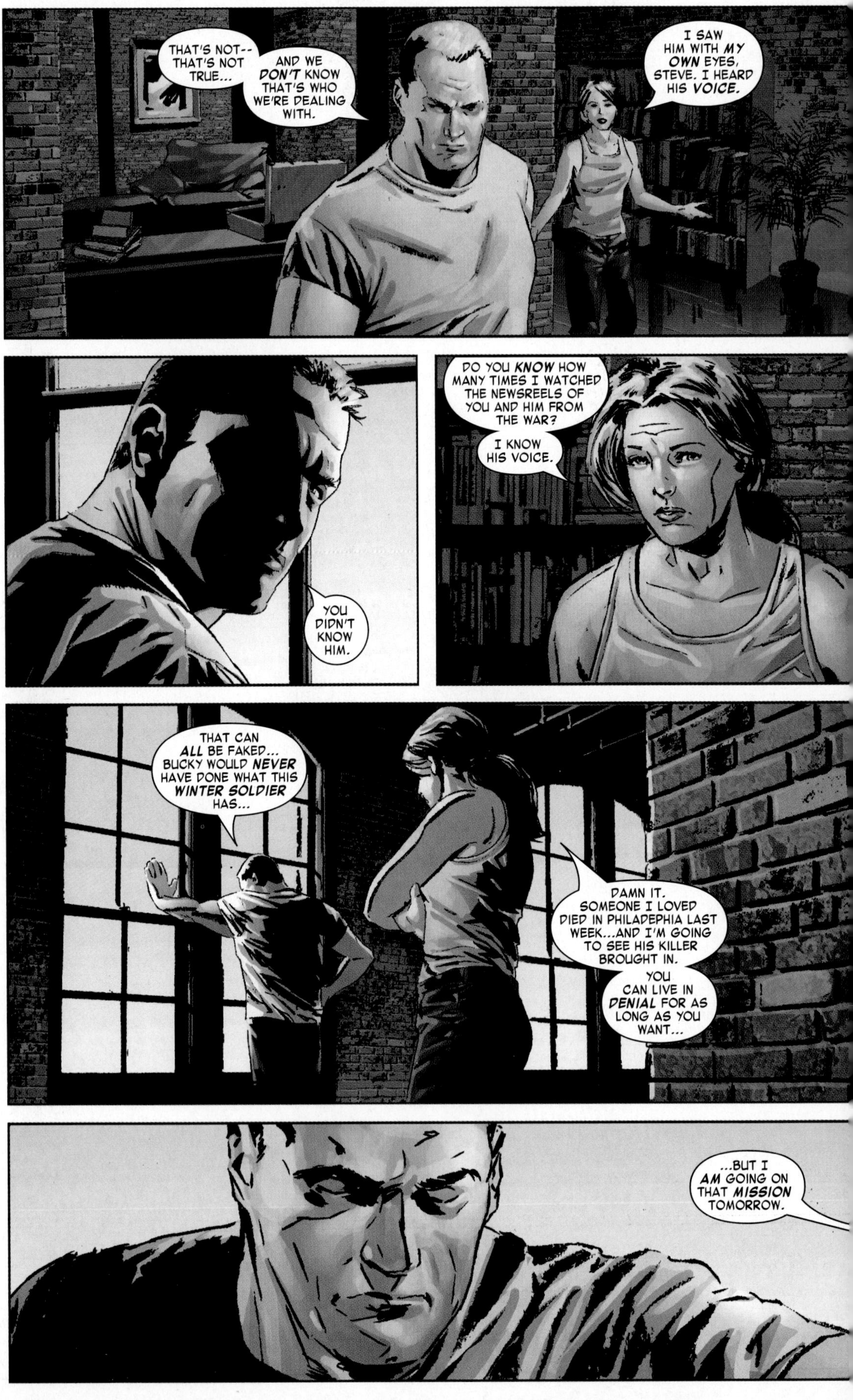
THAT'S NOT-- THAT'S NOT TRUE...
AND WE DON'T KNOW THAT'S WHO WE'RE DEALING WITH.
I SAW HIM WITH MY OWN EYES, STEVE. I HEARD HIS VOICE.
DO YOU KNOW HOW MANY TIMES I WATCHED THE NEWSREELS OF YOU AND HIM FROM THE WAR?
I KNOW HIS VOICE.
YOU DIDN'T KNOW HIM.
THAT CAN ALL BE FAKED... BUCKY WOULD NEVER HAVE DONE WHAT THIS WINTER SOLDIER HAS...
DAMN IT. SOMEONE I LOVED DIED IN PHILADEPHIA LAST WEEK...AND I'M GOING TO SEE HIS KILLER BROUGHT IN.
YOU CAN LIVE IN DENIAL FOR AS LONG AS YOU WANT...
...BUT I AM GOING ON THAT MISSION TOMORROW.

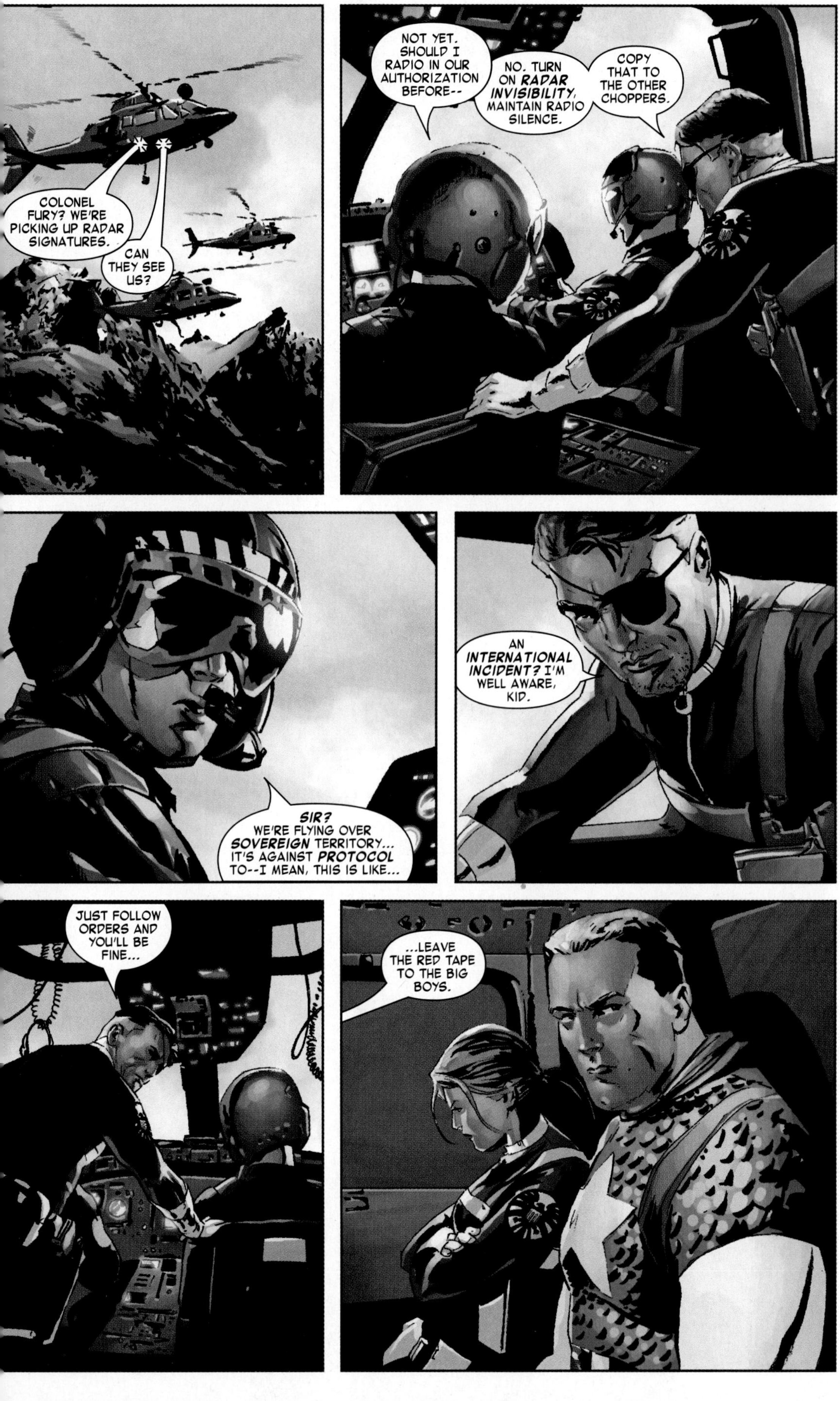
COLONEL FURY? WE'RE PICKING UP RADAR SIGNATURES.
CAN THEY SEE US?
NOT YET. SHOULD I RADIO IN OUR AUTHORIZATION BEFORE--
NO. TURN ON RADAR INVISIBILITY, MAINTAIN RADIO SILENCE.
COPY THAT TO THE OTHER CHOPPERS.
SIR? WE'RE FLYING OVER SOVEREIGN TERRITORY... IT'S AGAINST PROTOCOL TO--I MEAN, THIS IS LIKE...
AN INTERNATIONAL INCIDENT? I'M WELL AWARE, KID.
JUST FOLLOW ORDERS AND YOU'LL BE FINE...
...LEAVE THE RED TAPE TO THE BIG BOYS.

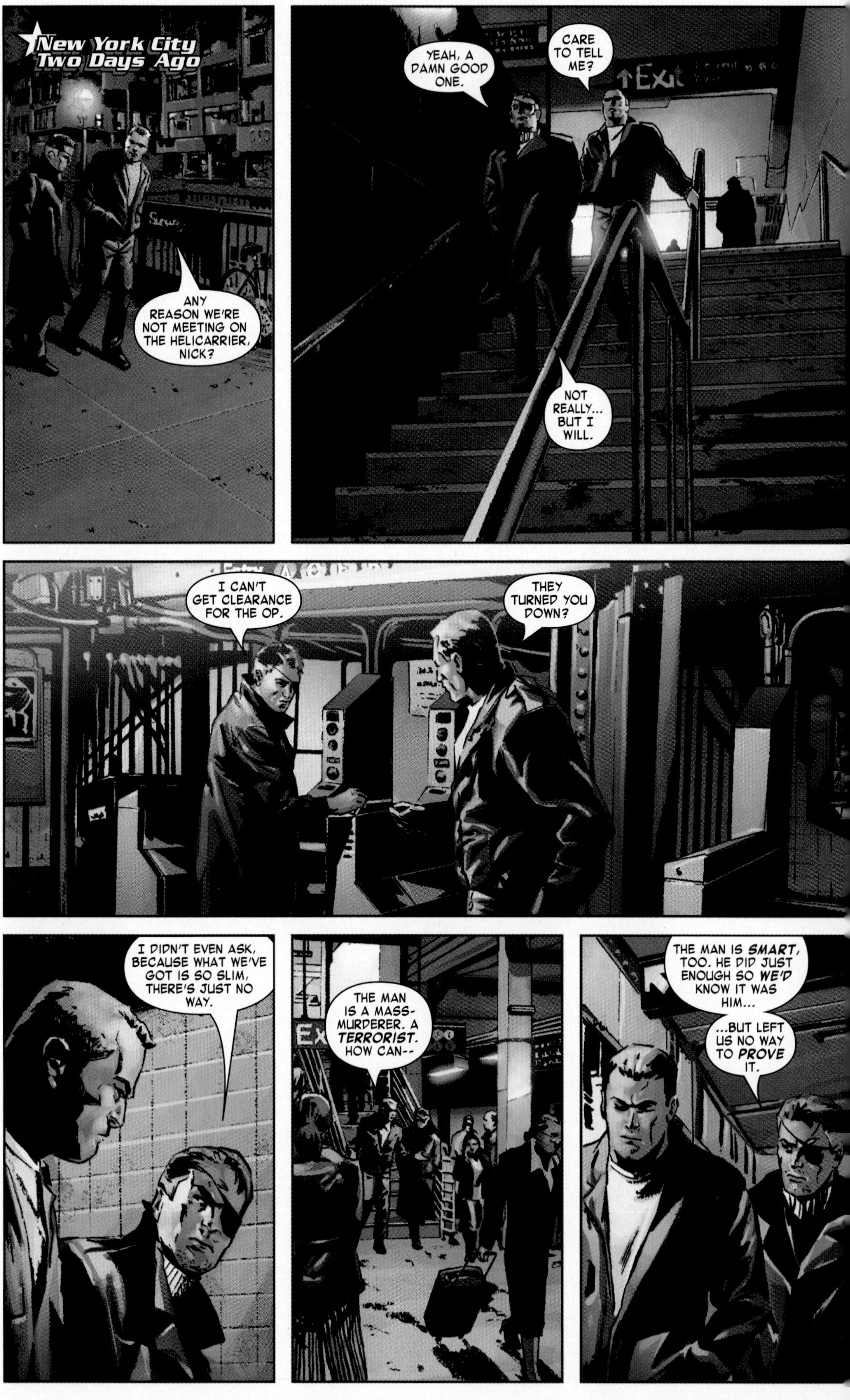
New York City Two Days Ago
ANY REASON WE'RE NOT MEETING ON THE HELICARRIER, NICK?
YEAH, A DAMN GOOD ONE.
CARE TO TELL ME?
NOT REALLY... BUT I WILL.
I CAN'T GET CLEARANCE FOR THE OP.
THEY TURNED YOU DOWN?
I DIDN'T EVEN ASK, BECAUSE WHAT WE'VE GOT IS SO SLIM, THERE'S JUST NO WAY.
THE MAN IS A MASS-MURDERER. A *TERRORIST*. HOW CAN--
THE MAN IS *SMART*, TOO. HE DID JUST ENOUGH SO *WE'D* KNOW IT WAS HIM...
...BUT LEFT US NO WAY TO *PROVE* IT.

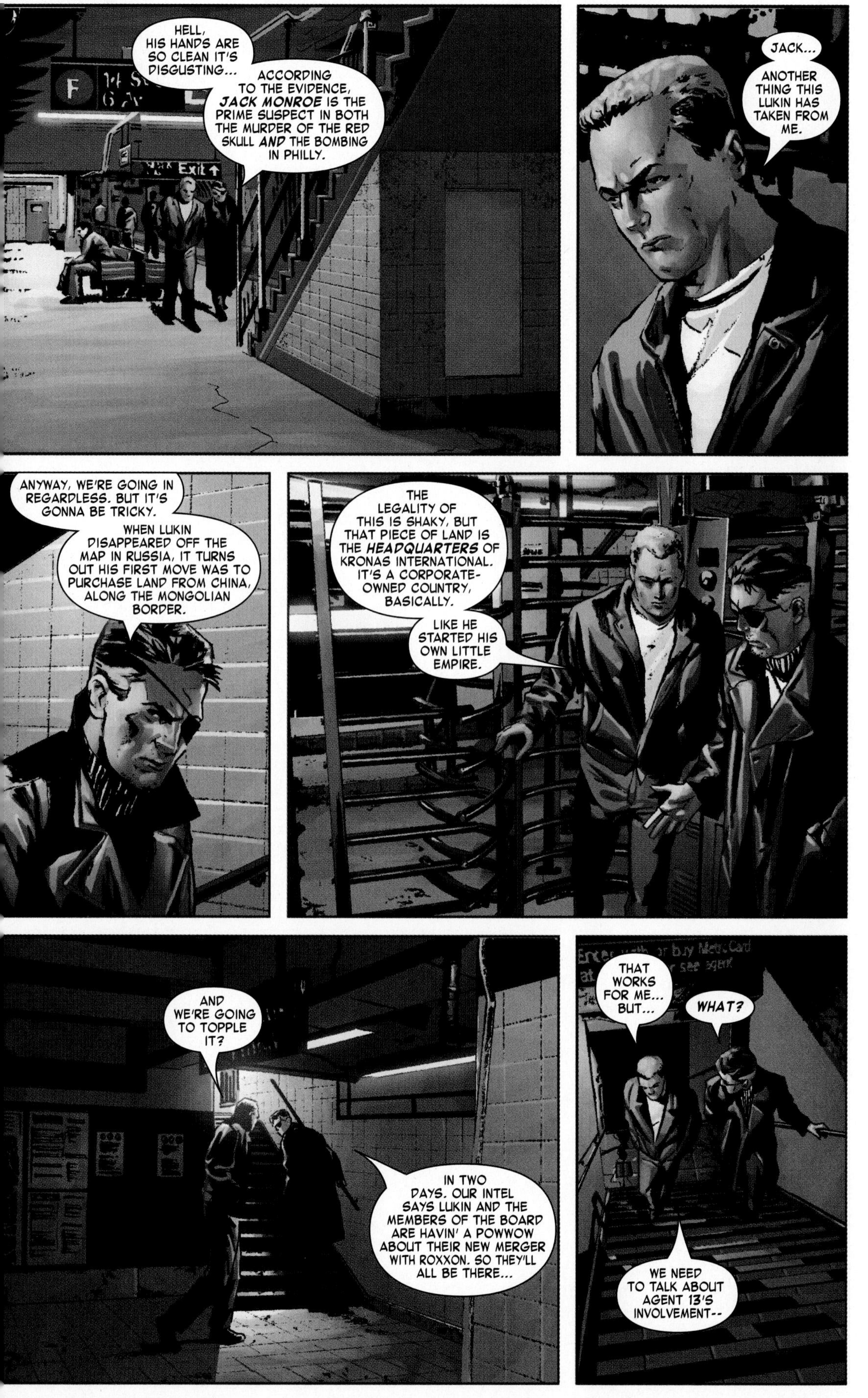
HELL, HIS HANDS ARE SO CLEAN IT'S DISGUSTING...
ACCORDING TO THE EVIDENCE, JACK MONROE IS THE PRIME SUSPECT IN BOTH THE MURDER OF THE RED SKULL AND THE BOMBING IN PHILLY.
JACK...
ANOTHER THING THIS LUKIN HAS TAKEN FROM ME.
ANYWAY, WE'RE GOING IN REGARDLESS. BUT IT'S GONNA BE TRICKY.
WHEN LUKIN DISAPPEARED OFF THE MAP IN RUSSIA, IT TURNS OUT HIS FIRST MOVE WAS TO PURCHASE LAND FROM CHINA, ALONG THE MONGOLIAN BORDER.
THE LEGALITY OF THIS IS SHAKY, BUT THAT PIECE OF LAND IS THE HEADQUARTERS OF KRONAS INTERNATIONAL. IT'S A CORPORATE-OWNED COUNTRY, BASICALLY.
LIKE HE STARTED HIS OWN LITTLE EMPIRE.
AND WE'RE GOING TO TOPPLE IT?
IN TWO DAYS. OUR INTEL SAYS LUKIN AND THE MEMBERS OF THE BOARD ARE HAVIN' A POWWOW ABOUT THEIR NEW MERGER WITH ROXXON. SO THEY'LL ALL BE THERE...
THAT WORKS FOR ME... BUT...
WHAT?
WE NEED TO TALK ABOUT AGENT 13'S INVOLVEMENT--

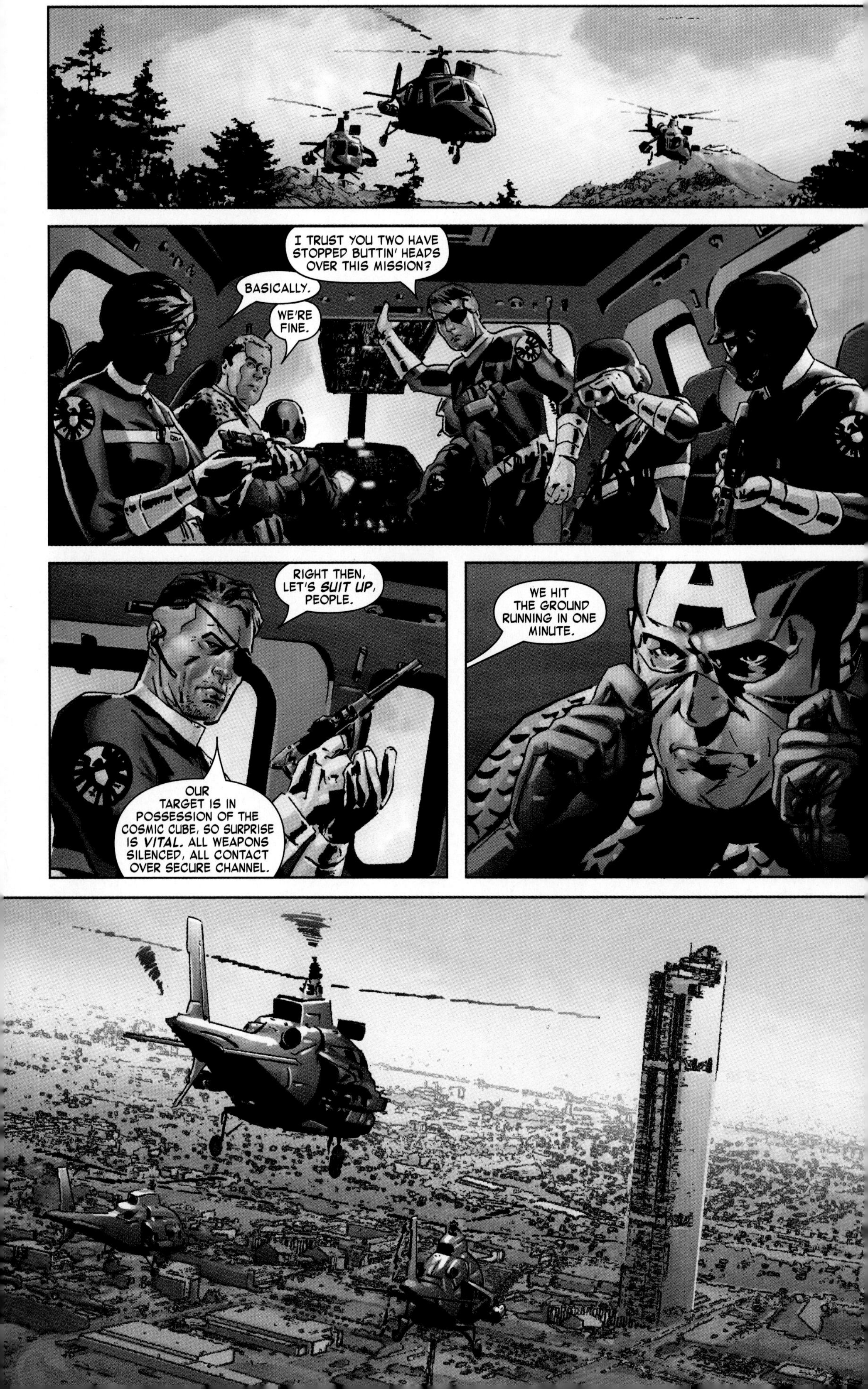
I TRUST YOU TWO HAVE STOPPED BUTTIN' HEADS OVER THIS MISSION?
BASICALLY.
WE'RE FINE.
RIGHT THEN, LET'S *SUIT UP*, PEOPLE.
OUR TARGET IS IN POSSESSION OF THE COSMIC CUBE, SO SURPRISE IS *VITAL*. ALL WEAPONS SILENCED, ALL CONTACT OVER SECURE CHANNEL.
WE HIT THE GROUND RUNNING IN ONE MINUTE.

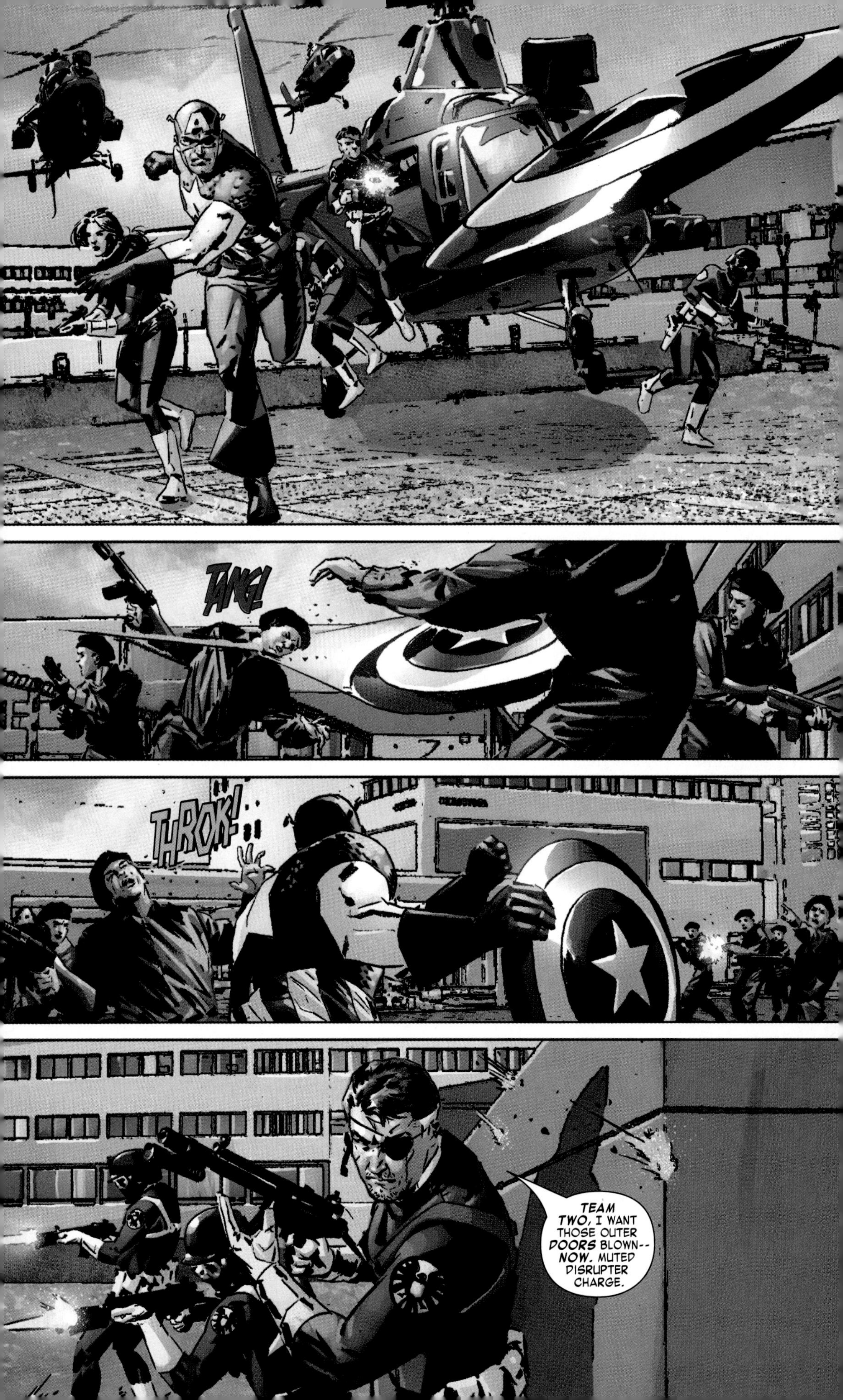

TANG!
THROK!
TEAM TWO, I WANT THOSE OUTER DOORS BLOWN-- NOW. MUTED DISRUPTER CHARGE.

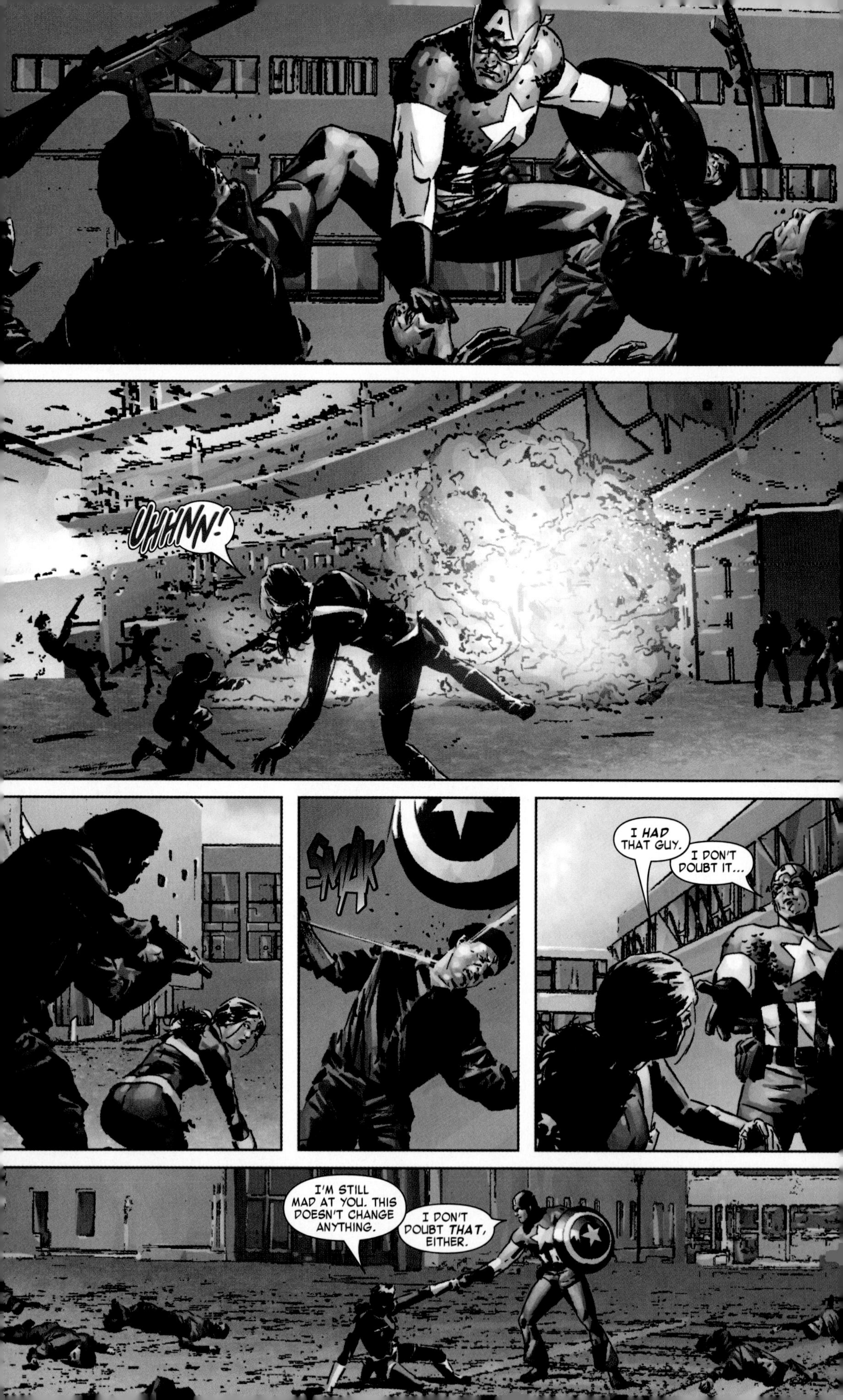
UHHNN!
SMAK
I HAD THAT GUY.
I DON'T DOUBT IT...
I'M STILL MAD AT YOU. THIS DOESN'T CHANGE ANYTHING.
I DON'T DOUBT THAT, EITHER.

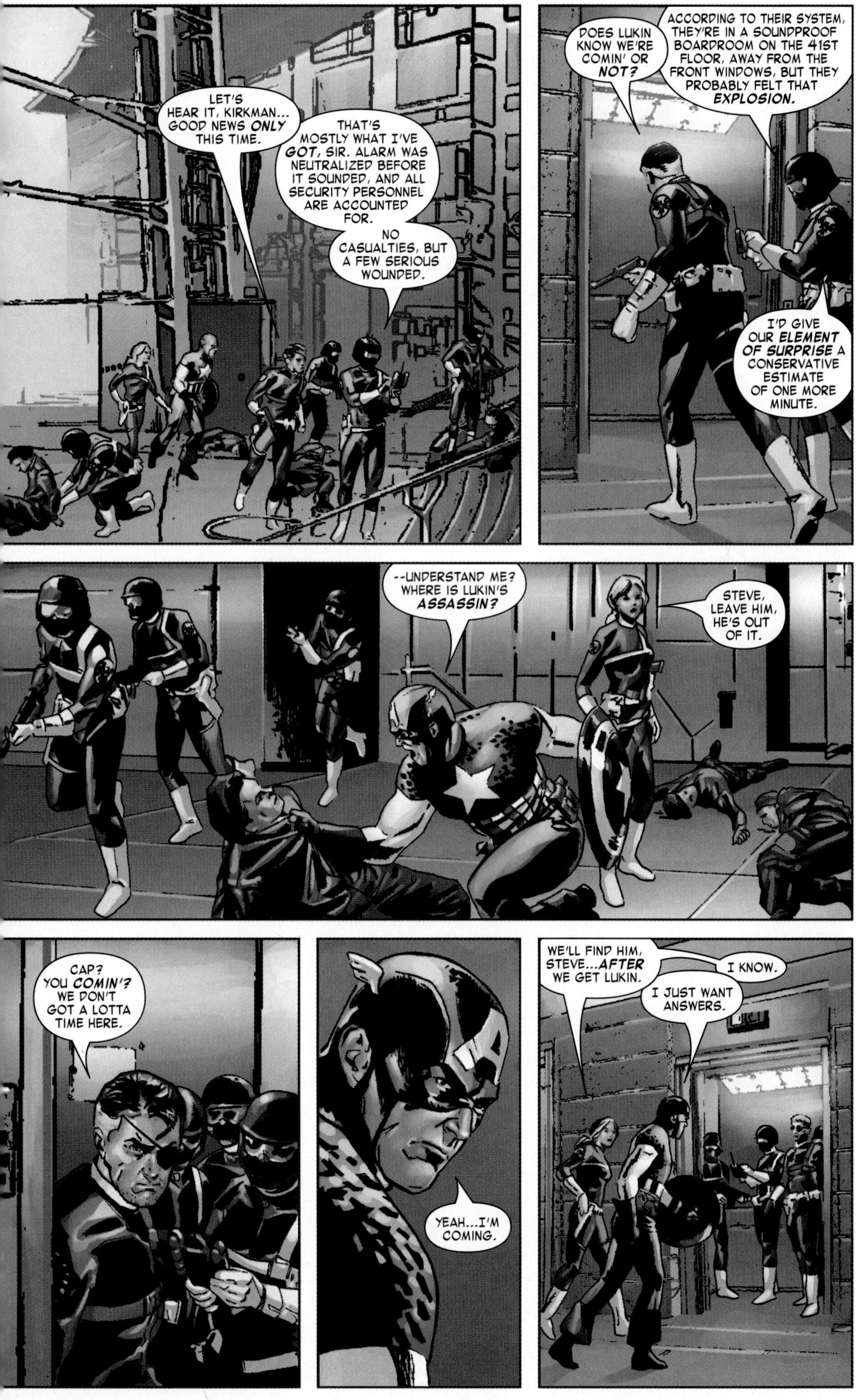
LET'S HEAR IT, KIRKMAN... GOOD NEWS ONLY THIS TIME.
THAT'S MOSTLY WHAT I'VE GOT, SIR. ALARM WAS NEUTRALIZED BEFORE IT SOUNDED, AND ALL SECURITY PERSONNEL ARE ACCOUNTED FOR.
NO CASUALTIES, BUT A FEW SERIOUS WOUNDED.
DOES LUKIN KNOW WE'RE COMIN' OR NOT?
ACCORDING TO THEIR SYSTEM, THEY'RE IN A SOUNDPROOF BOARDROOM ON THE 41ST FLOOR, AWAY FROM THE FRONT WINDOWS, BUT THEY PROBABLY FELT THAT EXPLOSION.
I'D GIVE OUR ELEMENT OF SURPRISE A CONSERVATIVE ESTIMATE OF ONE MORE MINUTE.
--UNDERSTAND ME? WHERE IS LUKIN'S ASSASSIN?
STEVE, LEAVE HIM, HE'S OUT OF IT.
CAP? YOU COMIN'? WE DON'T GOT A LOTTA TIME HERE.
YEAH...I'M COMING.
WE'LL FIND HIM, STEVE...AFTER WE GET LUKIN.
I KNOW.
I JUST WANT ANSWERS.

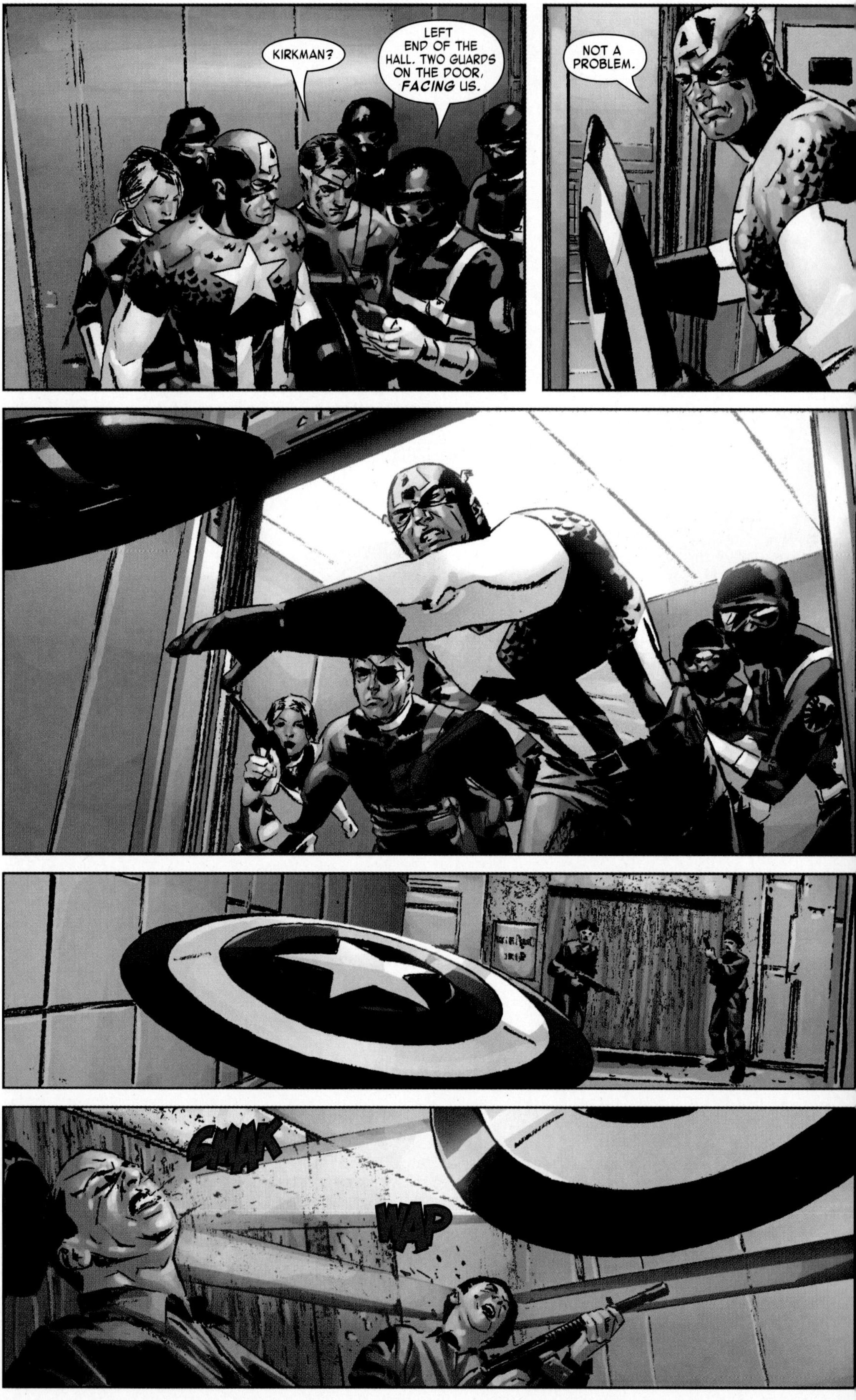
KIRKMAN?
LEFT END OF THE HALL. TWO GUARDS ON THE DOOR, *FACING* US.
NOT A PROBLEM.
SMAK
WAP

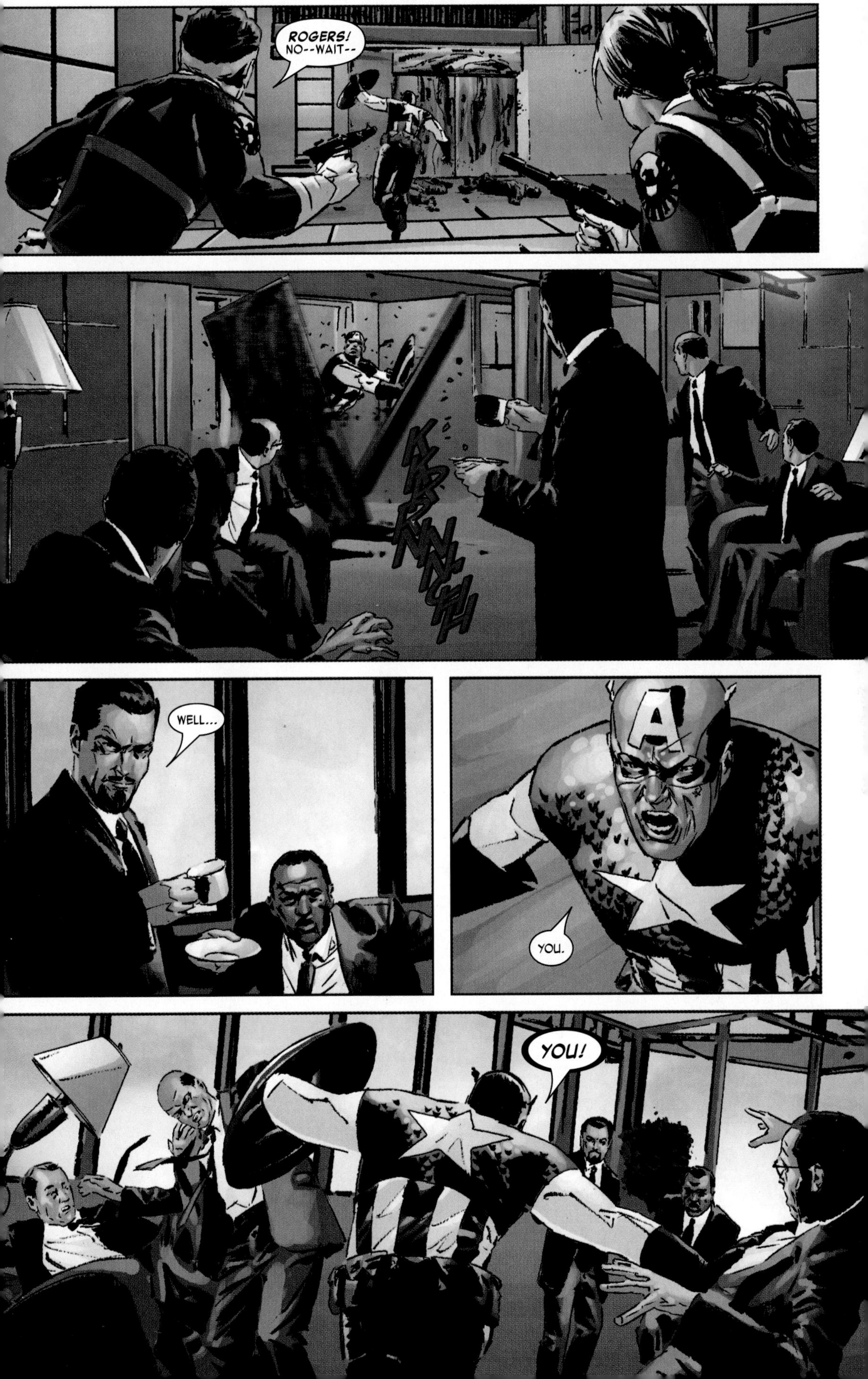
ROGERS! NO--WAIT--
WELL...
YOU.
YOU!

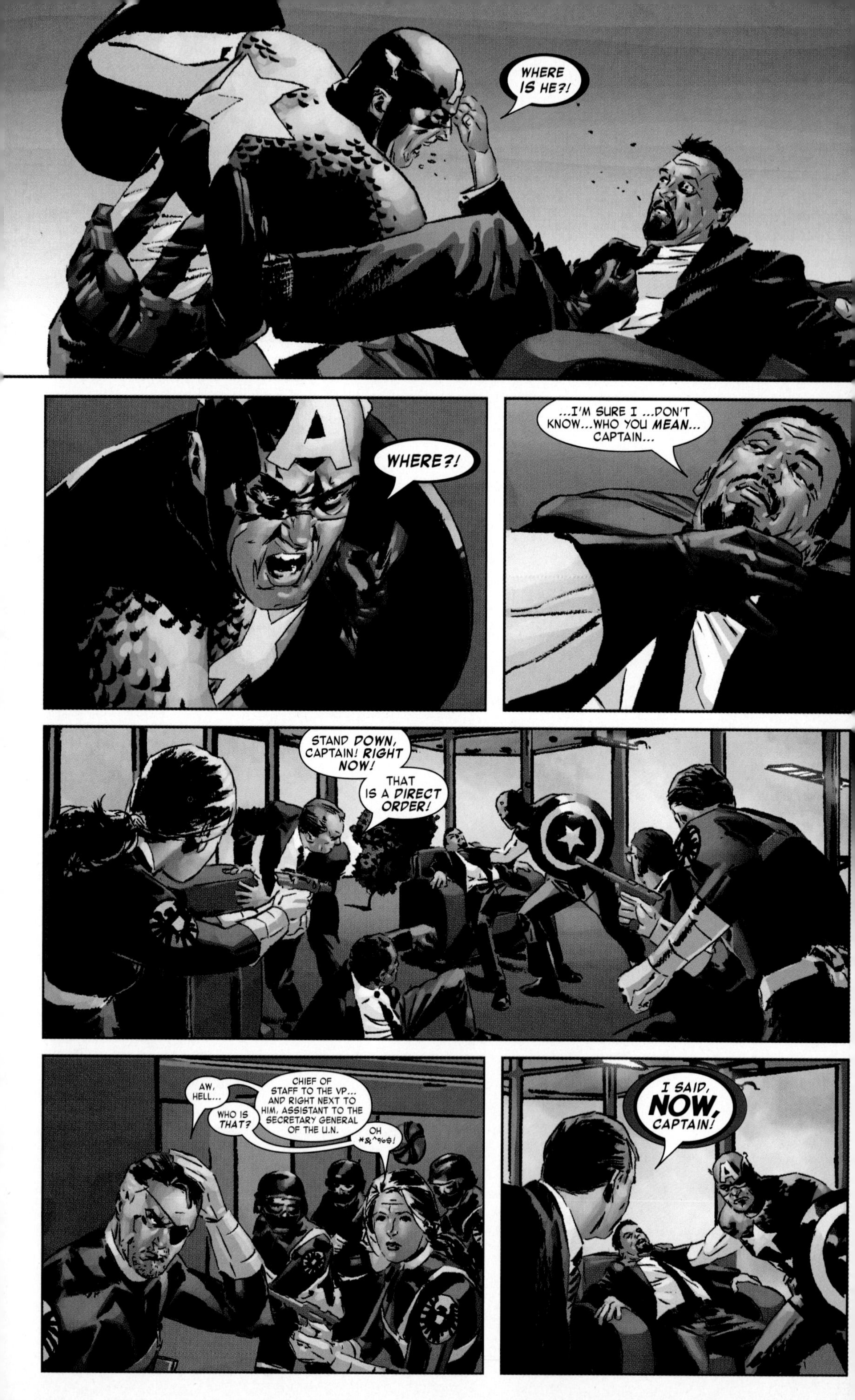
WHERE IS HE?!
WHERE?!
...I'M SURE I ...DON'T KNOW...WHO YOU MEAN... CAPTAIN...
STAND DOWN, CAPTAIN! RIGHT NOW!
THAT IS A DIRECT ORDER!
AW, HELL...
WHO IS THAT?
CHIEF OF STAFF TO THE VP... AND RIGHT NEXT TO HIM, ASSISTANT TO THE SECRETARY GENERAL OF THE U.N.
OH *&^%$!
I SAID, NOW, CAPTAIN!

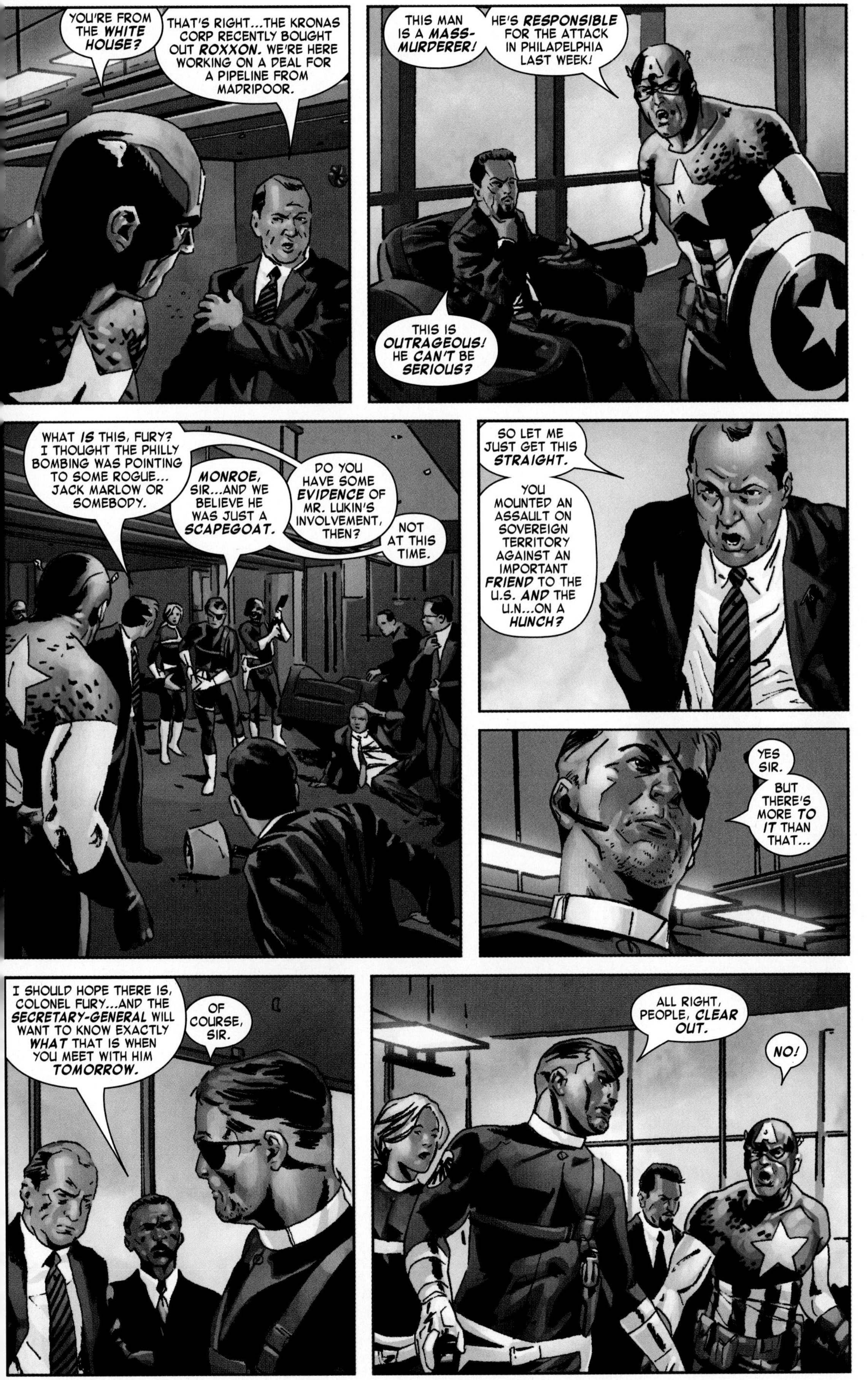
YOU'RE FROM THE WHITE HOUSE?
THAT'S RIGHT...THE KRONAS CORP RECENTLY BOUGHT OUT ROXXON. WE'RE HERE WORKING ON A DEAL FOR A PIPELINE FROM MADRIPOOR.
THIS MAN IS A MASS-MURDERER!
HE'S RESPONSIBLE FOR THE ATTACK IN PHILADELPHIA LAST WEEK!
THIS IS OUTRAGEOUS! HE CAN'T BE SERIOUS?
WHAT IS THIS, FURY? I THOUGHT THE PHILLY BOMBING WAS POINTING TO SOME ROGUE... JACK MARLOW OR SOMEBODY.
MONROE, SIR...AND WE BELIEVE HE WAS JUST A SCAPEGOAT.
DO YOU HAVE SOME EVIDENCE OF MR. LUKIN'S INVOLVEMENT, THEN?
NOT AT THIS TIME.
SO LET ME JUST GET THIS STRAIGHT.
YOU MOUNTED AN ASSAULT ON SOVEREIGN TERRITORY AGAINST AN IMPORTANT FRIEND TO THE U.S. AND THE U.N...ON A HUNCH?
YES SIR.
BUT THERE'S MORE TO IT THAN THAT...
I SHOULD HOPE THERE IS, COLONEL FURY...AND THE SECRETARY-GENERAL WILL WANT TO KNOW EXACTLY WHAT THAT IS WHEN YOU MEET WITH HIM TOMORROW.
OF COURSE, SIR.
ALL RIGHT, PEOPLE, CLEAR OUT.
NO!

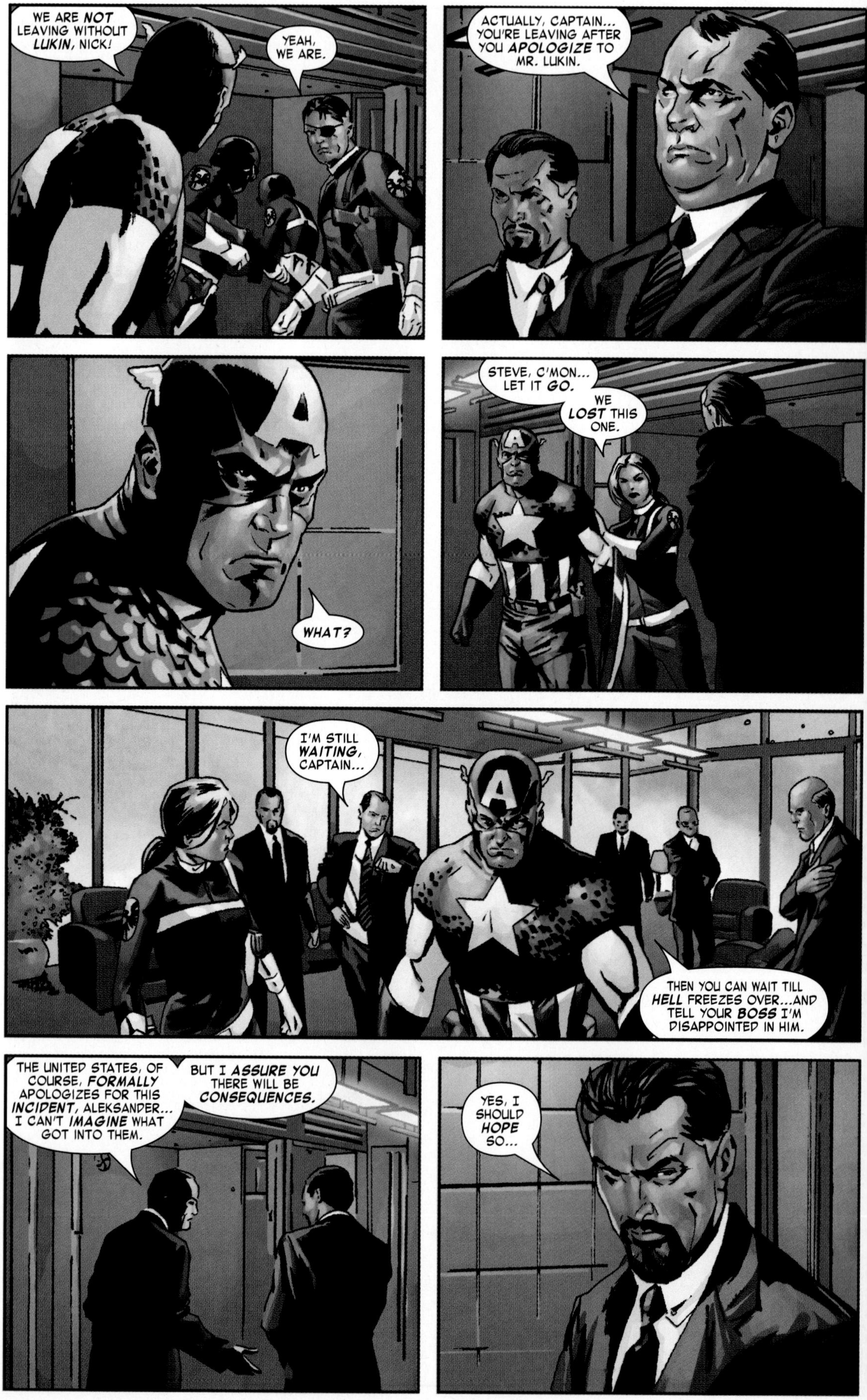
WE ARE NOT LEAVING WITHOUT LUKIN, NICK!
YEAH, WE ARE.
ACTUALLY, CAPTAIN... YOU'RE LEAVING AFTER YOU APOLOGIZE TO MR. LUKIN.
WHAT?
STEVE, C'MON... LET IT GO.
WE LOST THIS ONE.
I'M STILL WAITING, CAPTAIN...
THEN YOU CAN WAIT TILL HELL FREEZES OVER...AND TELL YOUR BOSS I'M DISAPPOINTED IN HIM.
THE UNITED STATES, OF COURSE, FORMALLY APOLOGIZES FOR THIS INCIDENT, ALEKSANDER... I CAN'T IMAGINE WHAT GOT INTO THEM.
BUT I ASSURE YOU THERE WILL BE CONSEQUENCES.
YES, I SHOULD HOPE SO...

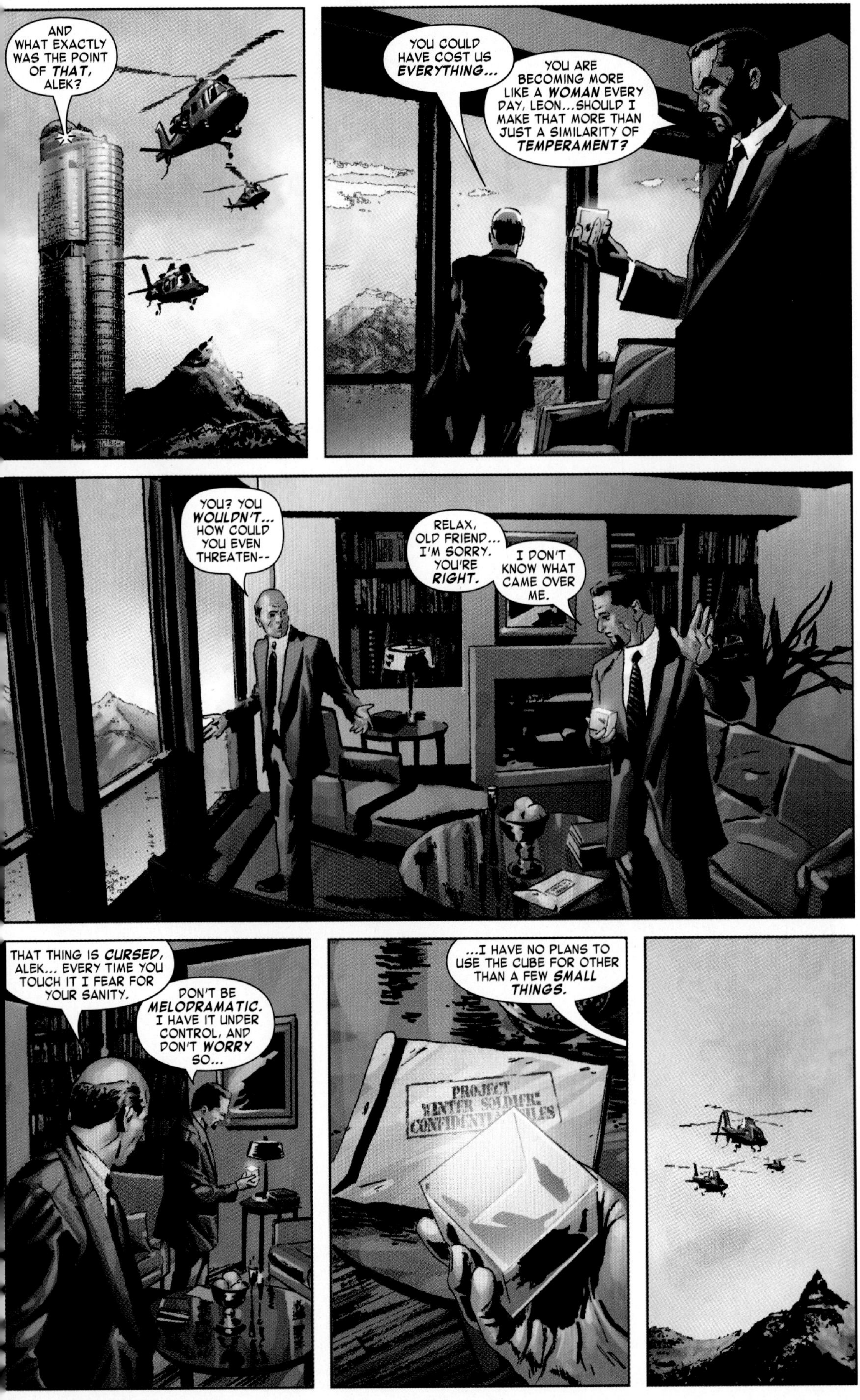
AND WHAT EXACTLY WAS THE POINT OF *THAT,* ALEK?
YOU COULD HAVE COST US *EVERYTHING...*
YOU ARE BECOMING MORE LIKE A *WOMAN* EVERY DAY, LEON...SHOULD I MAKE THAT MORE THAN JUST A SIMILARITY OF *TEMPERAMENT?*
YOU? YOU *WOULDN'T...* HOW COULD YOU EVEN THREATEN--
RELAX, OLD FRIEND... I'M SORRY. YOU'RE *RIGHT.*
I DON'T KNOW WHAT CAME OVER ME.
THAT THING IS *CURSED,* ALEK... EVERY TIME YOU TOUCH IT I FEAR FOR YOUR SANITY.
DON'T BE *MELODRAMATIC.* I HAVE IT UNDER CONTROL, AND DON'T *WORRY* SO...
...I HAVE NO PLANS TO USE THE CUBE FOR OTHER THAN A FEW *SMALL THINGS.*
PROJECT WINTER SOLDIER: CONFIDENTIAL FILES

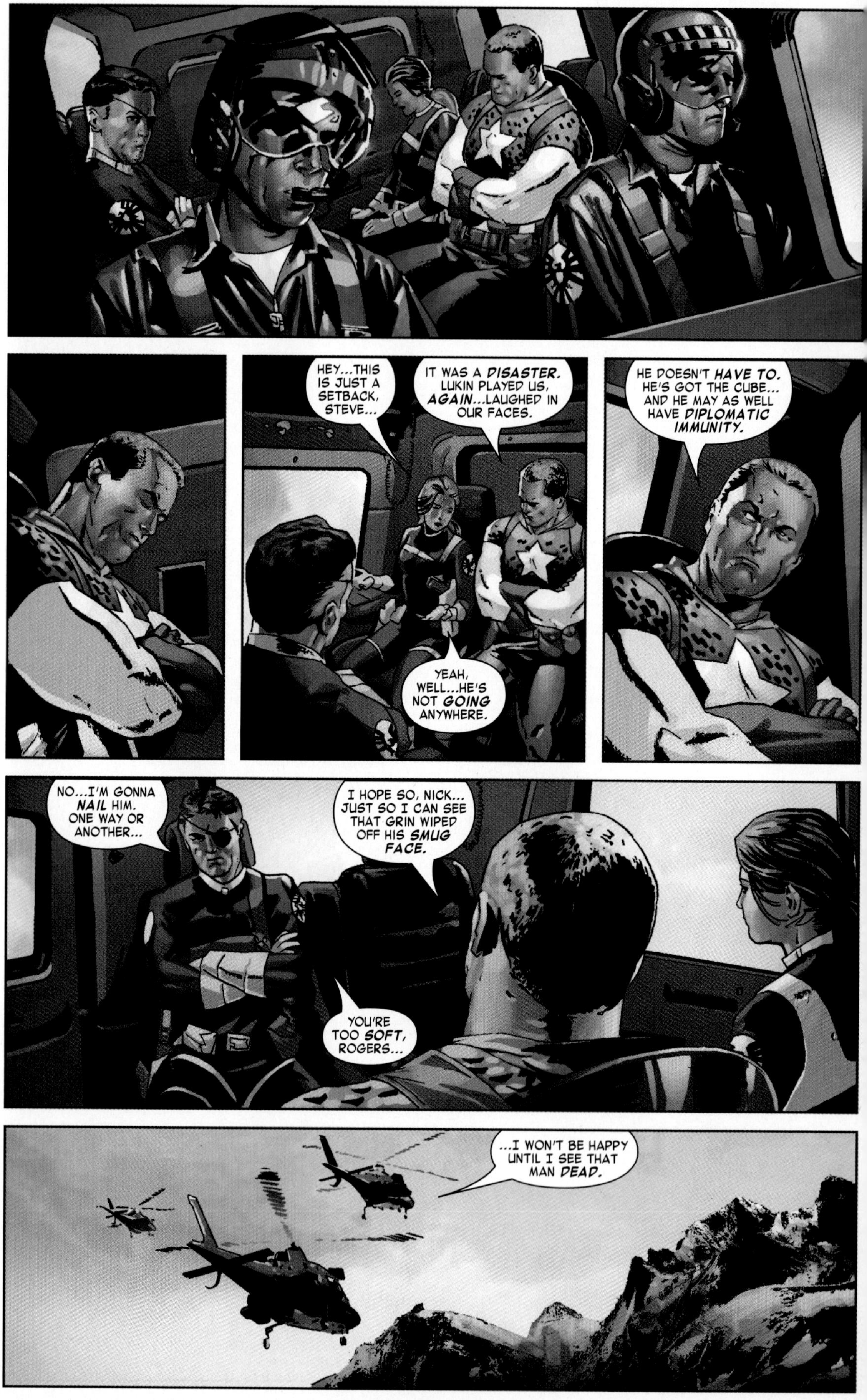
HEY...THIS IS JUST A SETBACK, STEVE...
IT WAS A DISASTER. LUKIN PLAYED US, AGAIN...LAUGHED IN OUR FACES.
YEAH, WELL...HE'S NOT GOING ANYWHERE.
HE DOESN'T HAVE TO. HE'S GOT THE CUBE... AND HE MAY AS WELL HAVE DIPLOMATIC IMMUNITY.
NO...I'M GONNA NAIL HIM. ONE WAY OR ANOTHER...
I HOPE SO, NICK... JUST SO I CAN SEE THAT GRIN WIPED OFF HIS SMUG FACE.
YOU'RE TOO SOFT, ROGERS...
...I WON'T BE HAPPY UNTIL I SEE THAT MAN DEAD.

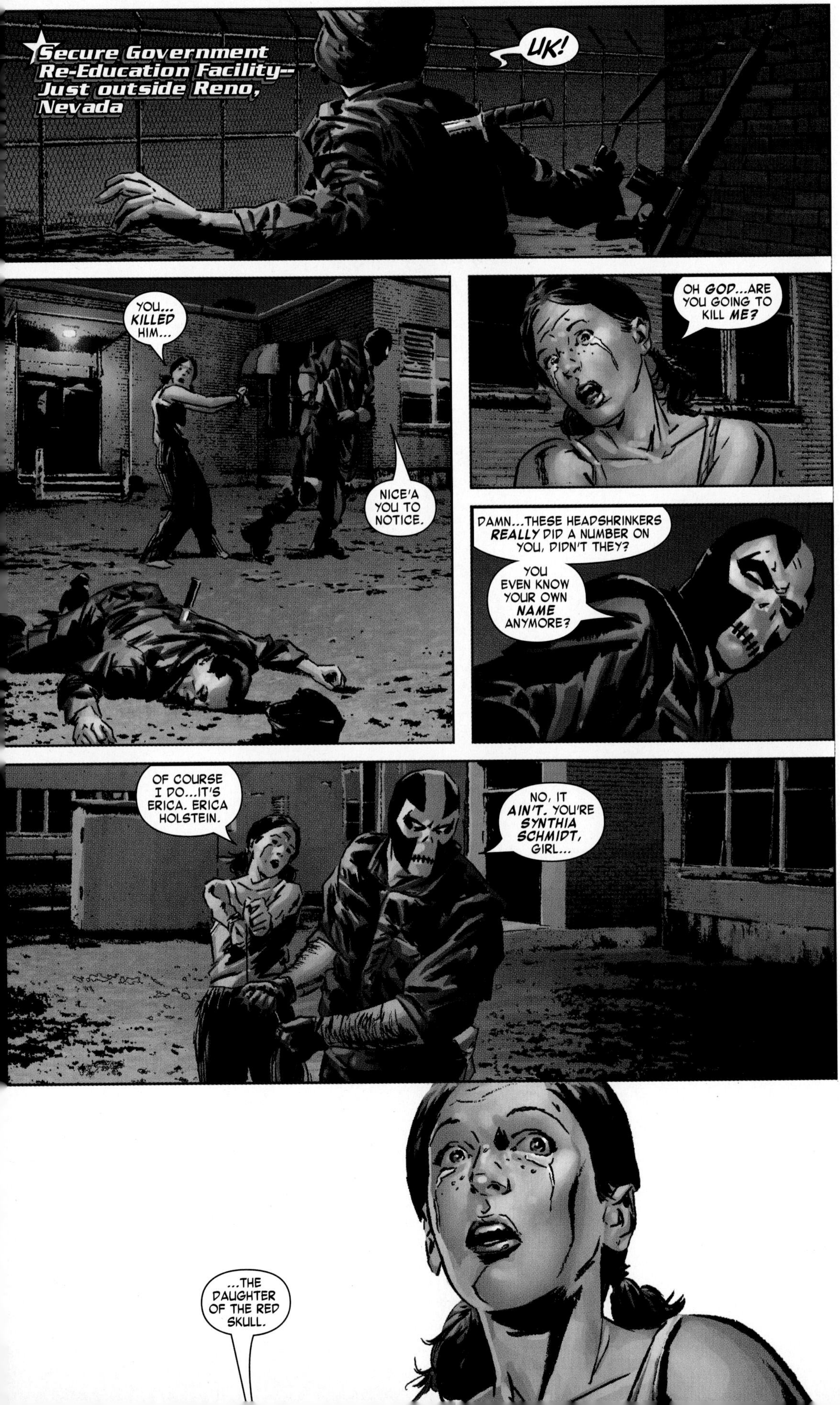
Secure Government Re-Education Facility-- Just outside Reno, Nevada
UK!
YOU... KILLED HIM...
NICE'A YOU TO NOTICE.
OH GOD...ARE YOU GOING TO KILL ME?
DAMN...THESE HEADSHRINKERS REALLY DID A NUMBER ON YOU, DIDN'T THEY?
YOU EVEN KNOW YOUR OWN NAME ANYMORE?
OF COURSE I DO...IT'S ERICA. ERICA HOLSTEIN.
NO, IT AIN'T. YOU'RE SYNTHIA SCHMIDT, GIRL...
...THE DAUGHTER OF THE RED SKULL.

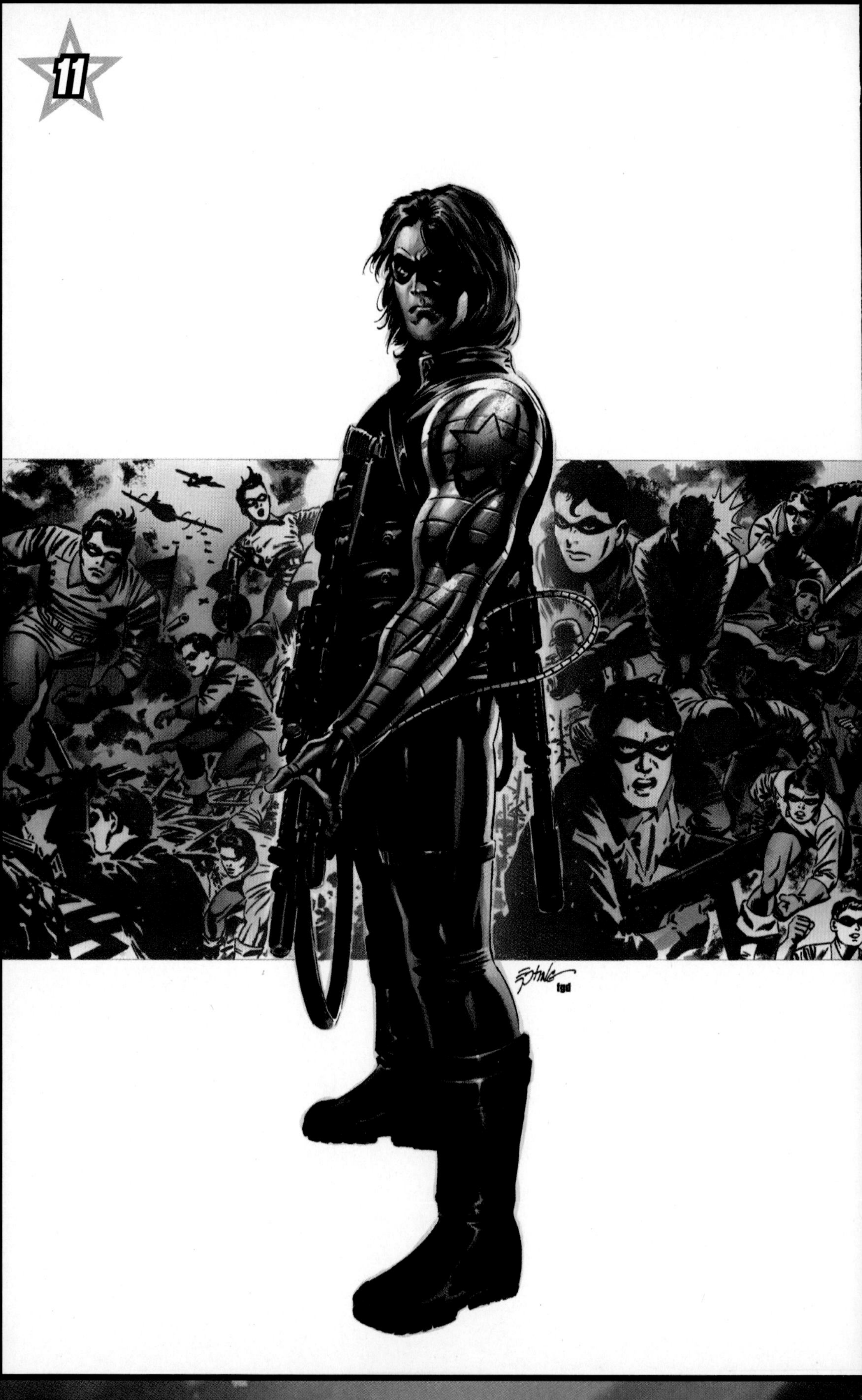
11

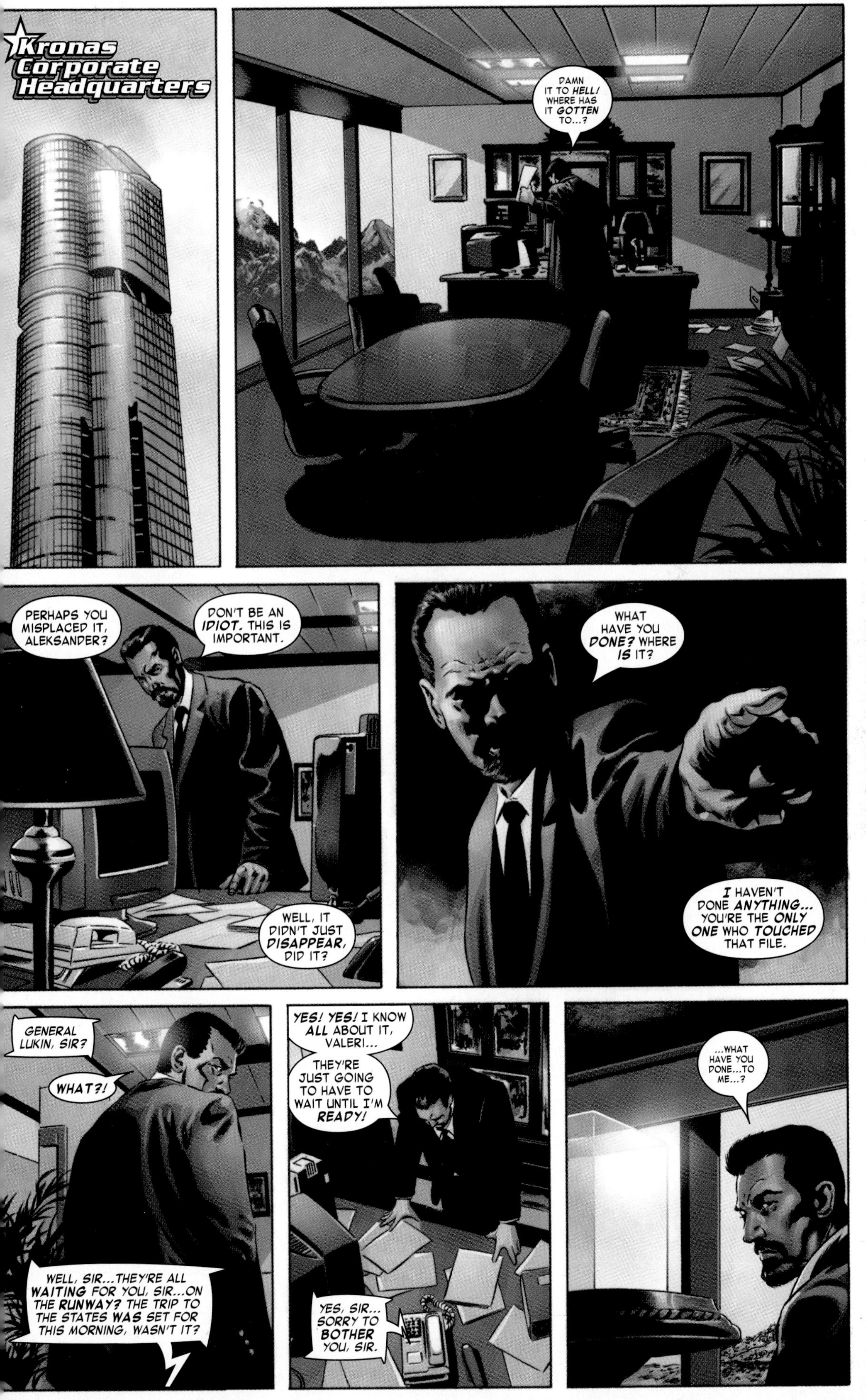

Kronas Corporate Headquarters
DAMN IT TO HELL! WHERE HAS IT GOTTEN TO...?
PERHAPS YOU MISPLACED IT, ALEKSANDER?
DON'T BE AN IDIOT. THIS IS IMPORTANT.
WELL, IT DIDN'T JUST DISAPPEAR, DID IT?
WHAT HAVE YOU DONE? WHERE IS IT?
I HAVEN'T DONE ANYTHING... YOU'RE THE ONLY ONE WHO TOUCHED THAT FILE.
GENERAL LUKIN, SIR?
WHAT?!
WELL, SIR...THEY'RE ALL WAITING FOR YOU, SIR...ON THE RUNWAY? THE TRIP TO THE STATES WAS SET FOR THIS MORNING, WASN'T IT?
YES! YES! I KNOW ALL ABOUT IT, VALERI...
THEY'RE JUST GOING TO HAVE TO WAIT UNTIL I'M READY!
YES, SIR... SORRY TO BOTHER YOU, SIR.
...WHAT HAVE YOU DONE...TO ME...?

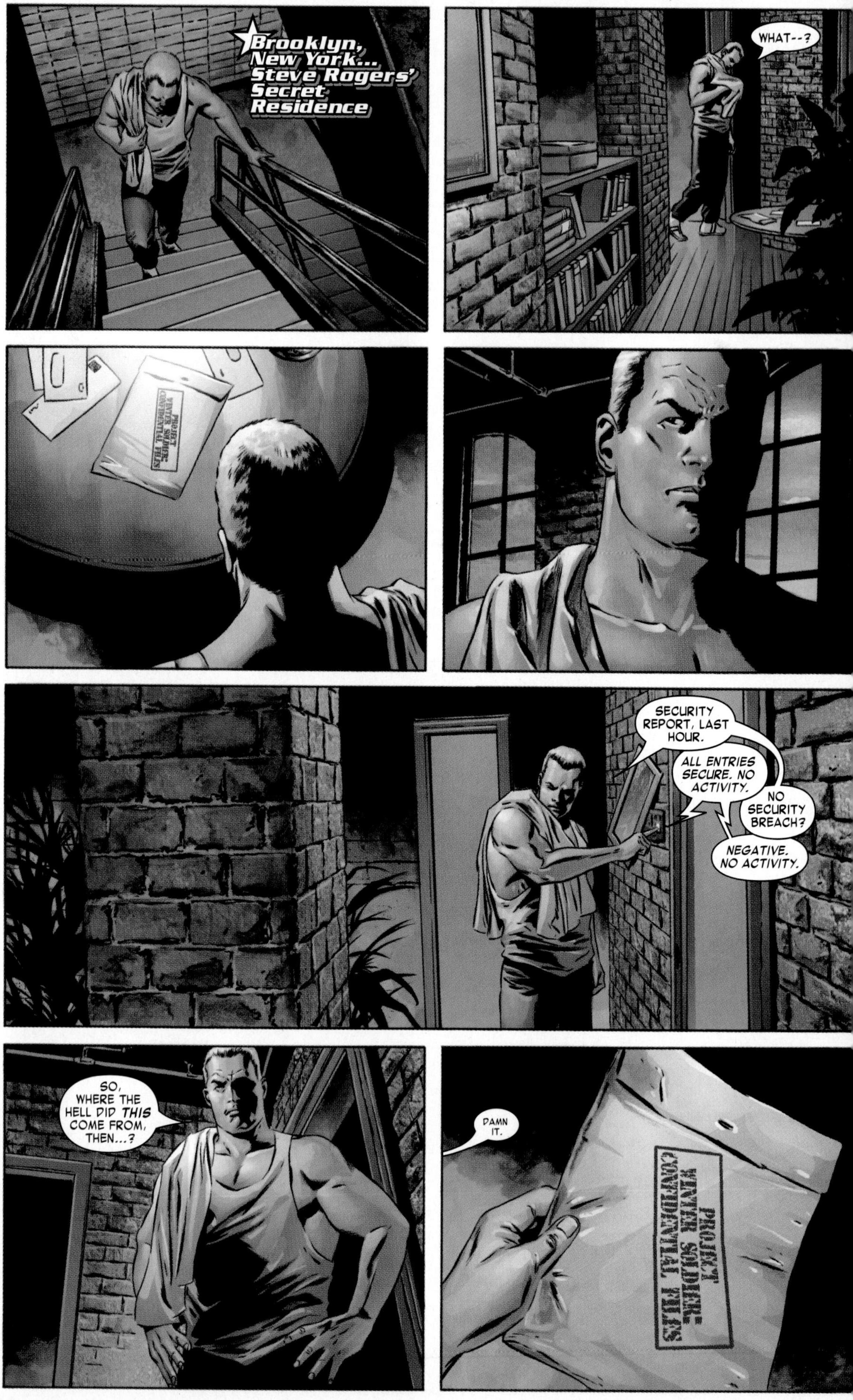
Brooklyn, New York... Steve Rogers' Secret Residence
WHAT--?
PROJECT WINTER SOLDIER CONFIDENTIAL FILES
SECURITY REPORT, LAST HOUR.
ALL ENTRIES SECURE. NO ACTIVITY.
NO SECURITY BREACH?
NEGATIVE. NO ACTIVITY.
SO, WHERE THE HELL DID *THIS* COME FROM, THEN...?
DAMN IT.
PROJECT WINTER SOLDIER CONFIDENTIAL FILES

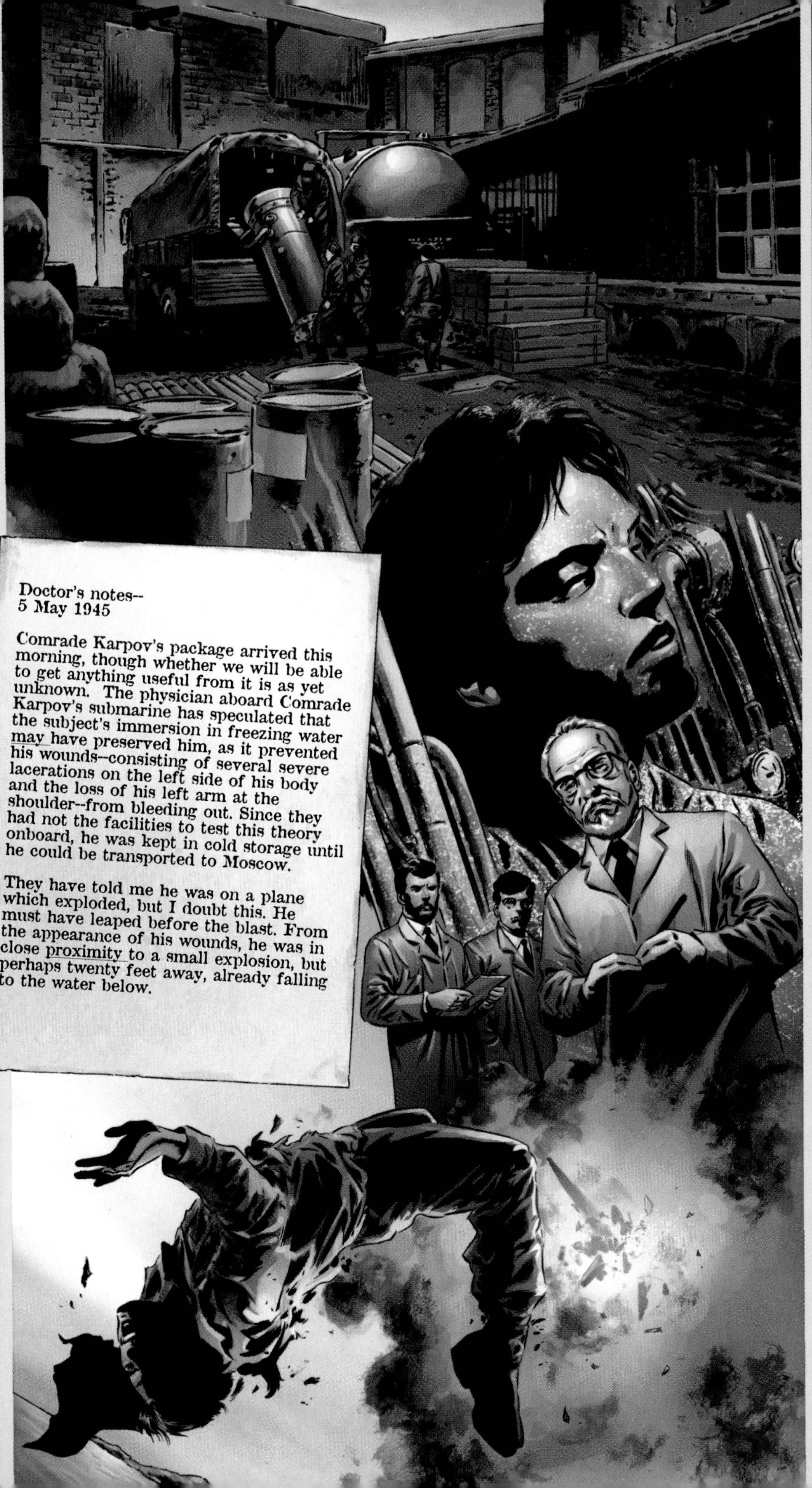
Doctor's notes--
5 May 1945
Comrade Karpov's package arrived this morning, though whether we will be able to get anything useful from it is as yet unknown. The physician aboard Comrade Karpov's submarine has speculated that the subject's immersion in freezing water may have preserved him, as it prevented his wounds--consisting of several severe lacerations on the left side of his body and the loss of his left arm at the shoulder--from bleeding out. Since they had not the facilities to test this theory onboard, he was kept in cold storage until he could be transported to Moscow.
They have told me he was on a plane which exploded, but I doubt this. He must have leaped before the blast. From the appearance of his wounds, he was in close proximity to a small explosion, but perhaps twenty feet away, already falling to the water below.

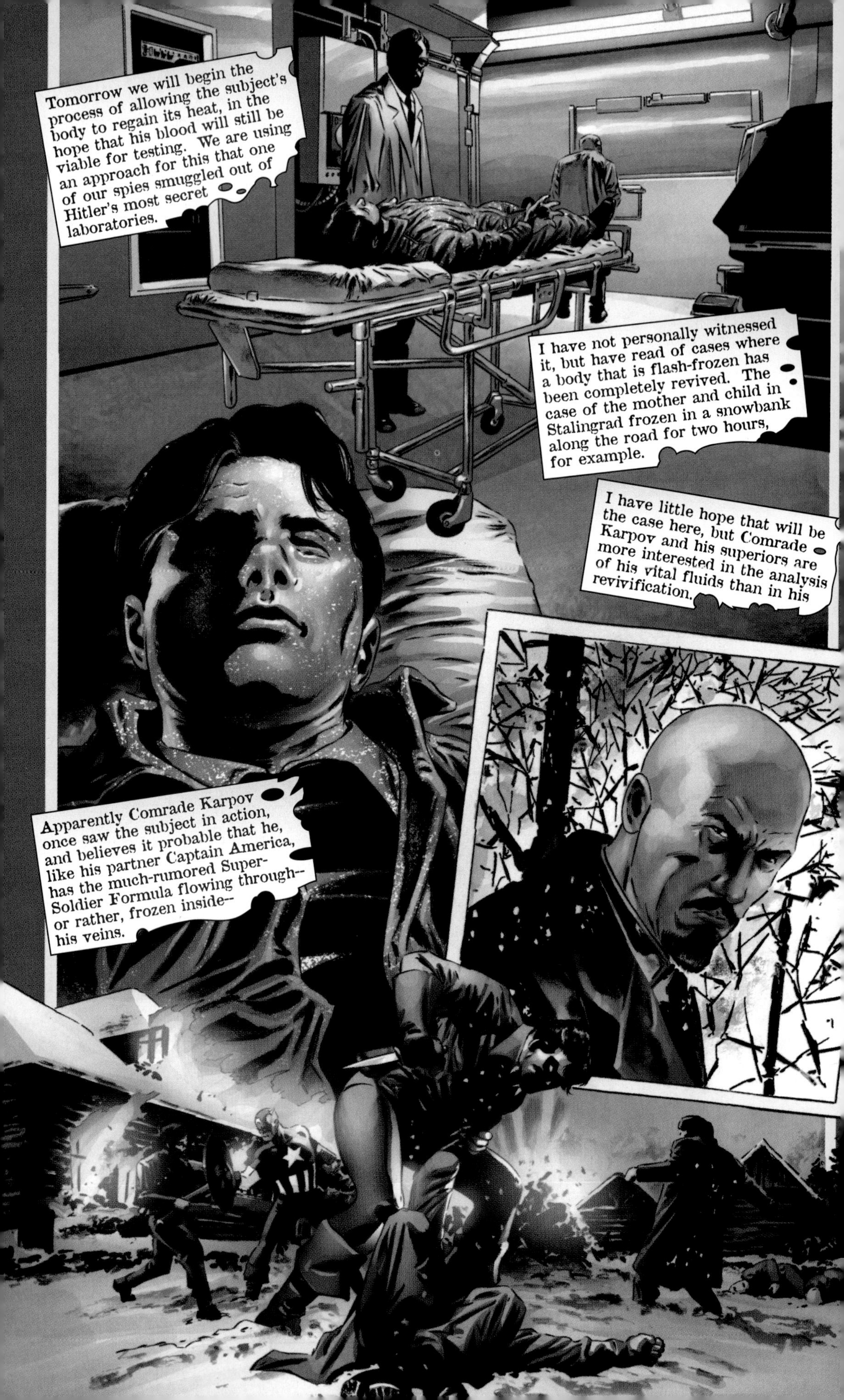
Tomorrow we will begin the process of allowing the subject's body to regain its heat, in the hope that his blood will still be viable for testing. We are using an approach for this that one of our spies smuggled out of Hitler's most secret laboratories.
I have not personally witnessed it, but have read of cases where a body that is flash-frozen has been completely revived. The case of the mother and child in Stalingrad frozen in a snowbank along the road for two hours, for example.
I have little hope that will be the case here, but Comrade Karpov and his superiors are more interested in the analysis of his vital fluids than in his revivification.
Apparently Comrade Karpov once saw the subject in action, and believes it probable that he, like his partner Captain America, has the much-rumored Super-Soldier Formula flowing through--or rather, frozen inside--his veins.

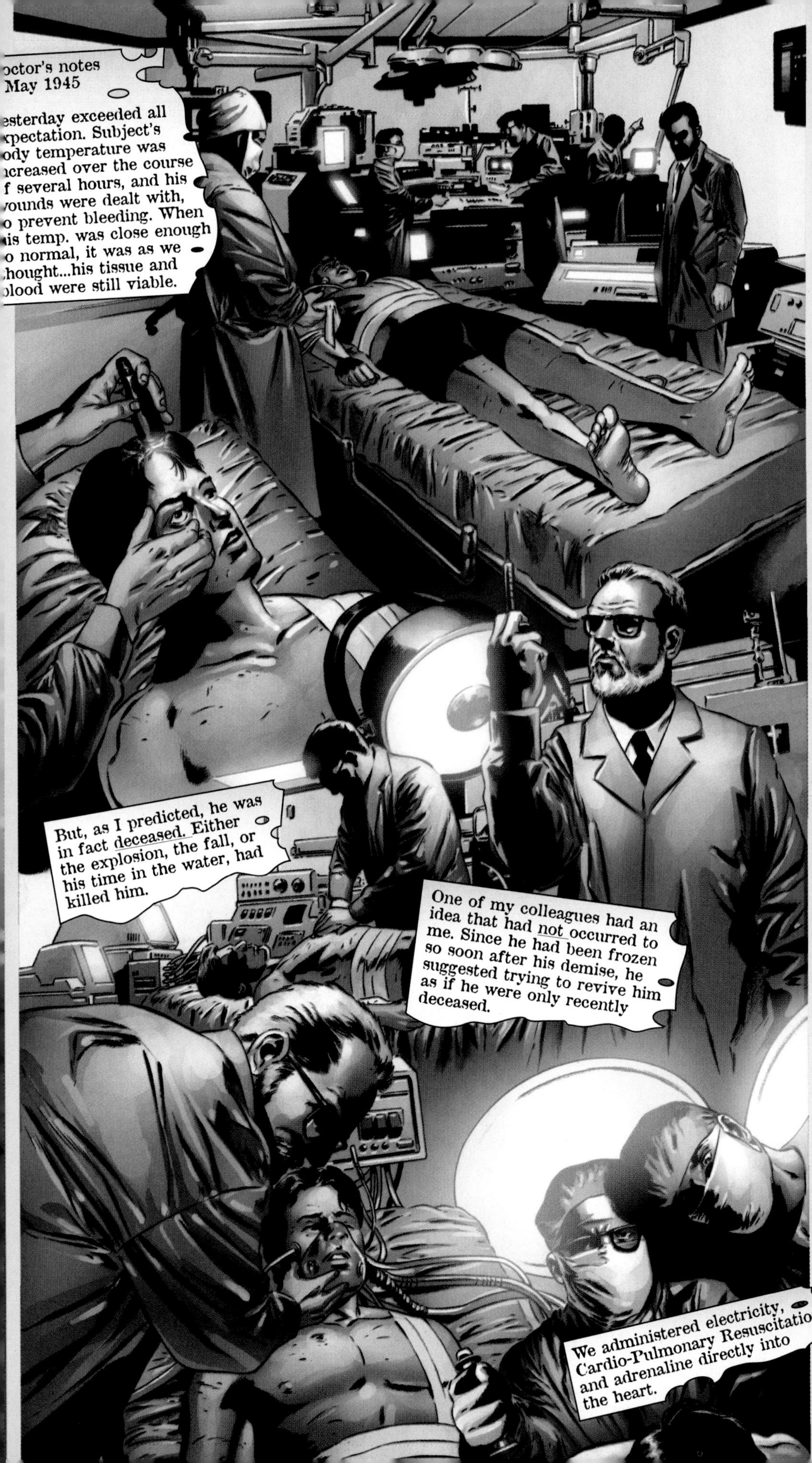

octor's notes
May 1945
esterday exceeded all xpectation. Subject's ody temperature was ncreased over the course f several hours, and his vounds were dealt with, o prevent bleeding. When is temp. was close enough o normal, it was as we hought...his tissue and lood were still viable.
But, as I predicted, he was in fact deceased. Either the explosion, the fall, or his time in the water, had killed him.
One of my colleagues had an idea that had not occurred to me. Since he had been frozen so soon after his demise, he suggested trying to revive him as if he were only recently deceased.
We administered electricity, Cardio-Pulmonary Resuscitation, and adrenaline directly into the heart.

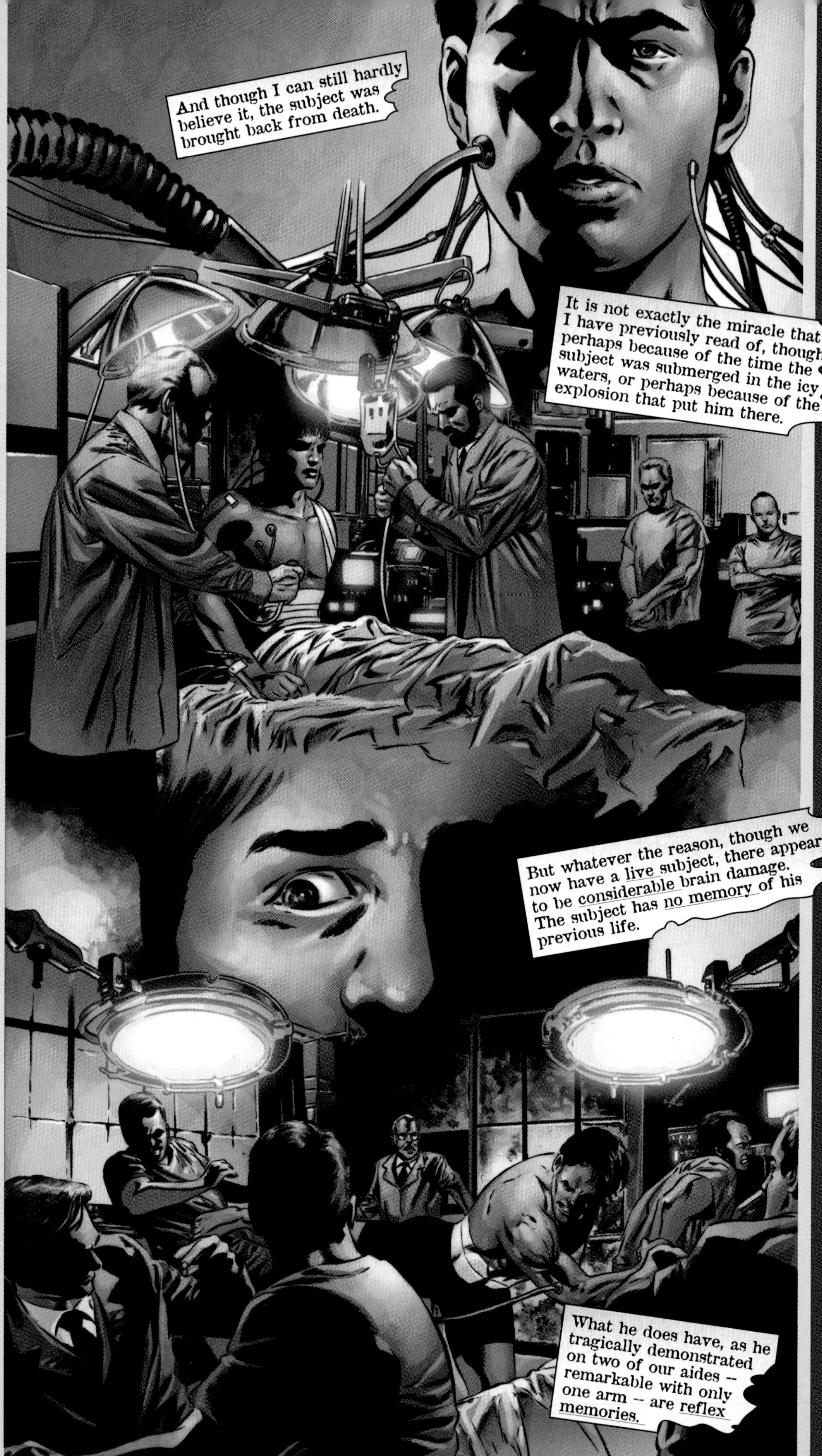
And though I can still hardly believe it, the subject was brought back from death.
It is not exactly the miracle that I have previously read of, though perhaps because of the time the subject was submerged in the icy waters, or perhaps because of the explosion that put him there.
But whatever the reason, though we now have a live subject, there appears to be considerable brain damage. The subject has no memory of his previous life.
What he does have, as he tragically demonstrated on two of our aides -- remarkable with only one arm -- are reflex memories.

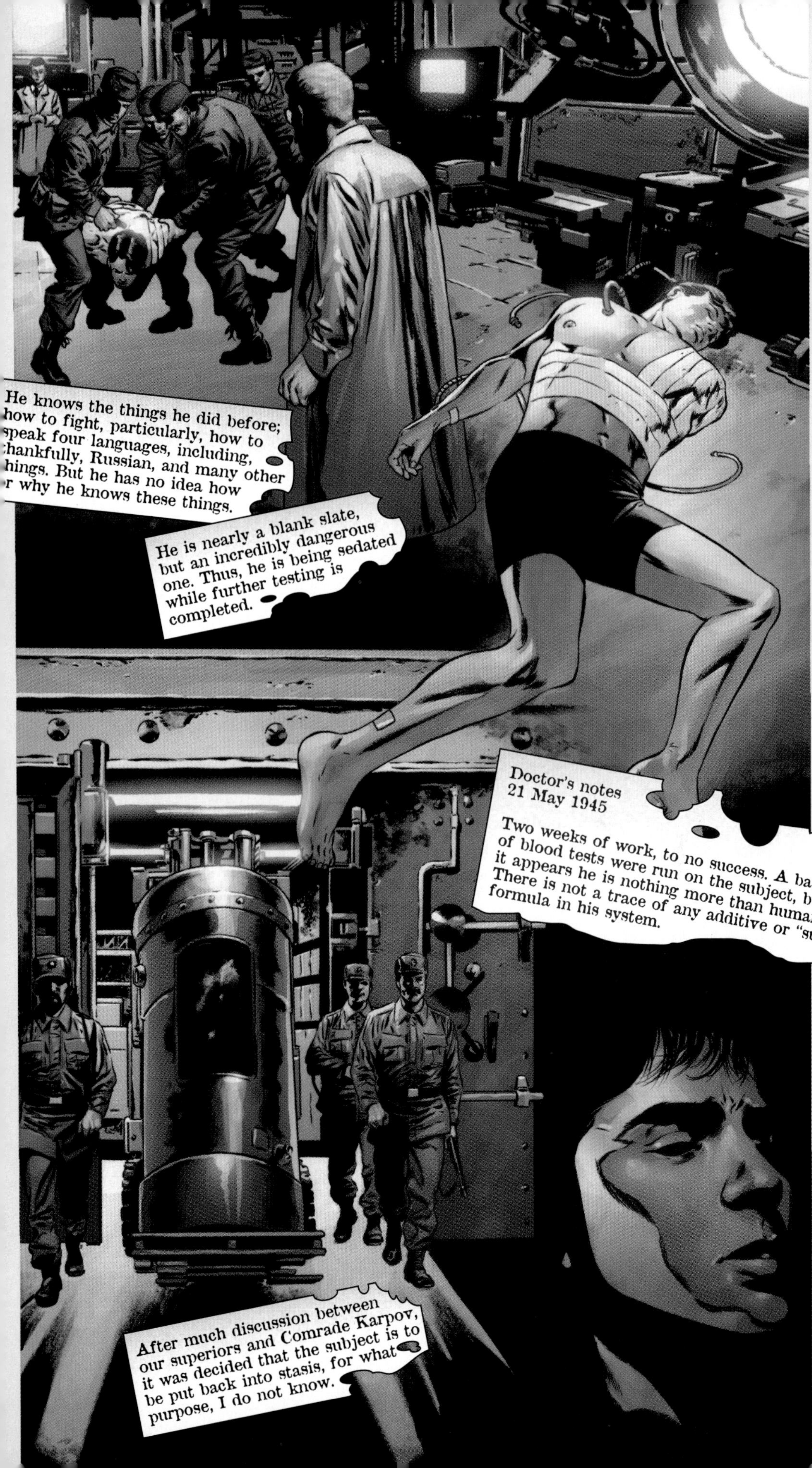
He knows the things he did before; how to fight, particularly, how to speak four languages, including, hankfully, Russian, and many other hings. But he has no idea how r why he knows these things.
He is nearly a blank slate, but an incredibly dangerous one. Thus, he is being sedated while further testing is completed.
Doctor's notes
21 May 1945
Two weeks of work, to no success. A battery of blood tests were run on the subject, but it appears he is nothing more than human. There is not a trace of any additive or "super" formula in his system.
After much discussion between our superiors and Comrade Karpov, it was decided that the subject is to be put back into stasis, for what purpose, I do not know.

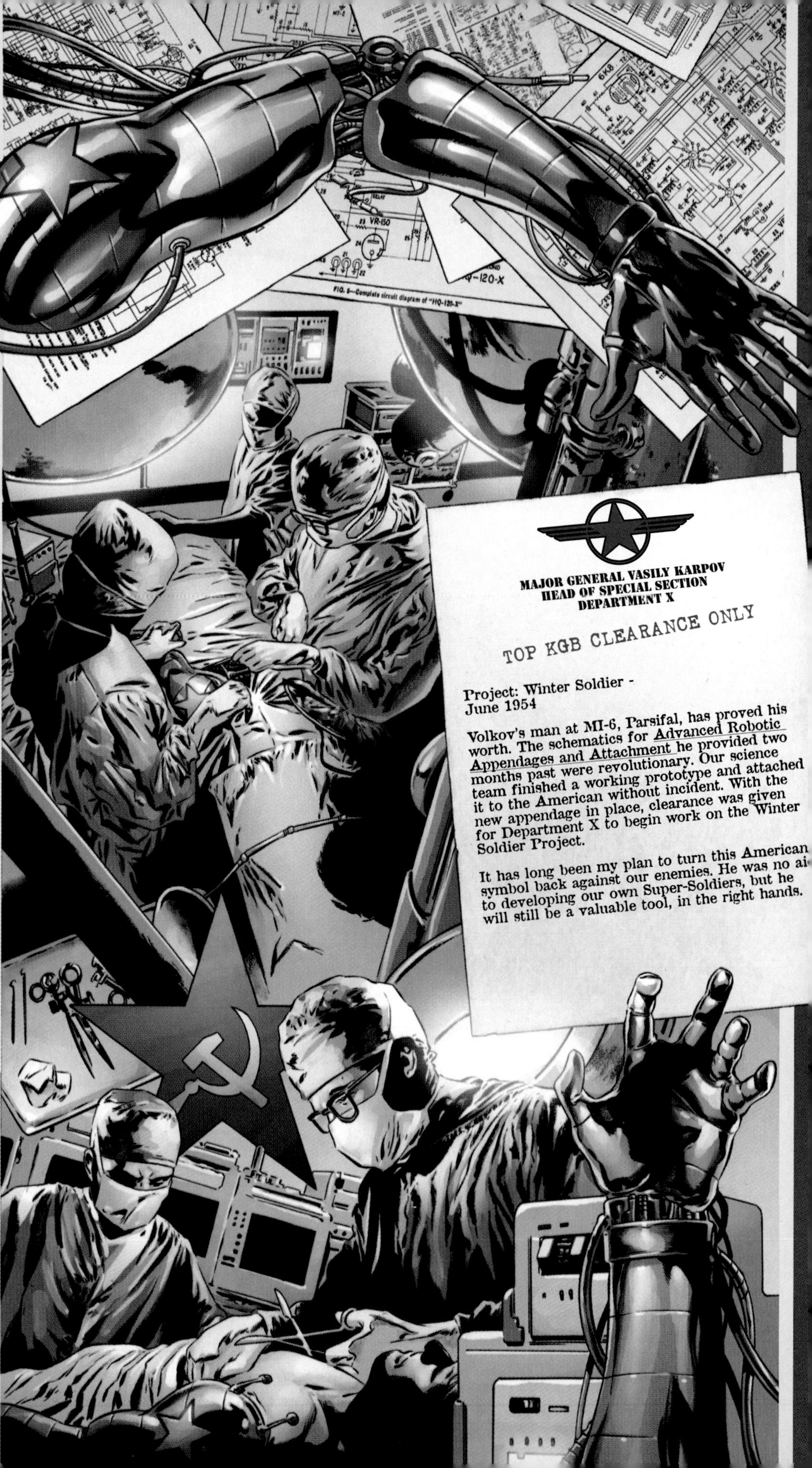

MAJOR GENERAL VASILY KARPOV
HEAD OF SPECIAL SECTION
DEPARTMENT X
TOP KGB CLEARANCE ONLY
Project: Winter Soldier -
June 1954
Volkov's man at MI-6, Parsifal, has proved his worth. The schematics for Advanced Robotic Appendages and Attachment he provided two months past were revolutionary. Our science team finished a working prototype and attached it to the American without incident. With the new appendage in place, clearance was given for Department X to begin work on the Winter Soldier Project.
It has long been my plan to turn this American symbol back against our enemies. He was no ai to developing our own Super-Soldiers, but he will still be a valuable tool, in the right hands.

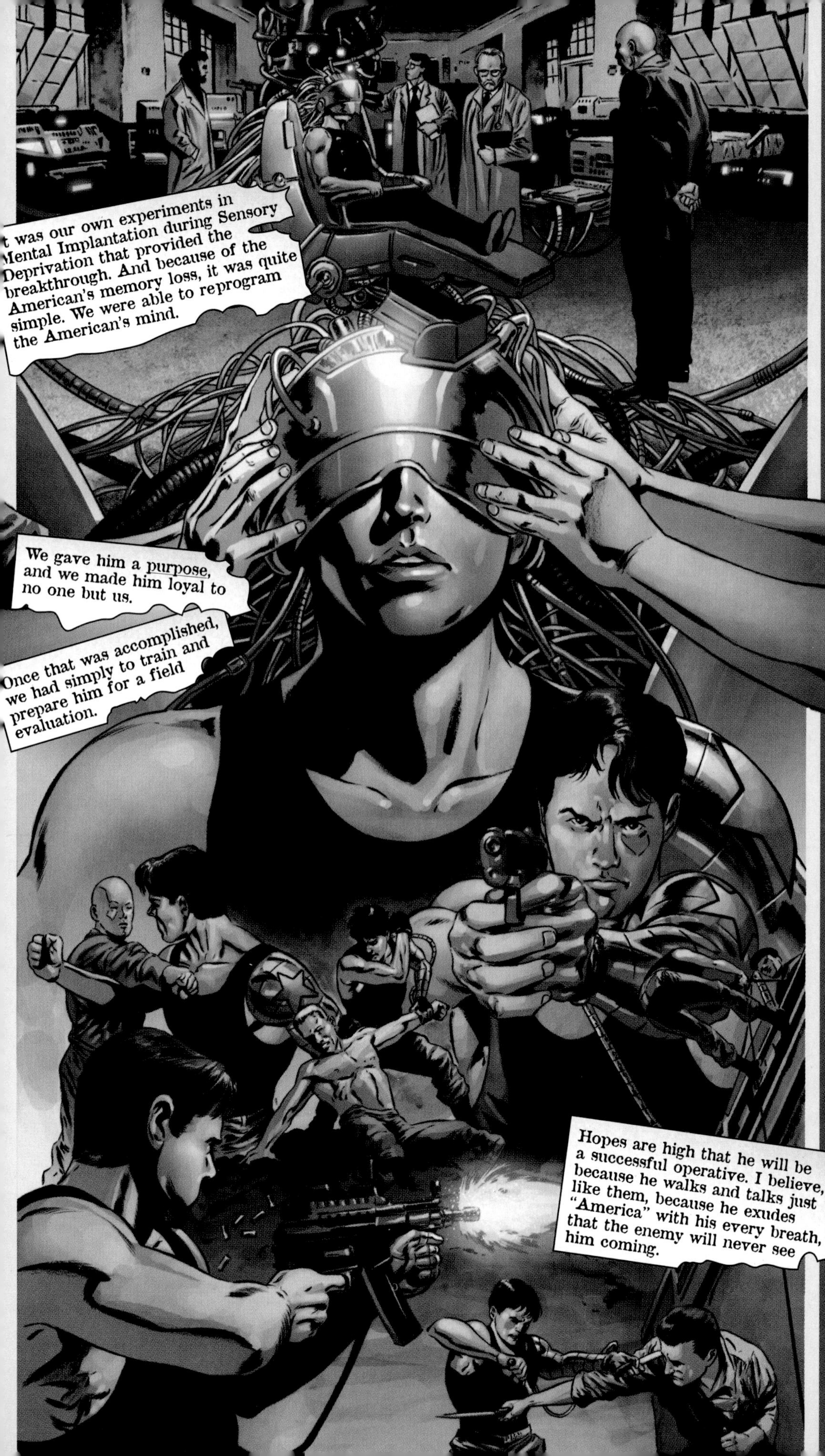
t was our own experiments in Mental Implantation during Sensory Deprivation that provided the breakthrough. And because of the American's memory loss, it was quite simple. We were able to reprogram the American's mind.
We gave him a purpose, and we made him loyal to no one but us.
Once that was accomplished, we had simply to train and prepare him for a field evaluation.
Hopes are high that he will be a successful operative. I believe, because he walks and talks just like them, because he exudes "America" with his every breath, that the enemy will never see him coming.

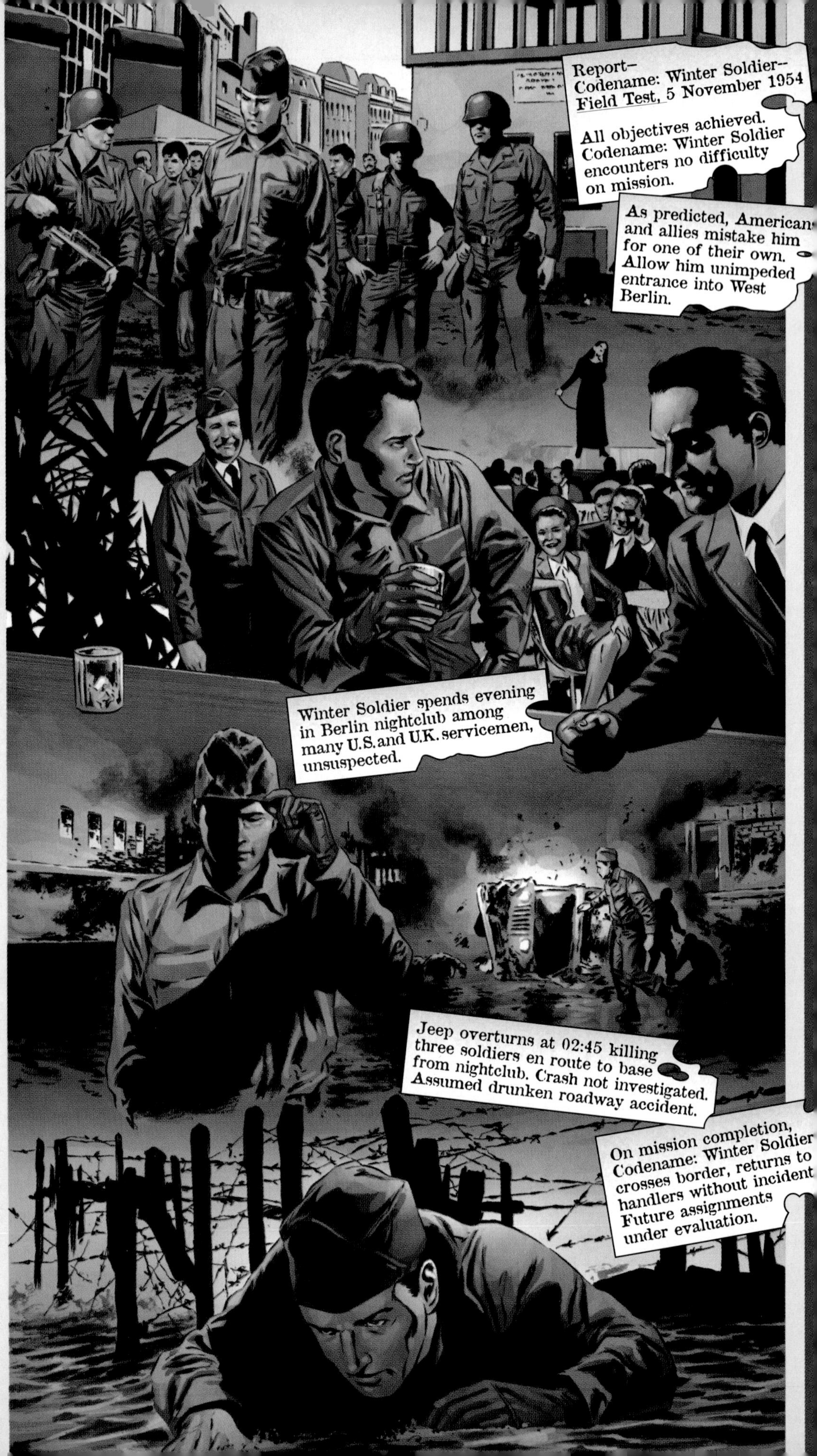
Report–
Codename: Winter Soldier--
Field Test, 5 November 1954
All objectives achieved. Codename: Winter Soldier encounters no difficulty on mission.
As predicted, American and allies mistake him for one of their own. Allow him unimpeded entrance into West Berlin.
Winter Soldier spends evening in Berlin nightclub among many U.S. and U.K. servicemen, unsuspected.
Jeep overturns at 02:45 killing three soldiers en route to base from nightclub. Crash not investigated. Assumed drunken roadway accident.
On mission completion, Codename: Winter Soldier crosses border, returns to handlers without incident. Future assignments under evaluation.

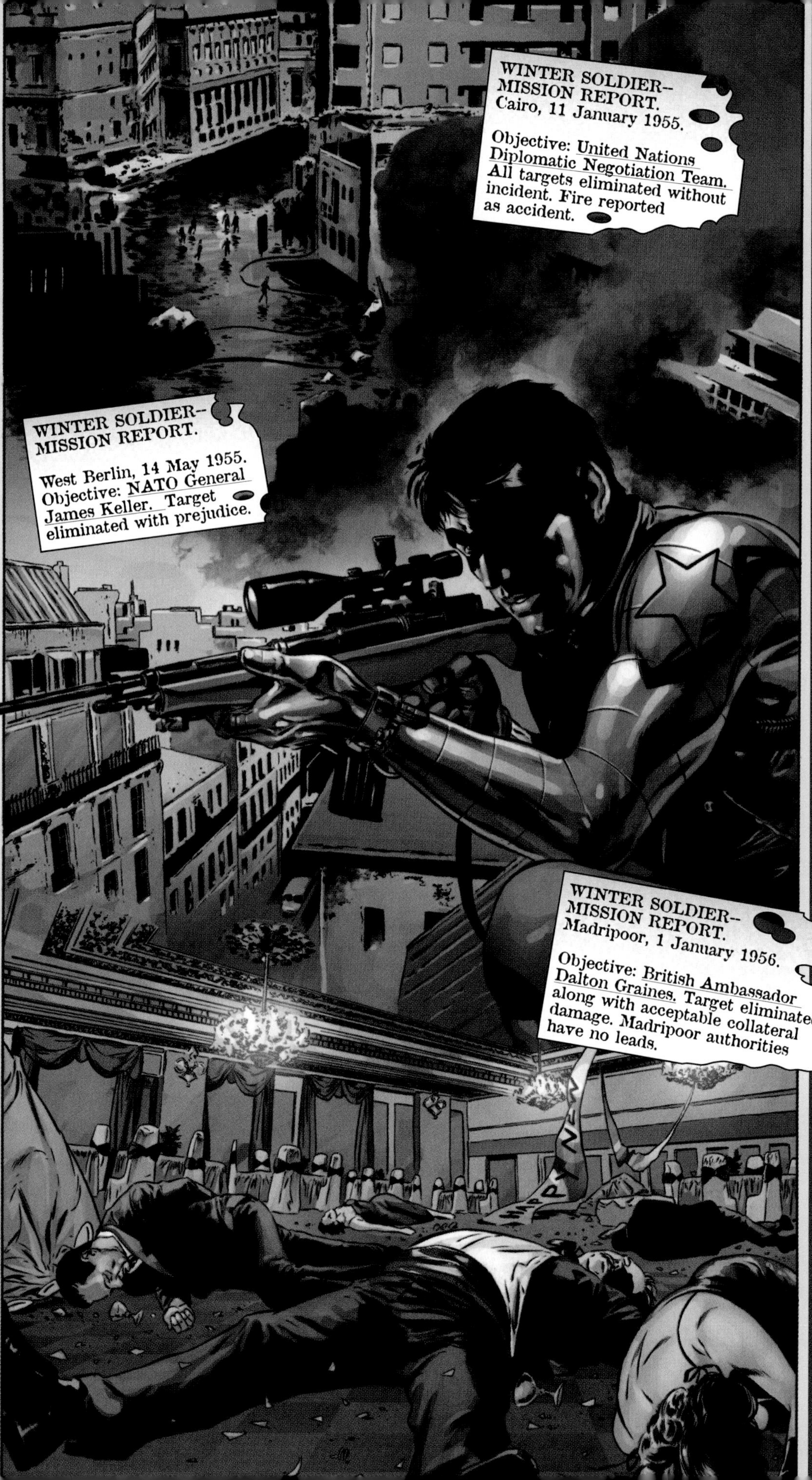

WINTER SOLDIER--
MISSION REPORT.
Cairo, 11 January 1955.
Objective: United Nations Diplomatic Negotiation Team. All targets eliminated without incident. Fire reported as accident.
WINTER SOLDIER--
MISSION REPORT.
West Berlin, 14 May 1955.
Objective: NATO General James Keller. Target eliminated with prejudice.
WINTER SOLDIER--
MISSION REPORT.
Madripoor, 1 January 1956.
Objective: British Ambassador Dalton Graines. Target eliminated, along with acceptable collateral damage. Madripoor authorities have no leads.

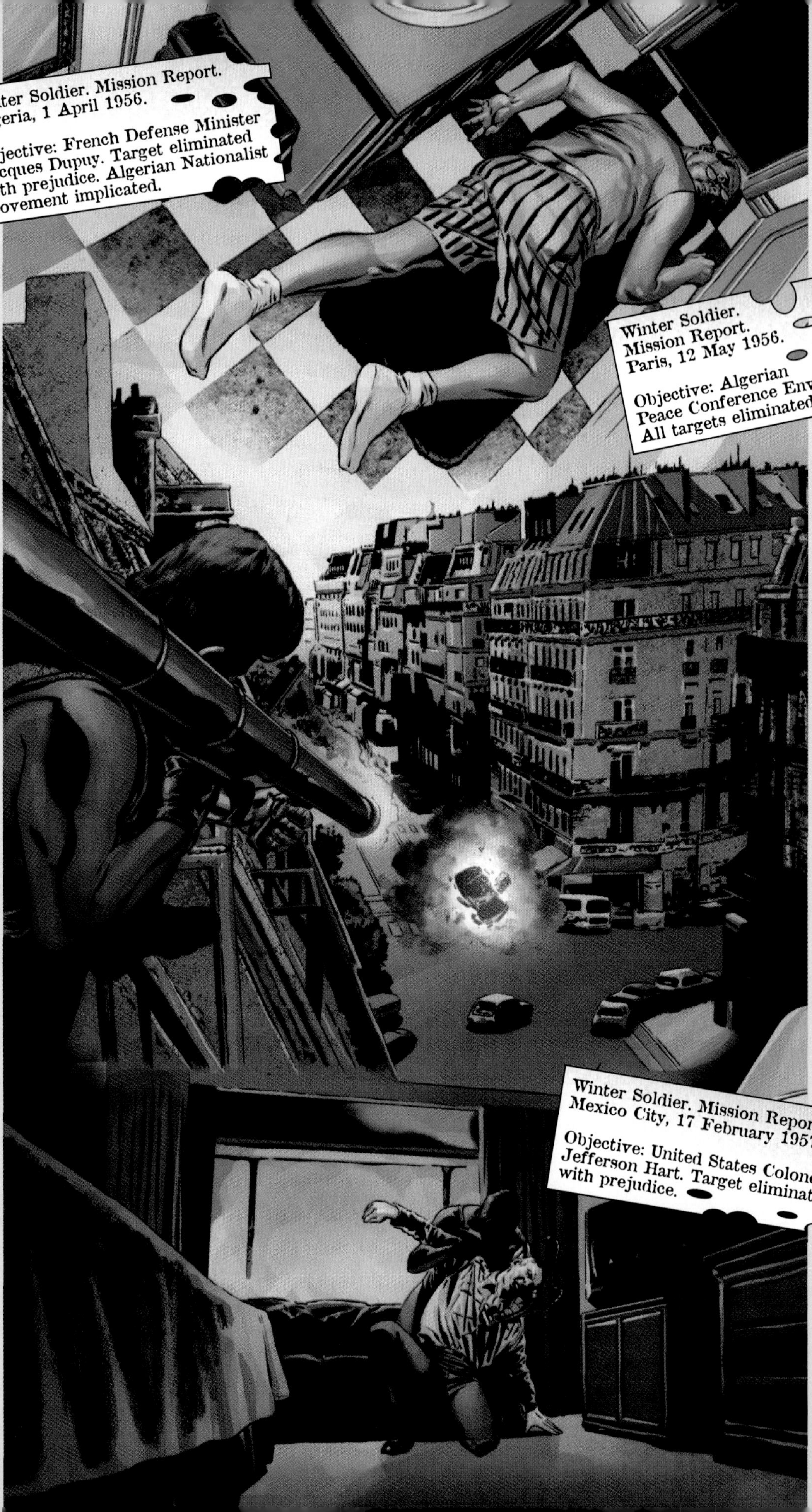
Winter Soldier. Mission Report. Algeria, 1 April 1956.
Objective: French Defense Minister Jacques Dupuy. Target eliminated with prejudice. Algerian Nationalist Movement implicated.
Winter Soldier. Mission Report. Paris, 12 May 1956.
Objective: Algerian Peace Conference Envo
All targets eliminated.
Winter Soldier. Mission Report. Mexico City, 17 February 1957.
Objective: United States Colonel Jefferson Hart. Target eliminate with prejudice.

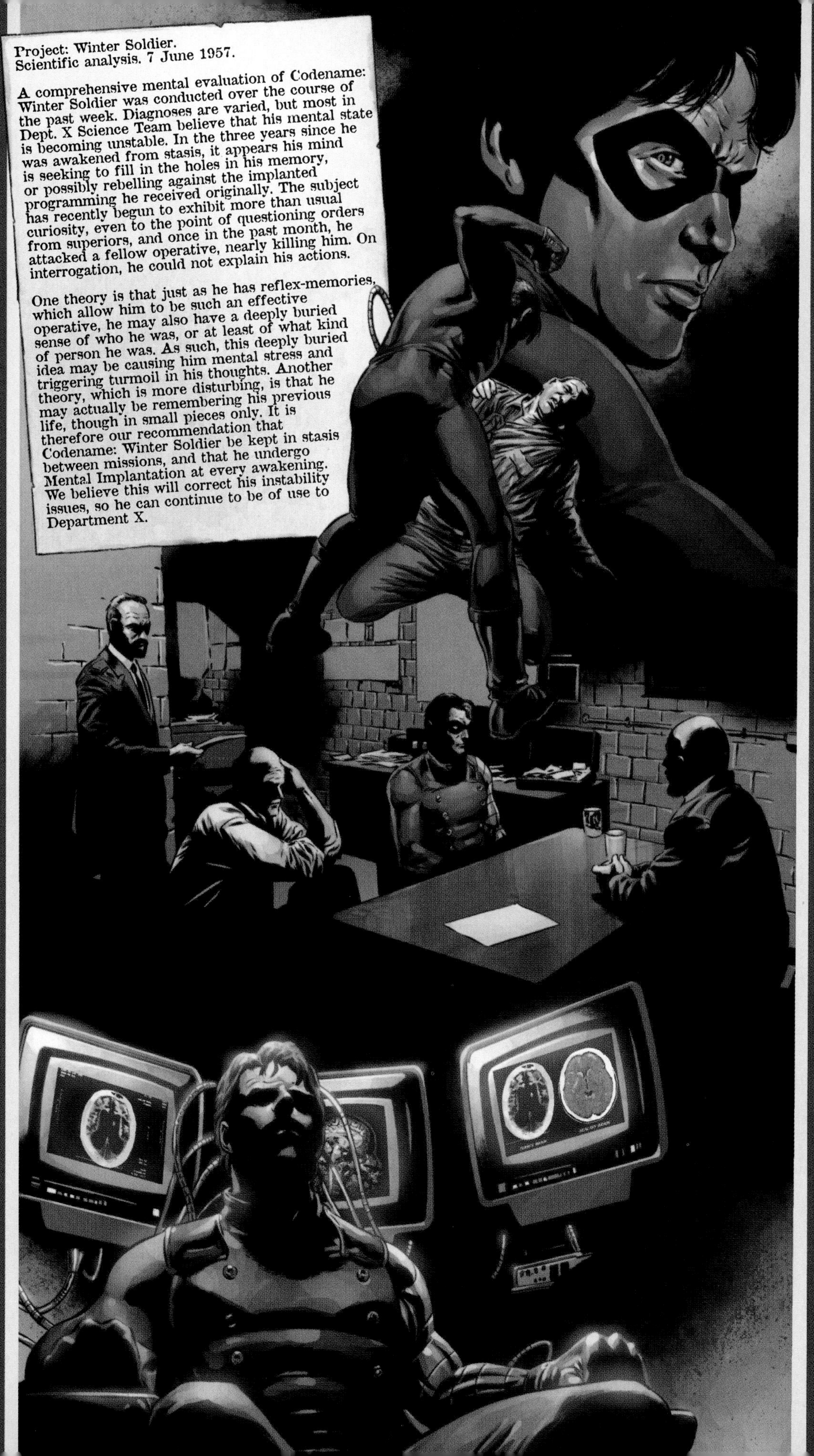

Project: Winter Soldier.
Scientific analysis. 7 June 1957.

A comprehensive mental evaluation of Codename: Winter Soldier was conducted over the course of the past week. Diagnoses are varied, but most in Dept. X Science Team believe that his mental state is becoming unstable. In the three years since he was awakened from stasis, it appears his mind is seeking to fill in the holes in his memory, or possibly rebelling against the implanted programming he received originally. The subject has recently begun to exhibit more than usual curiosity, even to the point of questioning orders from superiors, and once in the past month, he attacked a fellow operative, nearly killing him. On interrogation, he could not explain his actions.

One theory is that just as he has reflex-memories, which allow him to be such an effective operative, he may also have a deeply buried sense of who he was, or at least of what kind of person he was. As such, this deeply buried idea may be causing him mental stress and triggering turmoil in his thoughts. Another theory, which is more disturbing, is that he may actually be remembering his previous life, though in small pieces only. It is therefore our recommendation that Codename: Winter Soldier be kept in stasis between missions, and that he undergo Mental Implantation at every awakening. We believe this will correct his instability issues, so he can continue to be of use to Department X.

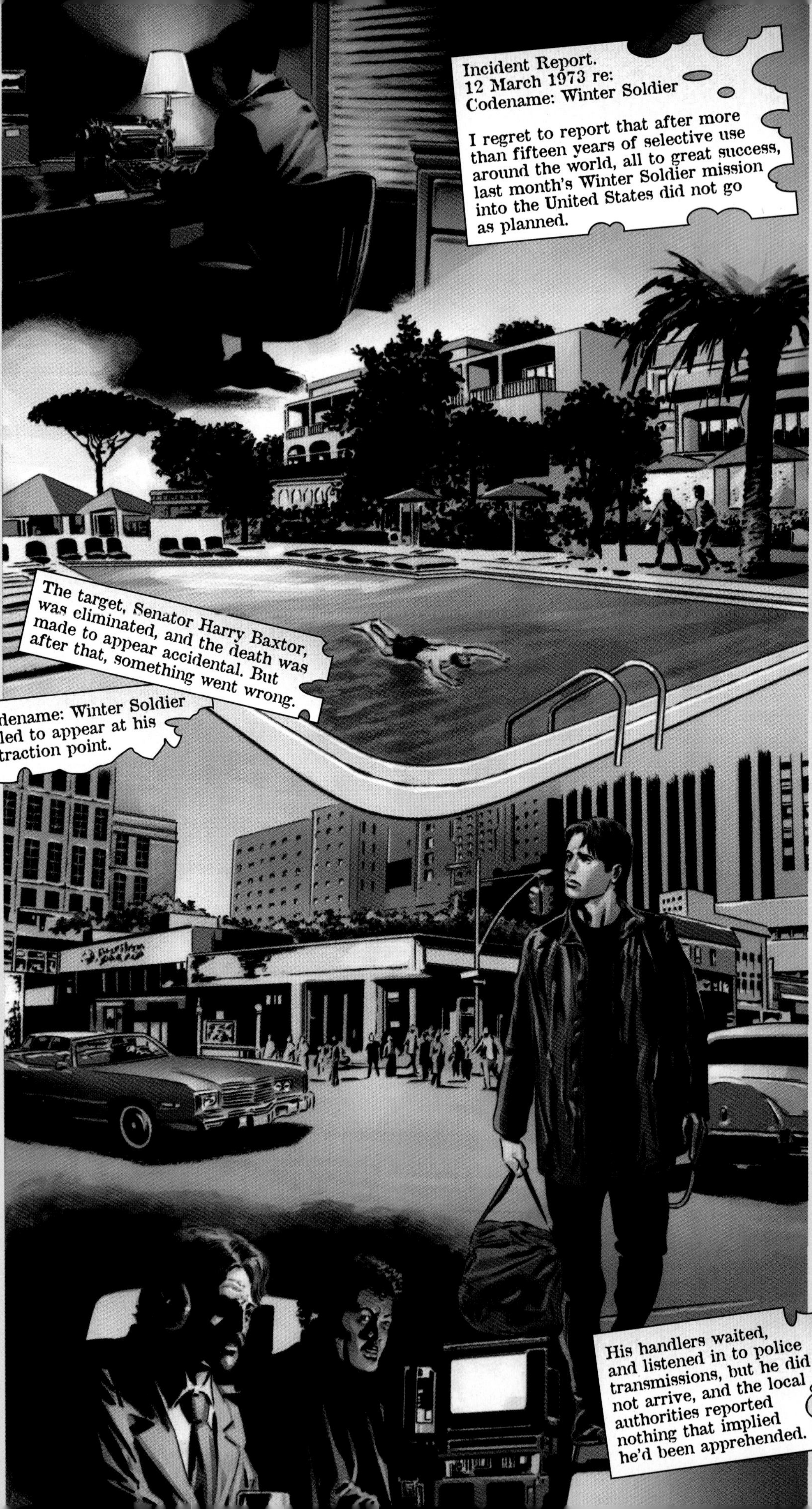
Incident Report.
12 March 1973 re:
Codename: Winter Soldier
I regret to report that after more than fifteen years of selective use around the world, all to great success, last month's Winter Soldier mission into the United States did not go as planned.
The target, Senator Harry Baxtor, was eliminated, and the death was made to appear accidental. But after that, something went wrong.
Codename: Winter Soldier failed to appear at his extraction point.
His handlers waited, and listened in to police transmissions, but he did not arrive, and the local authorities reported nothing that implied he'd been apprehended.

Following protocol, our agents in the U.S. began a wide search for Winter Soldier. All extremes were taken to recover this valuable asset, including several sleeper-agents breaking cover.

Through that considerable effort, we were able to track some of his movements. Security camera footage showed him in civilian garb at the Dallas train station, boarding a train to Chicago.

Interrogation of several passengers onboard the train left the impression that Winter Soldier was confused while onboard. He was apparently confused about what year it was, and appeared uneasy around the other passengers.

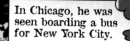

In Chicago, he was seen boarding a bus for New York City.

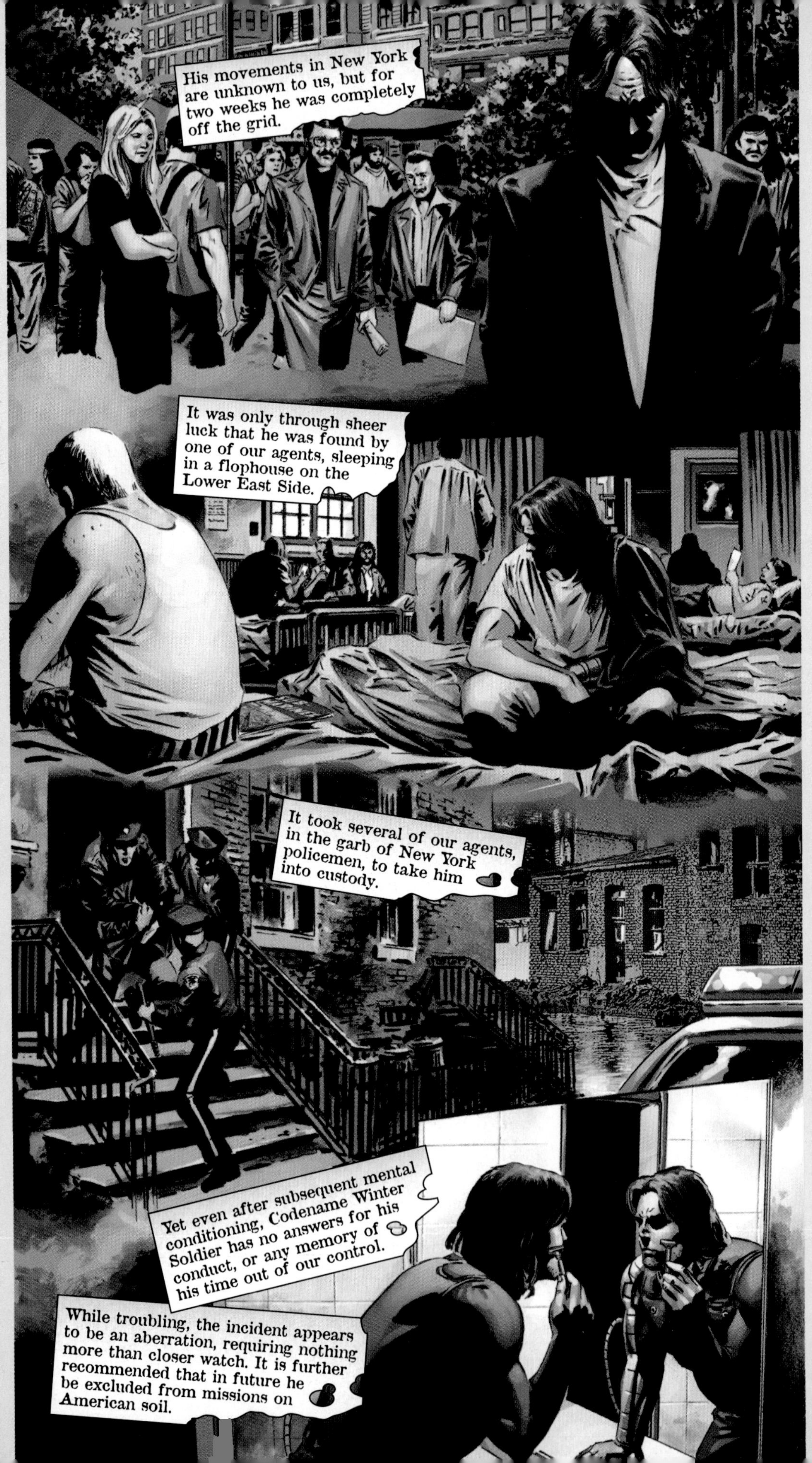
His movements in New York are unknown to us, but for two weeks he was completely off the grid.
It was only through sheer luck that he was found by one of our agents, sleeping in a flophouse on the Lower East Side.
It took several of our agents, in the garb of New York policemen, to take him into custody.
Yet even after subsequent mental conditioning, Codename Winter Soldier has no answers for his conduct, or any memory of his time out of our control.
While troubling, the incident appears to be an aberration, requiring nothing more than closer watch. It is further recommended that in future he be excluded from missions on American soil.

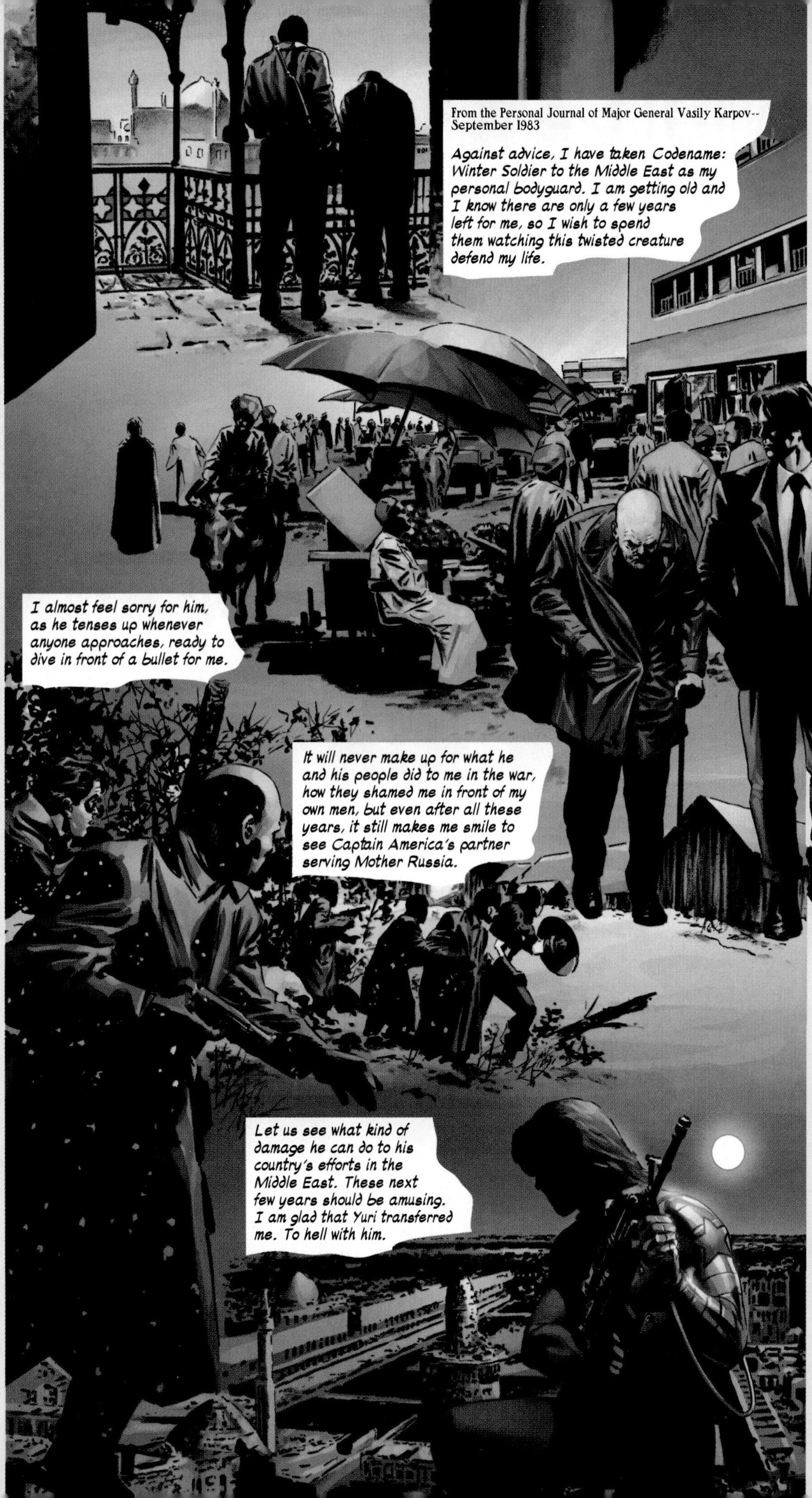
From the Personal Journal of Major General Vasily Karpov-- September 1983
Against advice, I have taken Codename: Winter Soldier to the Middle East as my personal bodyguard. I am getting old and I know there are only a few years left for me, so I wish to spend them watching this twisted creature defend my life.
I almost feel sorry for him, as he tenses up whenever anyone approaches, ready to dive in front of a bullet for me.
It will never make up for what he and his people did to me in the war, how they shamed me in front of my own men, but even after all these years, it still makes me smile to see Captain America's partner serving Mother Russia.
Let us see what kind of damage he can do to his country's efforts in the Middle East. These next few years should be amusing. I am glad that Yuri transferred me. To hell with him.

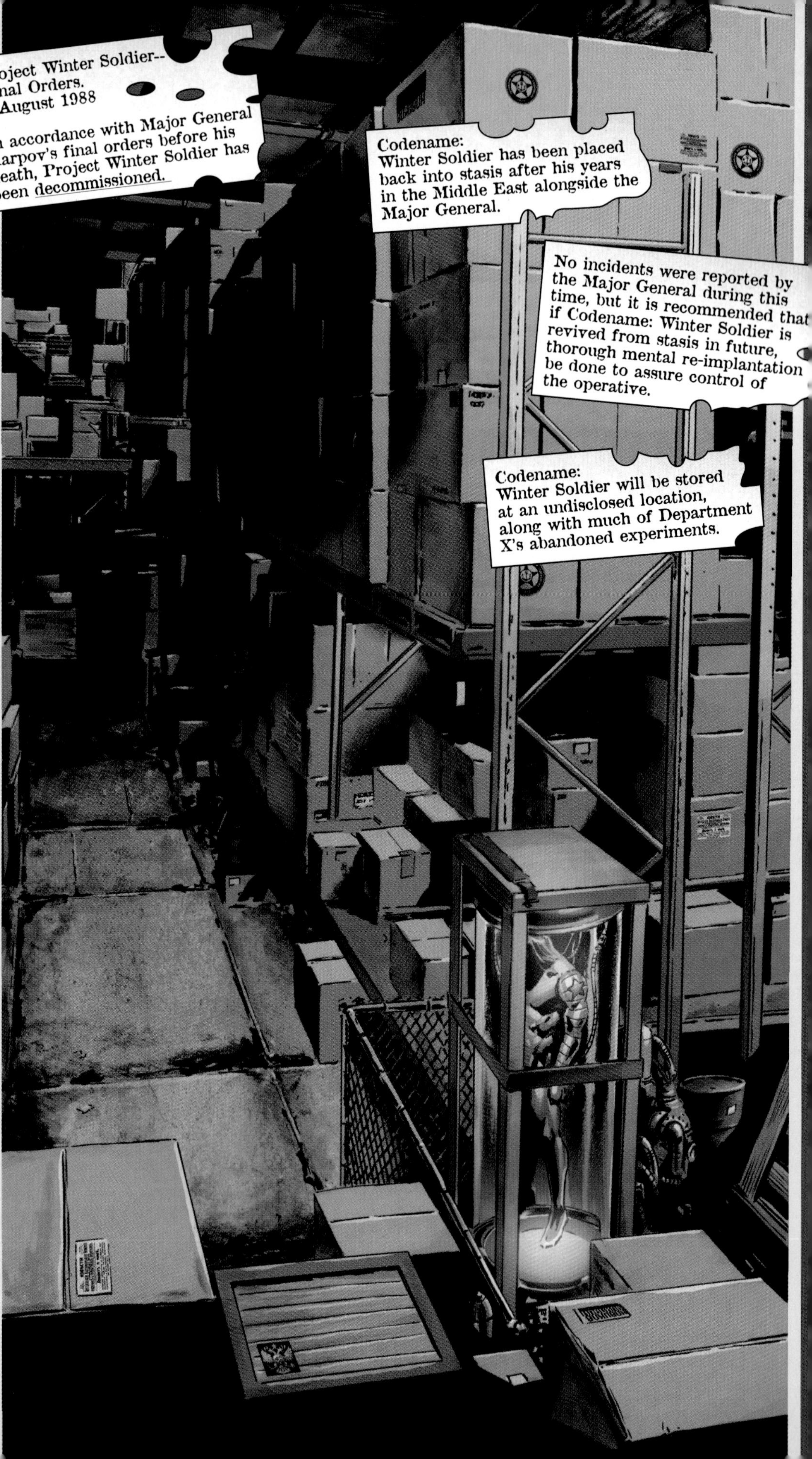
Project Winter Soldier--
Final Orders.
4 August 1988
In accordance with Major General Karpov's final orders before his death, Project Winter Soldier has been decommissioned.
Codename:
Winter Soldier has been placed back into stasis after his years in the Middle East alongside the Major General.
No incidents were reported by the Major General during this time, but it is recommended that if Codename: Winter Soldier is revived from stasis in future, thorough mental re-implantation be done to assure control of the operative.
Codename:
Winter Soldier will be stored at an undisclosed location, along with much of Department X's abandoned experiments.

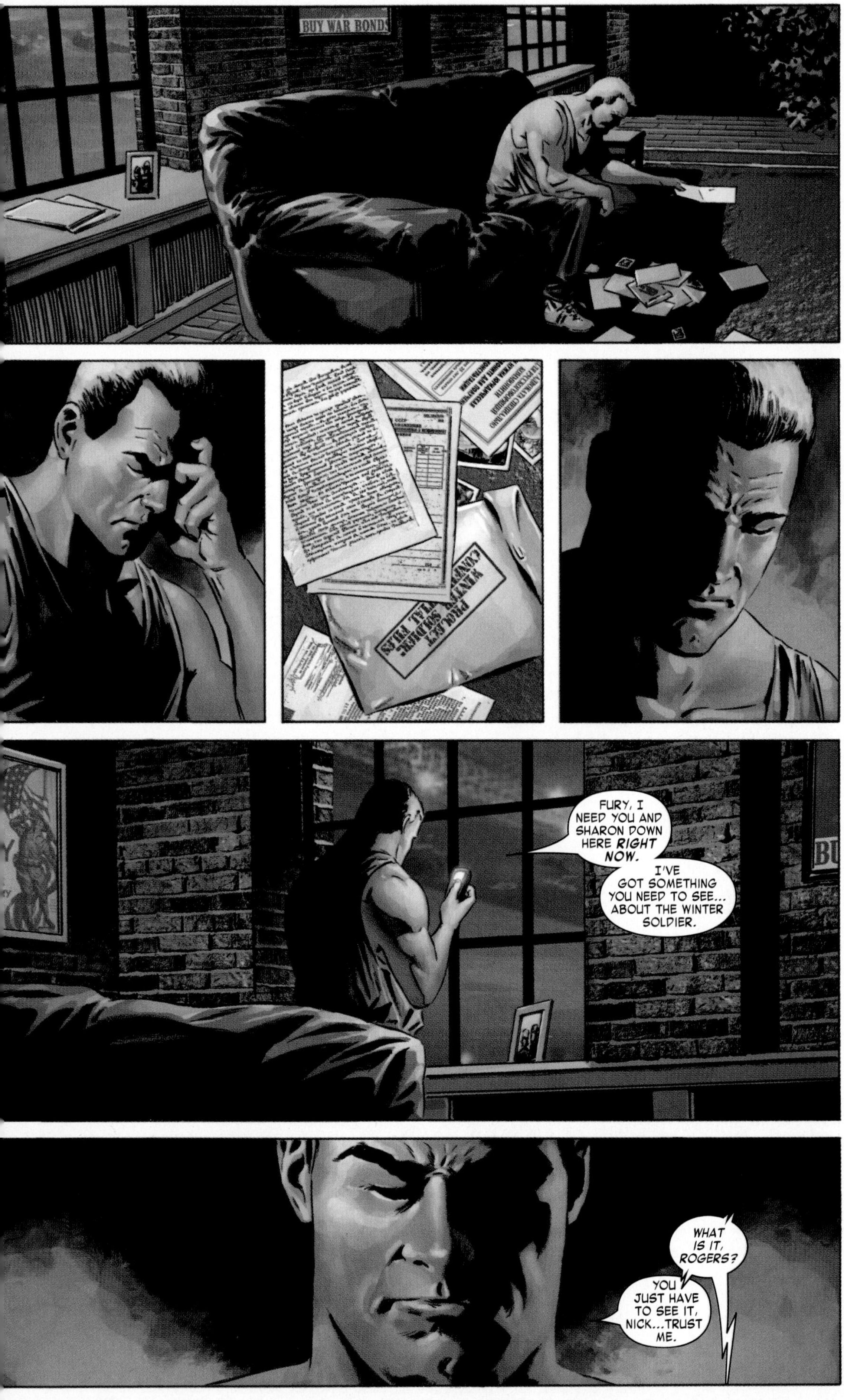
BUY WAR BONDS
FURY, I NEED YOU AND SHARON DOWN HERE RIGHT NOW.
I'VE GOT SOMETHING YOU NEED TO SEE... ABOUT THE WINTER SOLDIER.
WHAT IS IT, ROGERS?
YOU JUST HAVE TO SEE IT, NICK...TRUST ME.

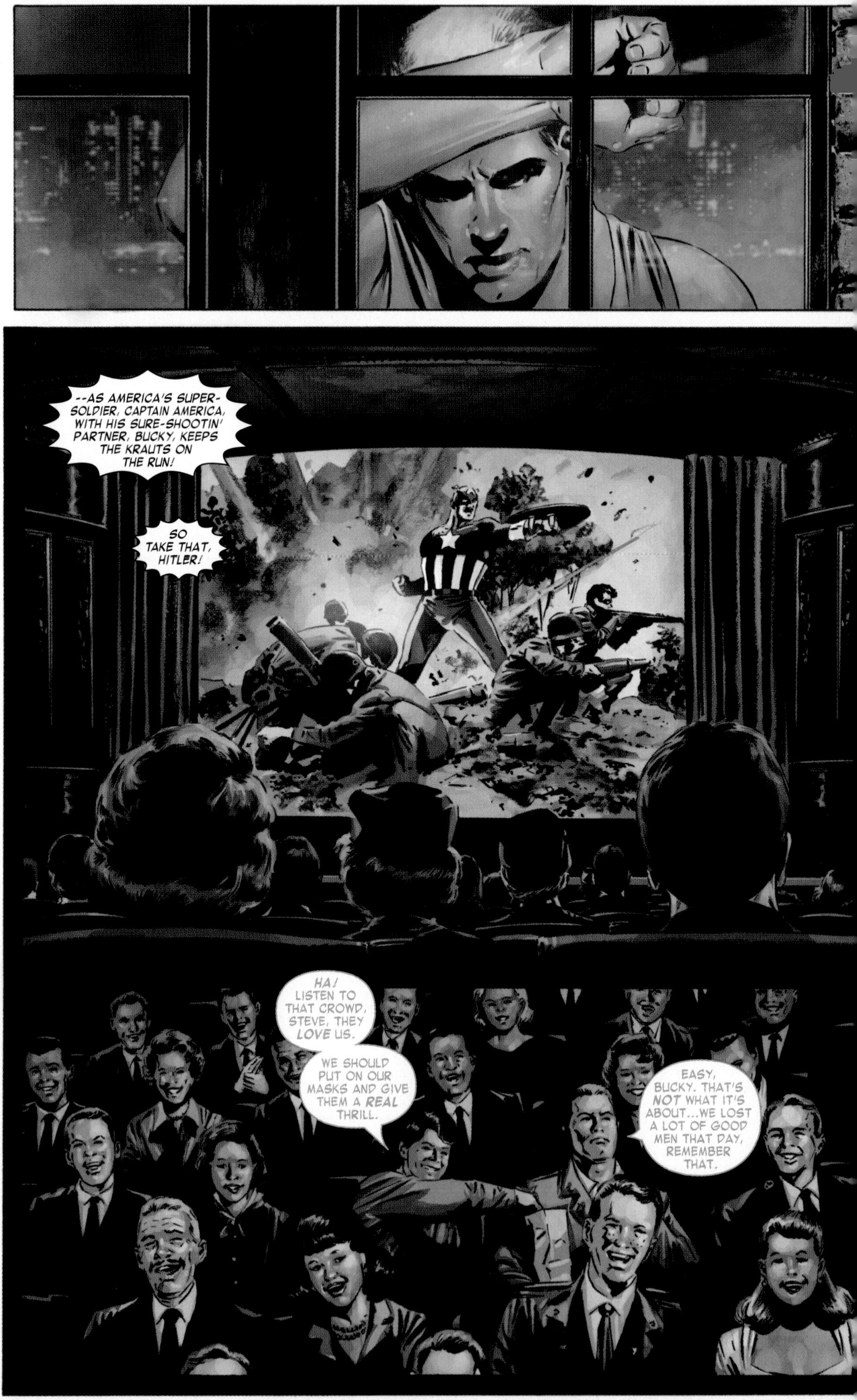
--AS AMERICA'S SUPER-SOLDIER, CAPTAIN AMERICA, WITH HIS SURE-SHOOTIN' PARTNER, BUCKY, KEEPS THE KRAUTS ON THE RUN!
SO TAKE THAT, HITLER!
HA! LISTEN TO THAT CROWD, STEVE, THEY LOVE US.
WE SHOULD PUT ON OUR MASKS AND GIVE THEM A REAL THRILL.
EASY, BUCKY. THAT'S NOT WHAT IT'S ABOUT...WE LOST A LOT OF GOOD MEN THAT DAY, REMEMBER THAT.

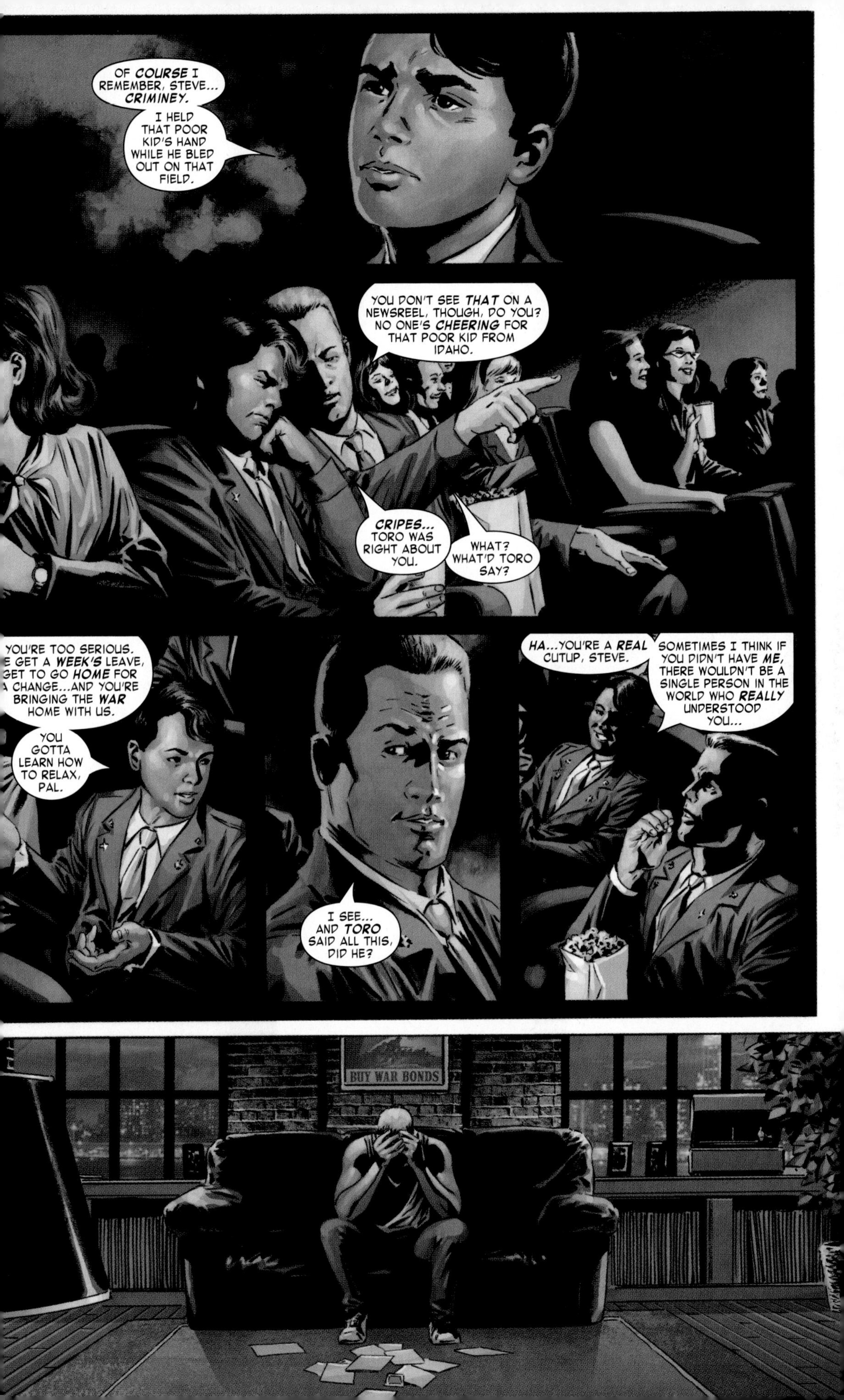
OF COURSE I REMEMBER, STEVE... CRIMINEY.
I HELD THAT POOR KID'S HAND WHILE HE BLED OUT ON THAT FIELD.
YOU DON'T SEE THAT ON A NEWSREEL, THOUGH, DO YOU? NO ONE'S CHEERING FOR THAT POOR KID FROM IDAHO.
CRIPES... TORO WAS RIGHT ABOUT YOU.
WHAT? WHAT'D TORO SAY?
YOU'RE TOO SERIOUS. E GET A WEEK'S LEAVE, GET TO GO HOME FOR A CHANGE...AND YOU'RE BRINGING THE WAR HOME WITH US.
YOU GOTTA LEARN HOW TO RELAX, PAL.
I SEE... AND TORO SAID ALL THIS, DID HE?
HA...YOU'RE A REAL CUTUP, STEVE.
SOMETIMES I THINK IF YOU DIDN'T HAVE ME, THERE WOULDN'T BE A SINGLE PERSON IN THE WORLD WHO REALLY UNDERSTOOD YOU...
BUY WAR BONDS

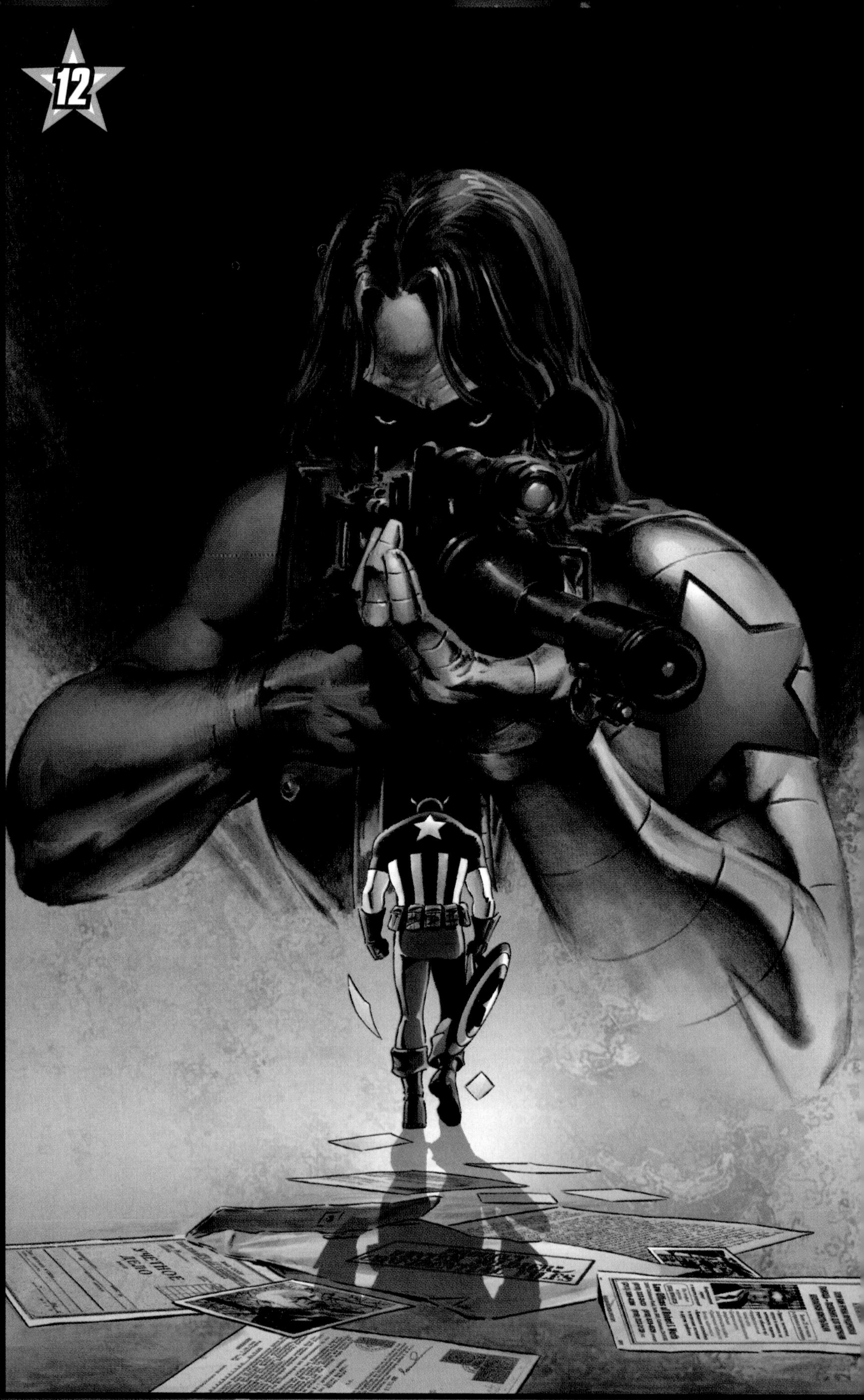
12

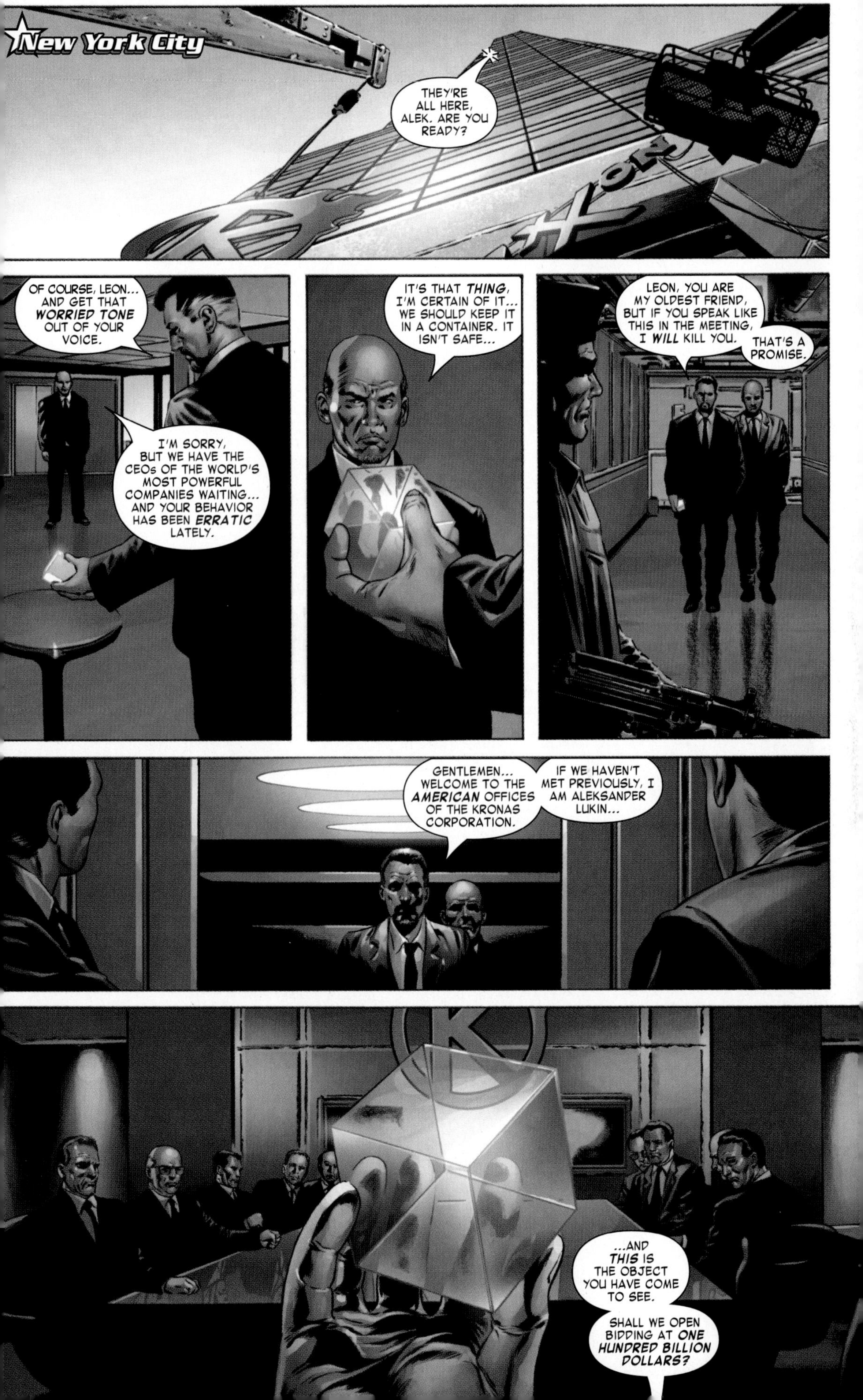
New York City
THEY'RE ALL HERE, ALEK. ARE YOU READY?
OF COURSE, LEON... AND GET THAT WORRIED TONE OUT OF YOUR VOICE.
I'M SORRY, BUT WE HAVE THE CEOs OF THE WORLD'S MOST POWERFUL COMPANIES WAITING... AND YOUR BEHAVIOR HAS BEEN ERRATIC LATELY.
IT'S THAT THING, I'M CERTAIN OF IT... WE SHOULD KEEP IT IN A CONTAINER. IT ISN'T SAFE...
LEON, YOU ARE MY OLDEST FRIEND, BUT IF YOU SPEAK LIKE THIS IN THE MEETING, I WILL KILL YOU.
THAT'S A PROMISE.
GENTLEMEN... WELCOME TO THE AMERICAN OFFICES OF THE KRONAS CORPORATION.
IF WE HAVEN'T MET PREVIOUSLY, I AM ALEKSANDER LUKIN...
...AND THIS IS THE OBJECT YOU HAVE COME TO SEE.
SHALL WE OPEN BIDDING AT ONE HUNDRED BILLION DOLLARS?

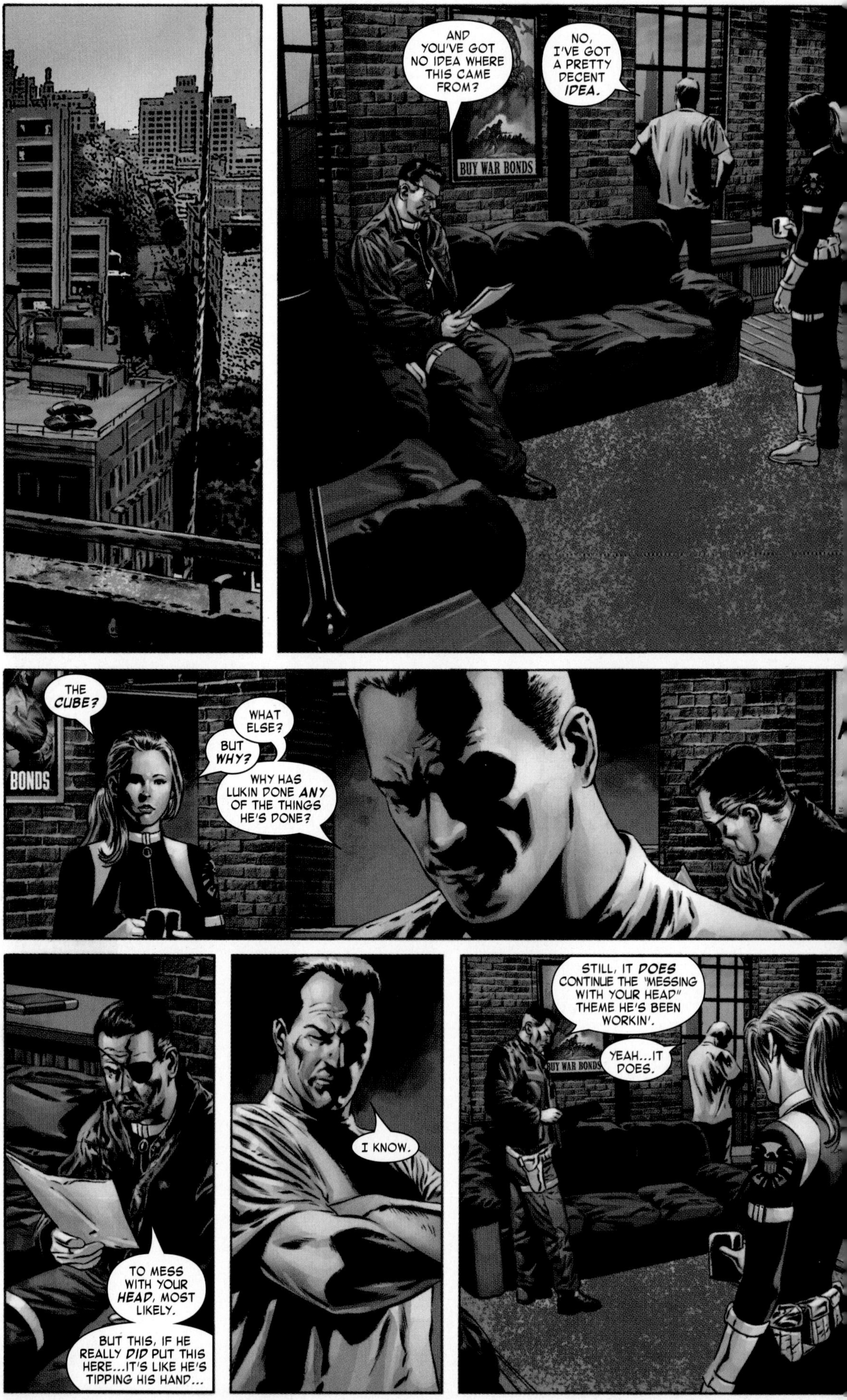
AND YOU'VE GOT NO IDEA WHERE THIS CAME FROM?
NO, I'VE GOT A PRETTY DECENT IDEA.
BUY WAR BONDS
THE CUBE?
WHAT ELSE?
BUT WHY?
WHY HAS LUKIN DONE ANY OF THE THINGS HE'S DONE?
BONDS
TO MESS WITH YOUR HEAD, MOST LIKELY.
BUT THIS, IF HE REALLY DID PUT THIS HERE...IT'S LIKE HE'S TIPPING HIS HAND...
I KNOW.
STILL, IT DOES CONTINUE THE "MESSING WITH YOUR HEAD" THEME HE'S BEEN WORKIN'.
BUY WAR BONDS
YEAH...IT DOES.

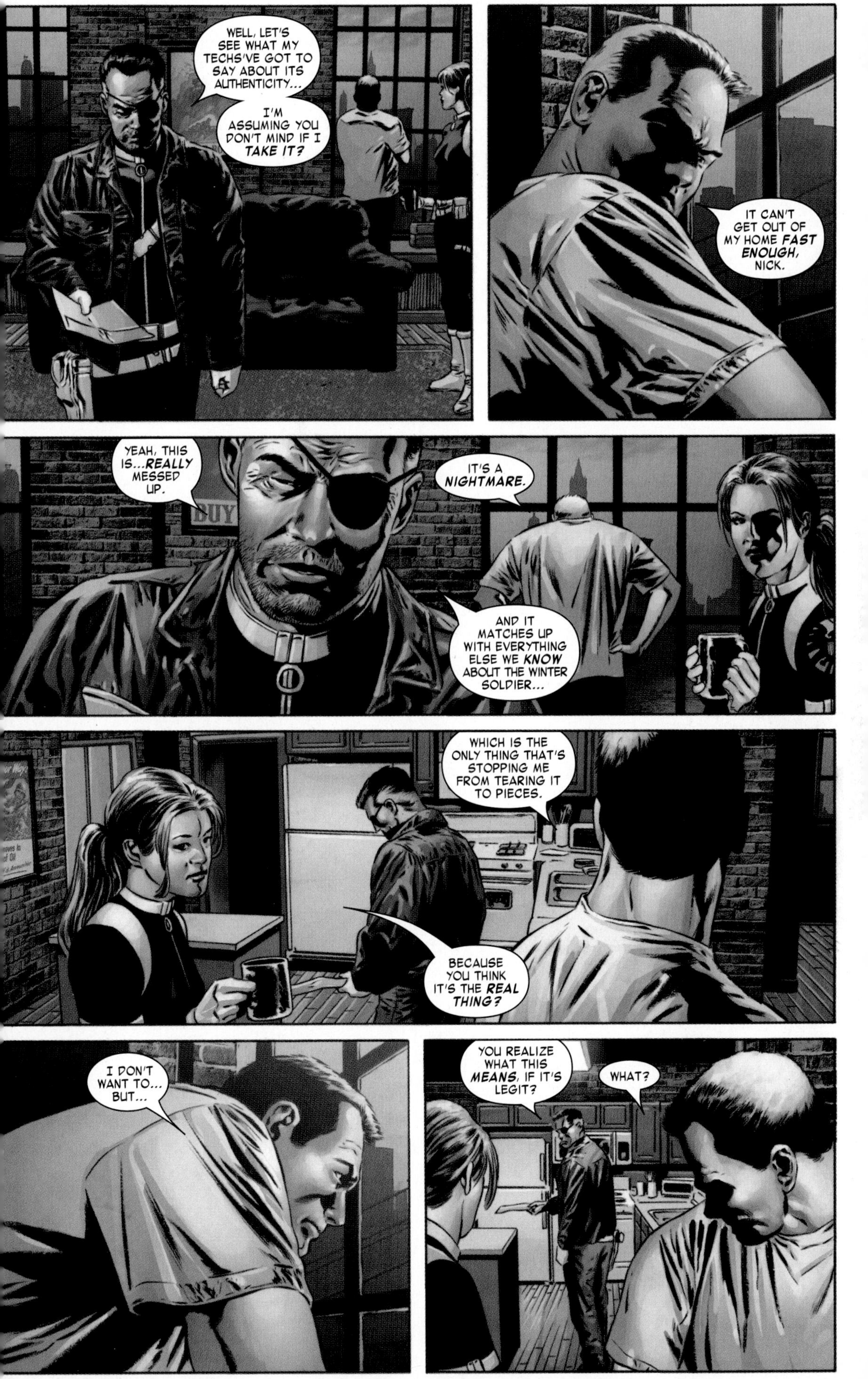
WELL, LET'S SEE WHAT MY TECHS'VE GOT TO SAY ABOUT ITS AUTHENTICITY...
I'M ASSUMING YOU DON'T MIND IF I TAKE IT?
IT CAN'T GET OUT OF MY HOME FAST ENOUGH, NICK.
YEAH, THIS IS...REALLY MESSED UP.
BUY
IT'S A NIGHTMARE.
AND IT MATCHES UP WITH EVERYTHING ELSE WE KNOW ABOUT THE WINTER SOLDIER...
WHICH IS THE ONLY THING THAT'S STOPPING ME FROM TEARING IT TO PIECES.
BECAUSE YOU THINK IT'S THE REAL THING?
I DON'T WANT TO... BUT...
YOU REALIZE WHAT THIS MEANS, IF IT'S LEGIT?
WHAT?

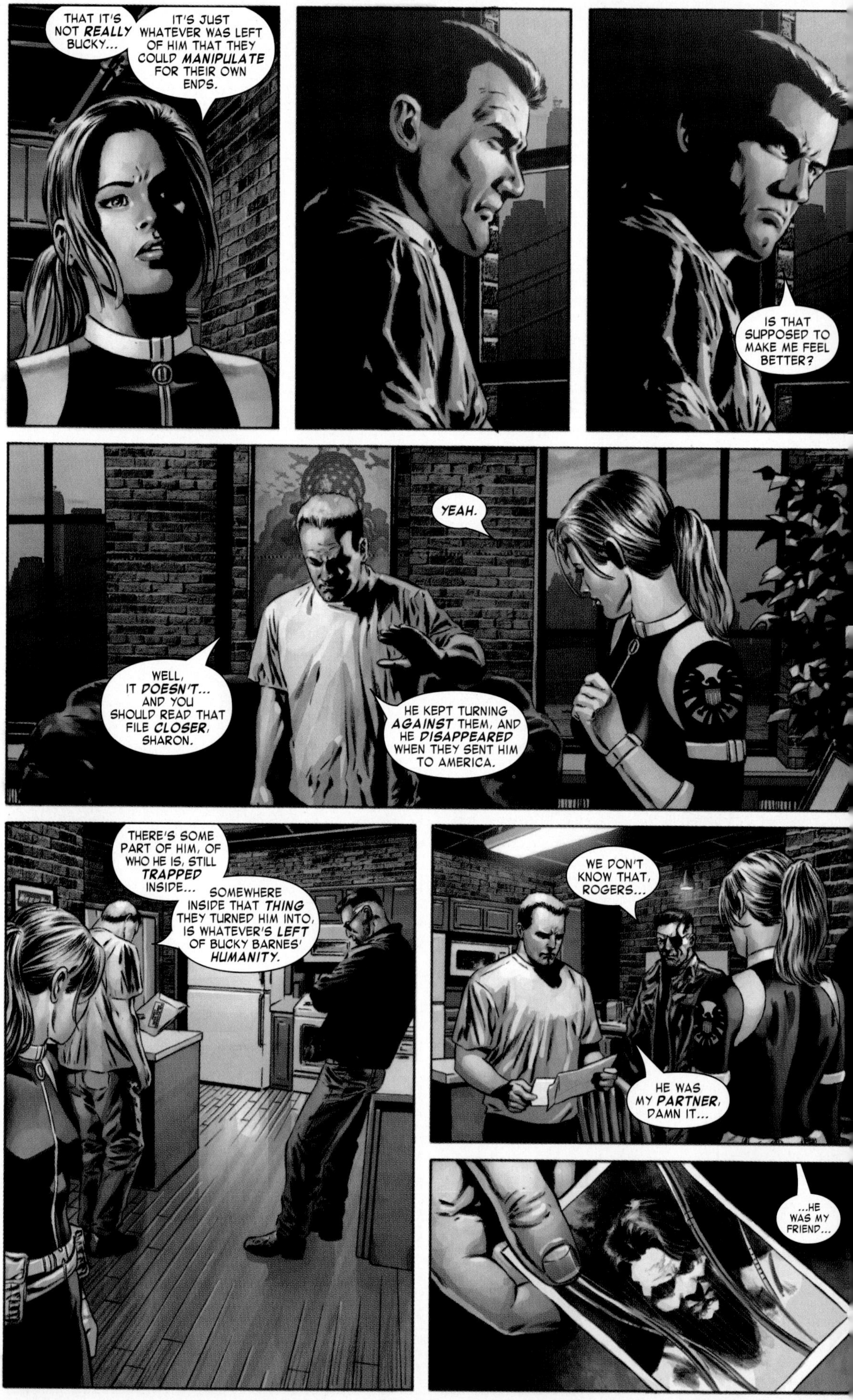

THAT IT'S NOT REALLY BUCKY...
IT'S JUST WHATEVER WAS LEFT OF HIM THAT THEY COULD MANIPULATE FOR THEIR OWN ENDS.
IS THAT SUPPOSED TO MAKE ME FEEL BETTER?
YEAH.
WELL, IT DOESN'T... AND YOU SHOULD READ THAT FILE CLOSER, SHARON.
HE KEPT TURNING AGAINST THEM, AND HE DISAPPEARED WHEN THEY SENT HIM TO AMERICA.
THERE'S SOME PART OF HIM, OF WHO HE IS, STILL TRAPPED INSIDE...
SOMEWHERE INSIDE THAT THING THEY TURNED HIM INTO, IS WHATEVER'S LEFT OF BUCKY BARNES' HUMANITY.
WE DON'T KNOW THAT, ROGERS...
HE WAS MY PARTNER, DAMN IT...
...HE WAS MY FRIEND...

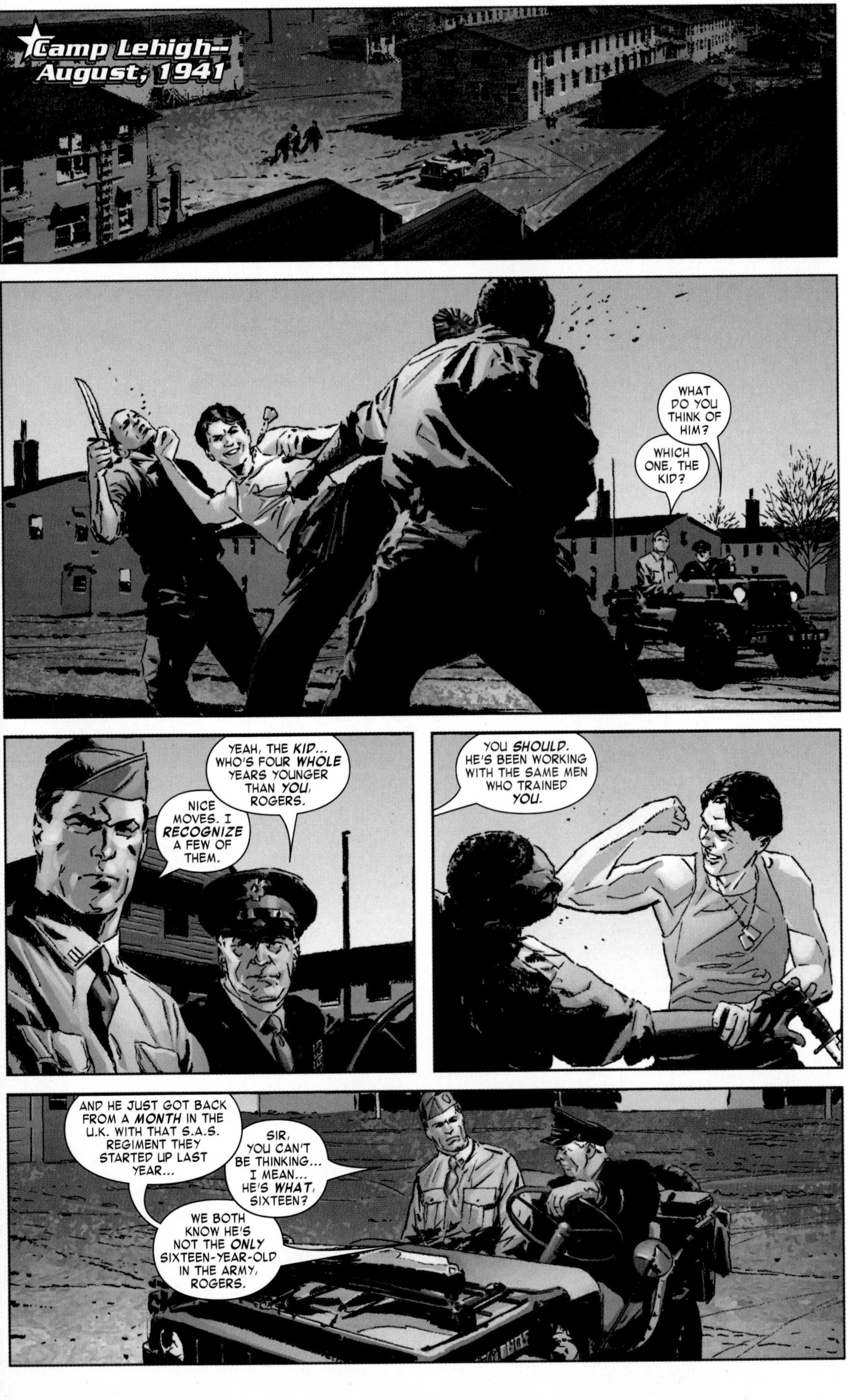
Camp Lehigh— August, 1941
WHAT DO YOU THINK OF HIM?
WHICH ONE, THE KID?
YEAH, THE *KID*... WHO'S FOUR *WHOLE* YEARS YOUNGER THAN *YOU*, ROGERS.
NICE MOVES. I *RECOGNIZE* A FEW OF THEM.
YOU *SHOULD*. HE'S BEEN WORKING WITH THE SAME MEN WHO TRAINED *YOU*.
AND HE JUST GOT BACK FROM A *MONTH* IN THE U.K. WITH THAT S.A.S. REGIMENT THEY STARTED UP LAST YEAR...
SIR, YOU CAN'T BE THINKING... I MEAN... HE'S *WHAT*, SIXTEEN?
WE BOTH KNOW HE'S NOT THE *ONLY* SIXTEEN-YEAR-OLD IN THE ARMY, ROGERS.

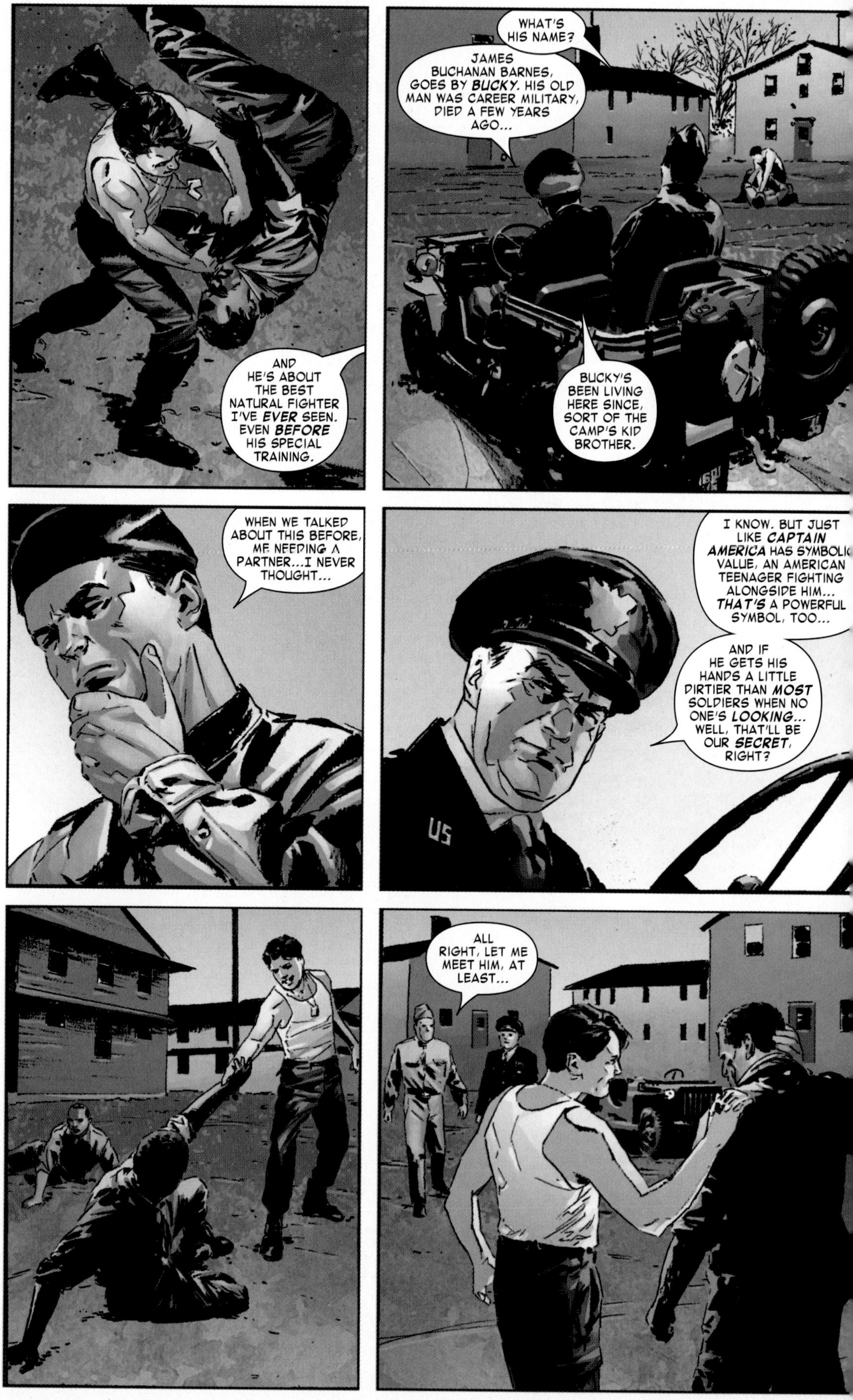
AND HE'S ABOUT THE BEST NATURAL FIGHTER I'VE *EVER* SEEN. EVEN *BEFORE* HIS SPECIAL TRAINING.
WHAT'S HIS NAME?
JAMES BUCHANAN BARNES, GOES BY *BUCKY.* HIS OLD MAN WAS CAREER MILITARY, DIED A FEW YEARS AGO...
BUCKY'S BEEN LIVING HERE SINCE, SORT OF THE CAMP'S KID BROTHER.
WHEN WE TALKED ABOUT THIS BEFORE, ME NEEDING A PARTNER...I NEVER THOUGHT...
I KNOW. BUT JUST LIKE *CAPTAIN AMERICA* HAS SYMBOLIC VALUE, AN AMERICAN TEENAGER FIGHTING ALONGSIDE HIM... *THAT'S* A POWERFUL SYMBOL, TOO...
AND IF HE GETS HIS HANDS A LITTLE DIRTIER THAN *MOST* SOLDIERS WHEN NO ONE'S *LOOKING...* WELL, THAT'LL BE OUR *SECRET*, RIGHT?
US
ALL RIGHT, LET ME MEET HIM, AT LEAST...

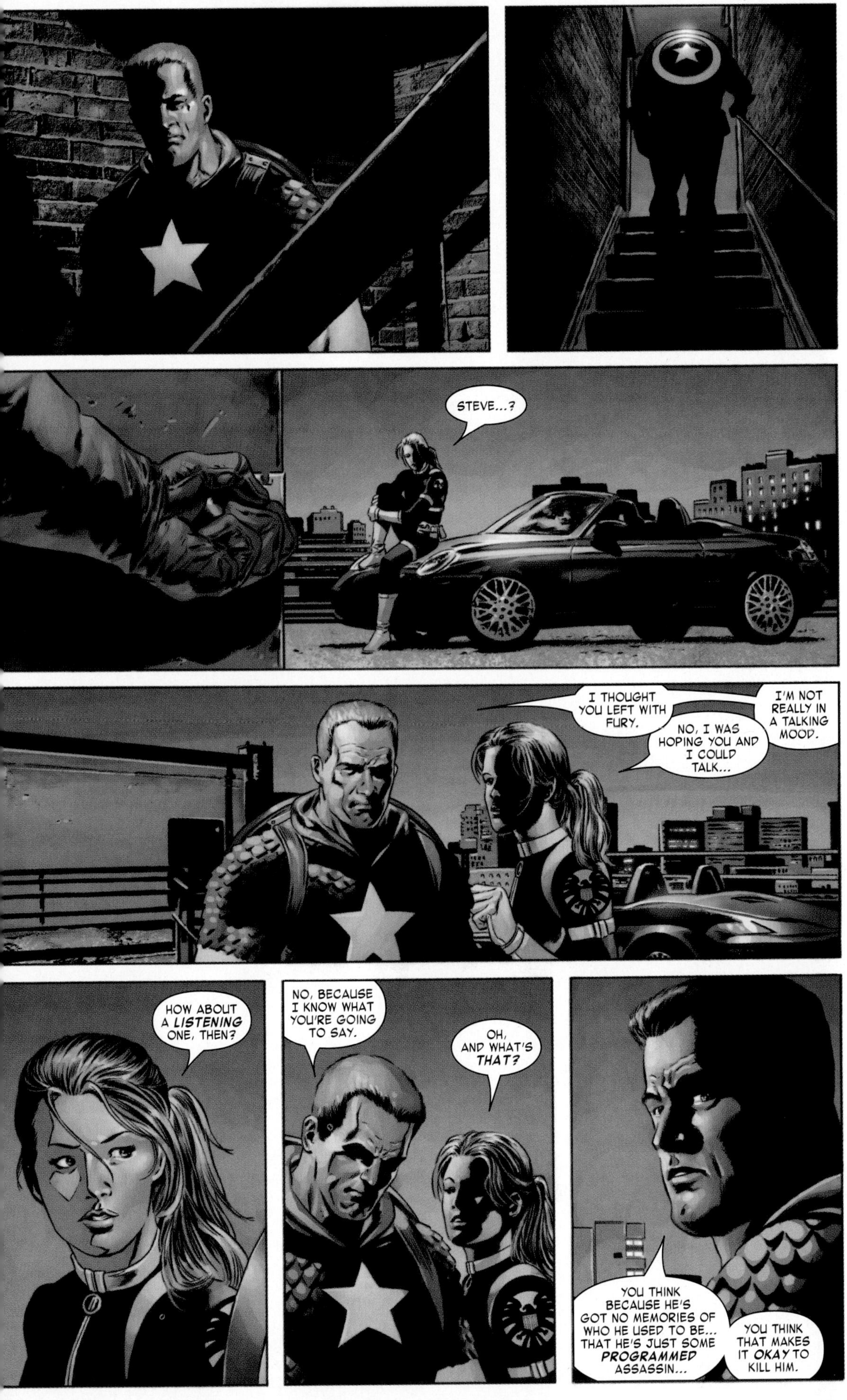
STEVE...?
I THOUGHT YOU LEFT WITH FURY.
NO, I WAS HOPING YOU AND I COULD TALK...
I'M NOT REALLY IN A TALKING MOOD.
HOW ABOUT A *LISTENING* ONE, THEN?
NO, BECAUSE I KNOW WHAT YOU'RE GOING TO SAY.
OH, AND WHAT'S *THAT?*
YOU THINK BECAUSE HE'S GOT NO MEMORIES OF WHO HE USED TO BE... THAT HE'S JUST SOME *PROGRAMMED* ASSASSIN...
YOU THINK THAT MAKES IT *OKAY* TO KILL HIM.

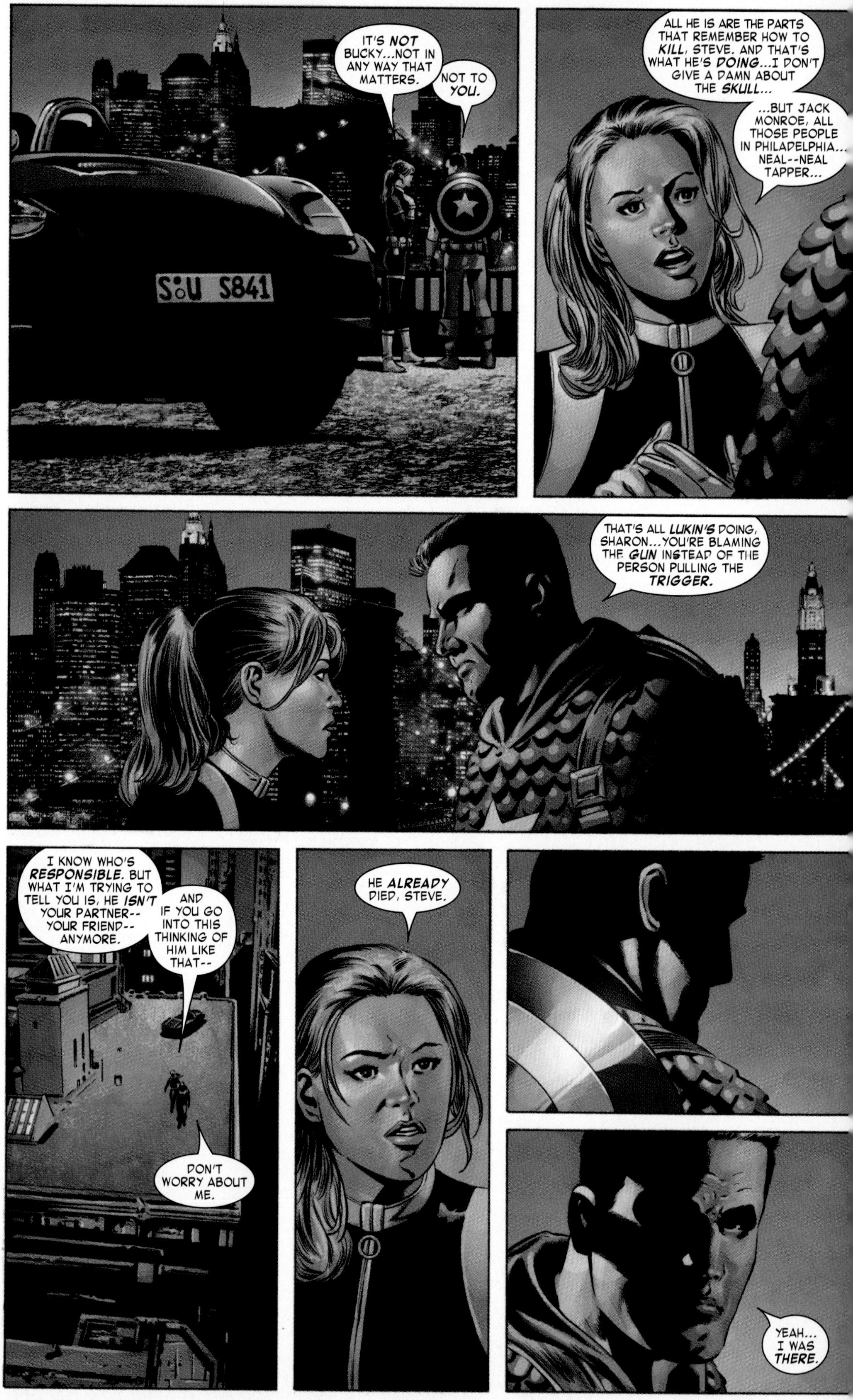
IT'S NOT BUCKY...NOT IN ANY WAY THAT MATTERS.
NOT TO YOU.
ALL HE IS ARE THE PARTS THAT REMEMBER HOW TO KILL, STEVE. AND THAT'S WHAT HE'S DOING...I DON'T GIVE A DAMN ABOUT THE SKULL...
...BUT JACK MONROE, ALL THOSE PEOPLE IN PHILADELPHIA... NEAL--NEAL TAPPER...
THAT'S ALL LUKIN'S DOING, SHARON...YOU'RE BLAMING THE GUN INSTEAD OF THE PERSON PULLING THE TRIGGER.
I KNOW WHO'S RESPONSIBLE. BUT WHAT I'M TRYING TO TELL YOU IS, HE ISN'T YOUR PARTNER-- YOUR FRIEND-- ANYMORE.
AND IF YOU GO INTO THIS THINKING OF HIM LIKE THAT--
DON'T WORRY ABOUT ME.
HE ALREADY DIED, STEVE.
YEAH... I WAS THERE.

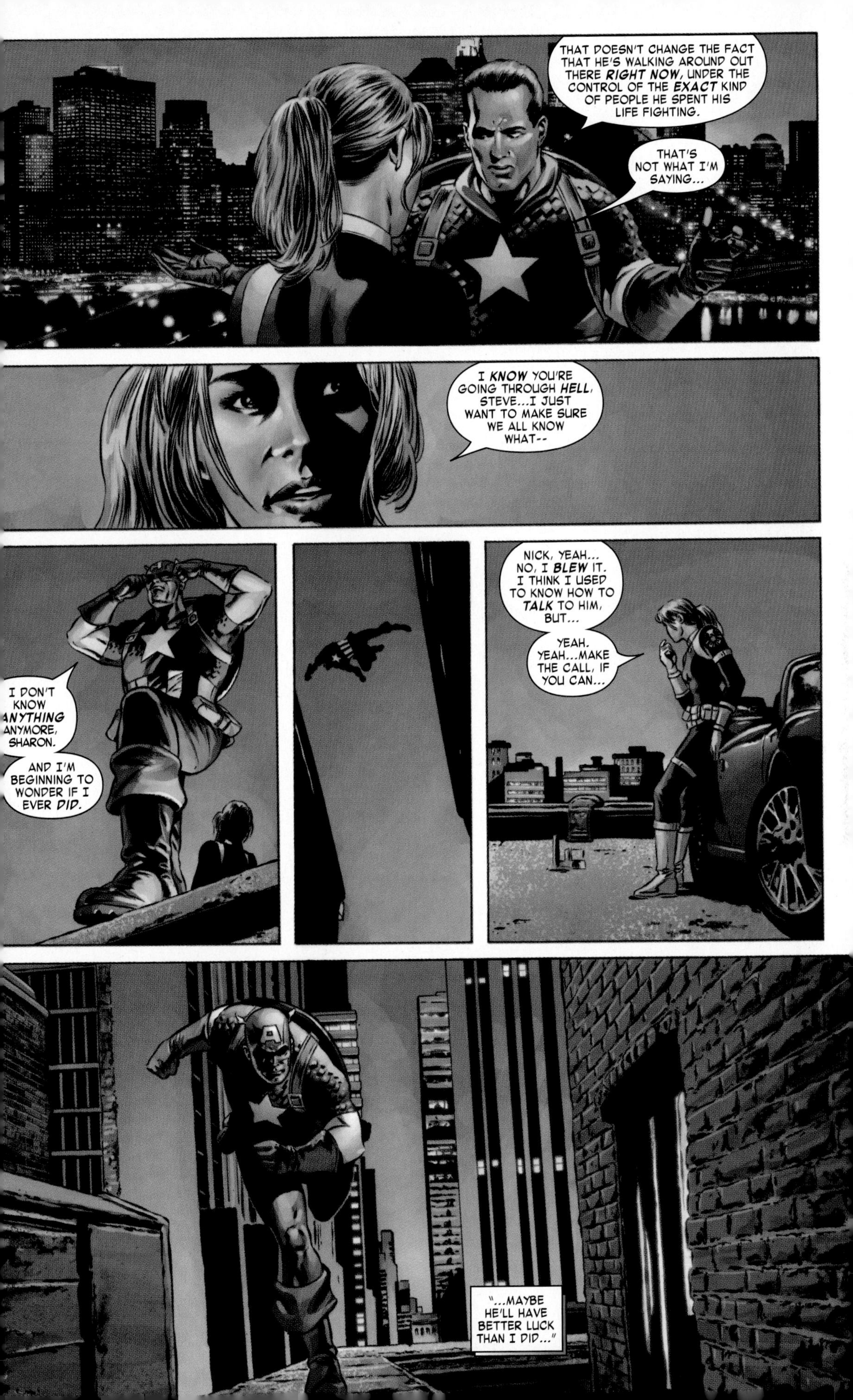
THAT DOESN'T CHANGE THE FACT THAT HE'S WALKING AROUND OUT THERE *RIGHT NOW*, UNDER THE CONTROL OF THE *EXACT* KIND OF PEOPLE HE SPENT HIS LIFE FIGHTING.
THAT'S NOT WHAT I'M SAYING...
I *KNOW* YOU'RE GOING THROUGH *HELL*, STEVE...I JUST WANT TO MAKE SURE WE ALL KNOW WHAT--
I DON'T KNOW *ANYTHING* ANYMORE, SHARON.
AND I'M BEGINNING TO WONDER IF I EVER *DID*.
NICK, YEAH... NO, I *BLEW* IT. I THINK I USED TO KNOW HOW TO *TALK* TO HIM, BUT...
YEAH. YEAH...MAKE THE CALL, IF YOU CAN...
"...MAYBE HE'LL HAVE BETTER LUCK THAN I DID..."

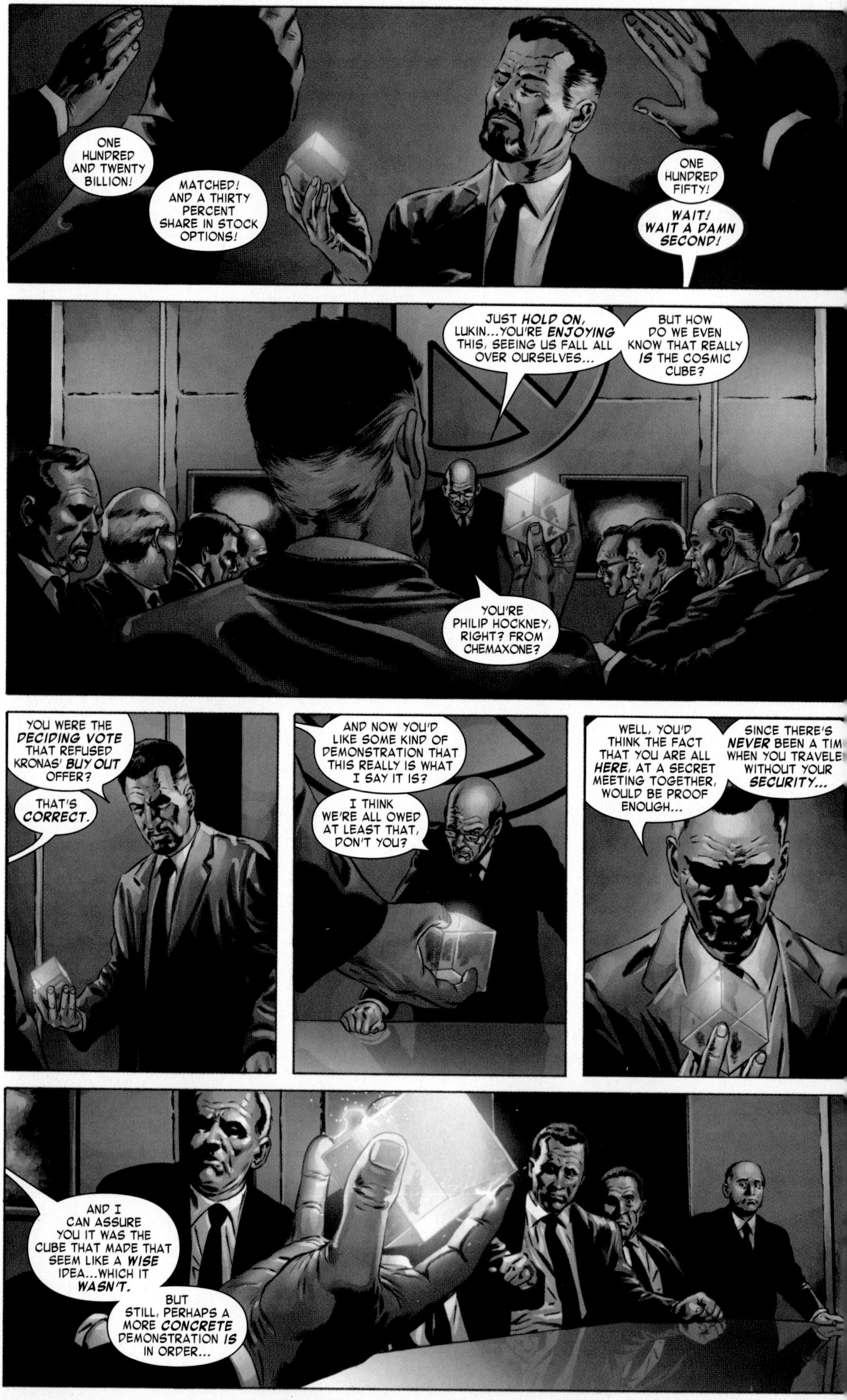
ONE HUNDRED AND TWENTY BILLION!
MATCHED! AND A THIRTY PERCENT SHARE IN STOCK OPTIONS!
ONE HUNDRED FIFTY!
WAIT! WAIT A DAMN SECOND!
JUST HOLD ON, LUKIN...YOU'RE ENJOYING THIS, SEEING US FALL ALL OVER OURSELVES...
BUT HOW DO WE EVEN KNOW THAT REALLY IS THE COSMIC CUBE?
YOU'RE PHILIP HOCKNEY, RIGHT? FROM CHEMAXONE?
YOU WERE THE DECIDING VOTE THAT REFUSED KRONAS' BUY OUT OFFER?
THAT'S CORRECT.
AND NOW YOU'D LIKE SOME KIND OF DEMONSTRATION THAT THIS REALLY IS WHAT I SAY IT IS?
I THINK WE'RE ALL OWED AT LEAST THAT, DON'T YOU?
WELL, YOU'D THINK THE FACT THAT YOU ARE ALL HERE, AT A SECRET MEETING TOGETHER, WOULD BE PROOF ENOUGH...
SINCE THERE'S NEVER BEEN A TIM WHEN YOU TRAVELE WITHOUT YOUR SECURITY...
AND I CAN ASSURE YOU IT WAS THE CUBE THAT MADE THAT SEEM LIKE A WISE IDEA...WHICH IT WASN'T.
BUT STILL, PERHAPS A MORE CONCRETE DEMONSTRATION IS IN ORDER...

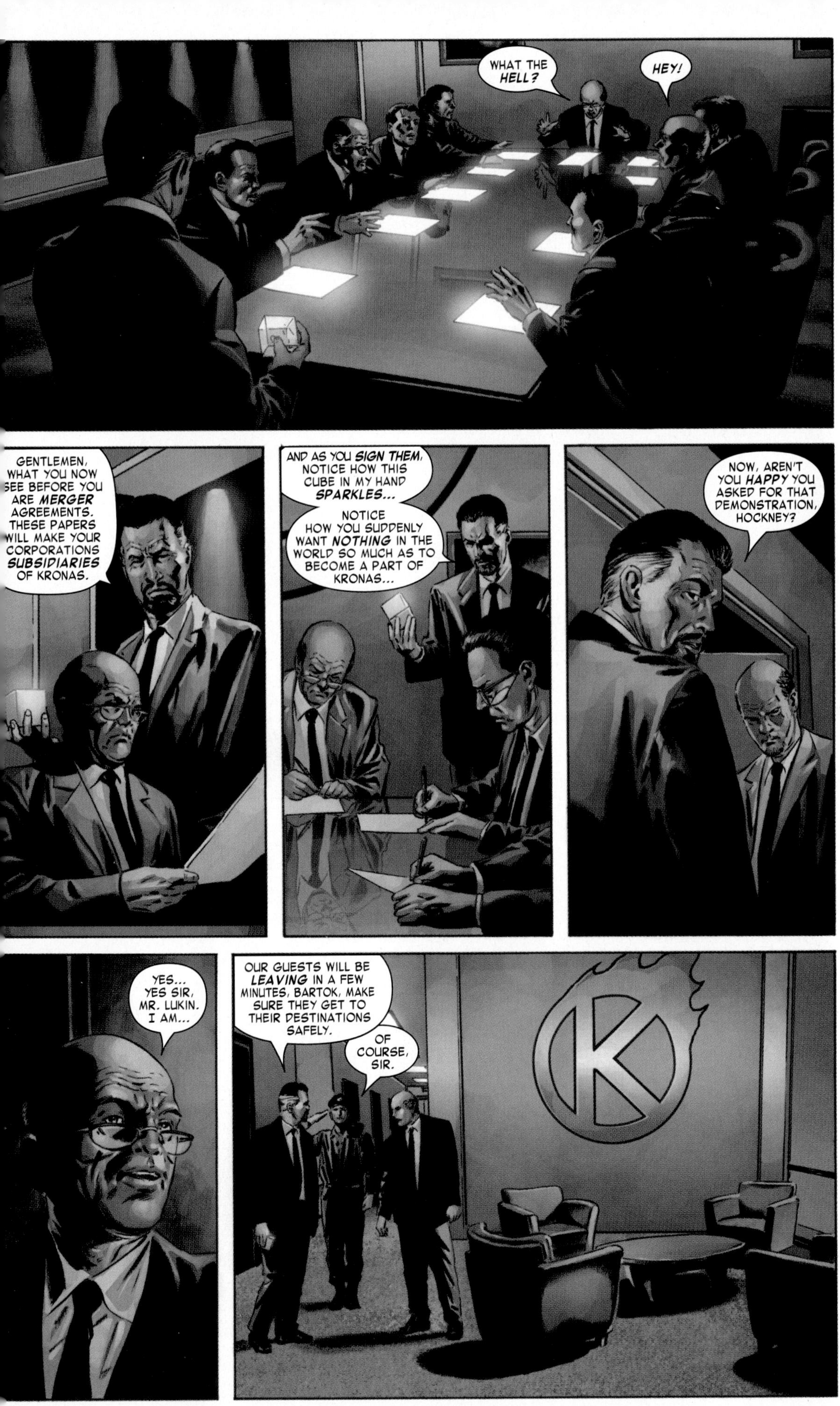

WHAT THE HELL?
HEY!
GENTLEMEN, WHAT YOU NOW SEE BEFORE YOU ARE MERGER AGREEMENTS. THESE PAPERS WILL MAKE YOUR CORPORATIONS SUBSIDIARIES OF KRONAS.
AND AS YOU SIGN THEM, NOTICE HOW THIS CUBE IN MY HAND SPARKLES...
NOTICE HOW YOU SUDDENLY WANT NOTHING IN THE WORLD SO MUCH AS TO BECOME A PART OF KRONAS...
NOW, AREN'T YOU HAPPY YOU ASKED FOR THAT DEMONSTRATION, HOCKNEY?
YES... YES SIR, MR. LUKIN. I AM...
OUR GUESTS WILL BE LEAVING IN A FEW MINUTES, BARTOK, MAKE SURE THEY GET TO THEIR DESTINATIONS SAFELY.
OF COURSE, SIR.

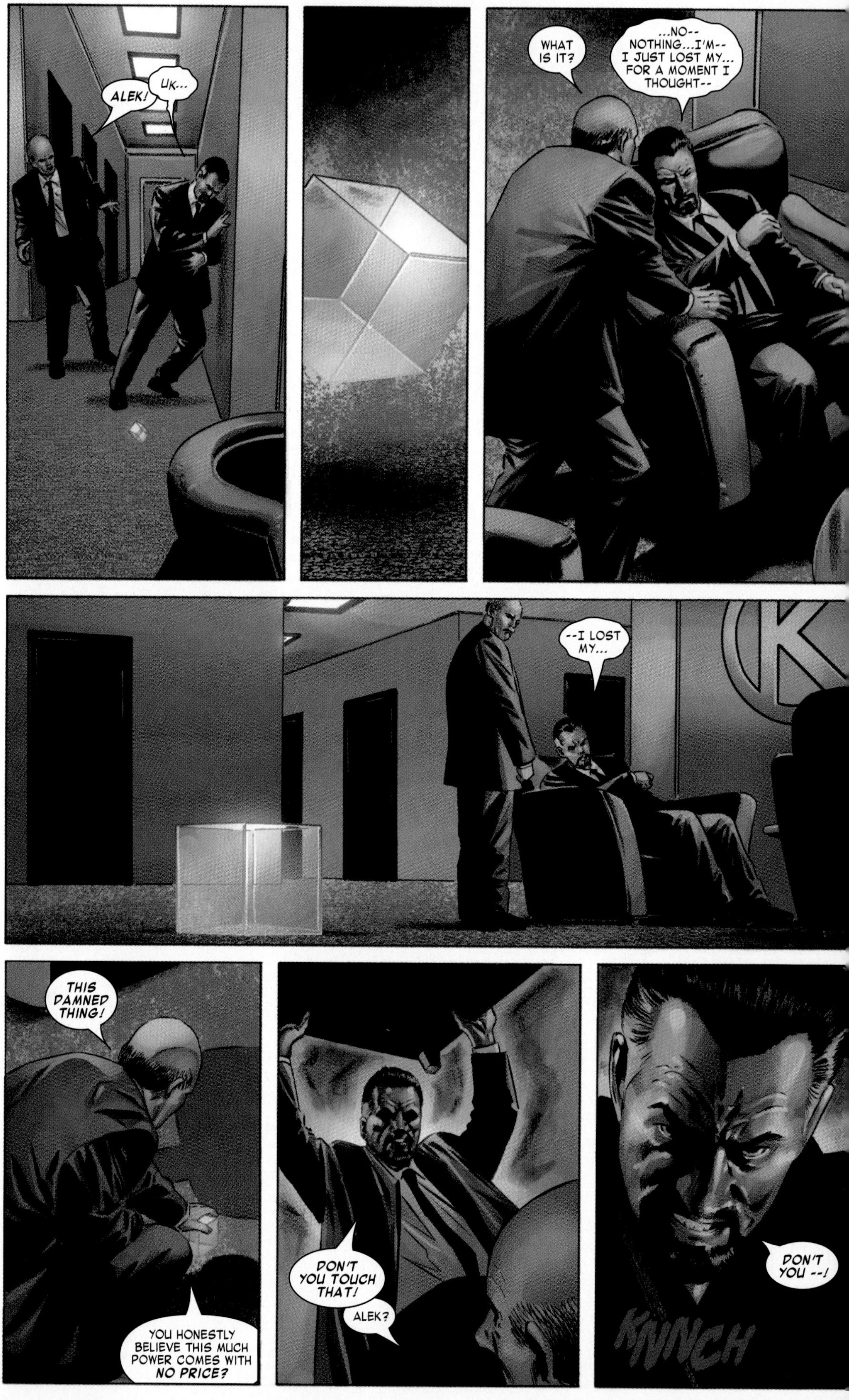
ALEK!
UK...
WHAT IS IT?
...NO-- NOTHING...I'M-- I JUST LOST MY... FOR A MOMENT I THOUGHT--
--I LOST MY...
THIS DAMNED THING!
YOU HONESTLY BELIEVE THIS MUCH POWER COMES WITH NO PRICE?
DON'T YOU TOUCH THAT!
ALEK?
DON'T YOU --!
KNNCH

DAMN IT.

THIS IS NO WAY TO FUNCTION... WORK THROUGH IT, STEVE.

ANGER WILL NOT HELP YOU DEAL WITH THIS.

IT'LL JUST MAKE SURE THAT *WHATEVER* YOU DO NEXT IS THE WRONG MOVE.

AND YOU CAN'T AFFORD THAT.

YOU'VE LET LUKIN PUSH ALL YOUR BUTTONS TOO EASILY SO FAR... YOU CAN'T AFFORD ANYTHING BUT A CLEAR HEAD FROM THIS POINT ON...

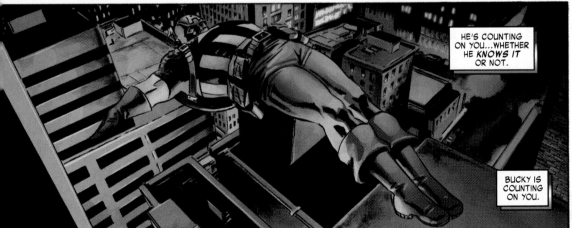

HE'S COUNTING ON YOU...WHETHER HE *KNOWS IT* OR NOT.

BUCKY IS COUNTING ON YOU.

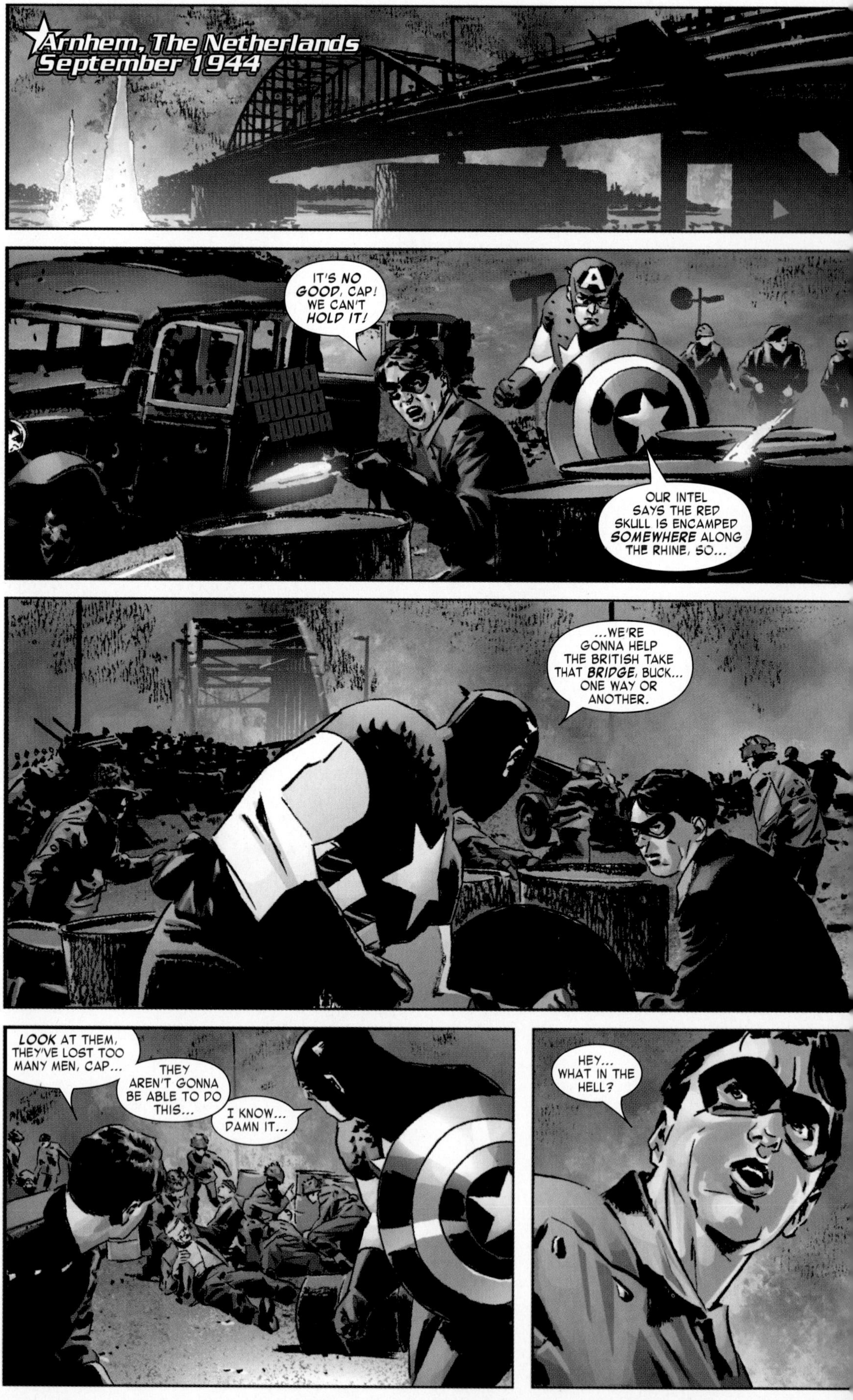
Arnhem, The Netherlands
September 1944
IT'S NO GOOD, CAP! WE CAN'T HOLD IT!
BUDDA BUDDA BUDDA
OUR INTEL SAYS THE RED SKULL IS ENCAMPED SOMEWHERE ALONG THE RHINE, SO...
...WE'RE GONNA HELP THE BRITISH TAKE THAT BRIDGE, BUCK... ONE WAY OR ANOTHER.
LOOK AT THEM, THEY'VE LOST TOO MANY MEN, CAP...
THEY AREN'T GONNA BE ABLE TO DO THIS...
I KNOW... DAMN IT...
HEY... WHAT IN THE HELL?

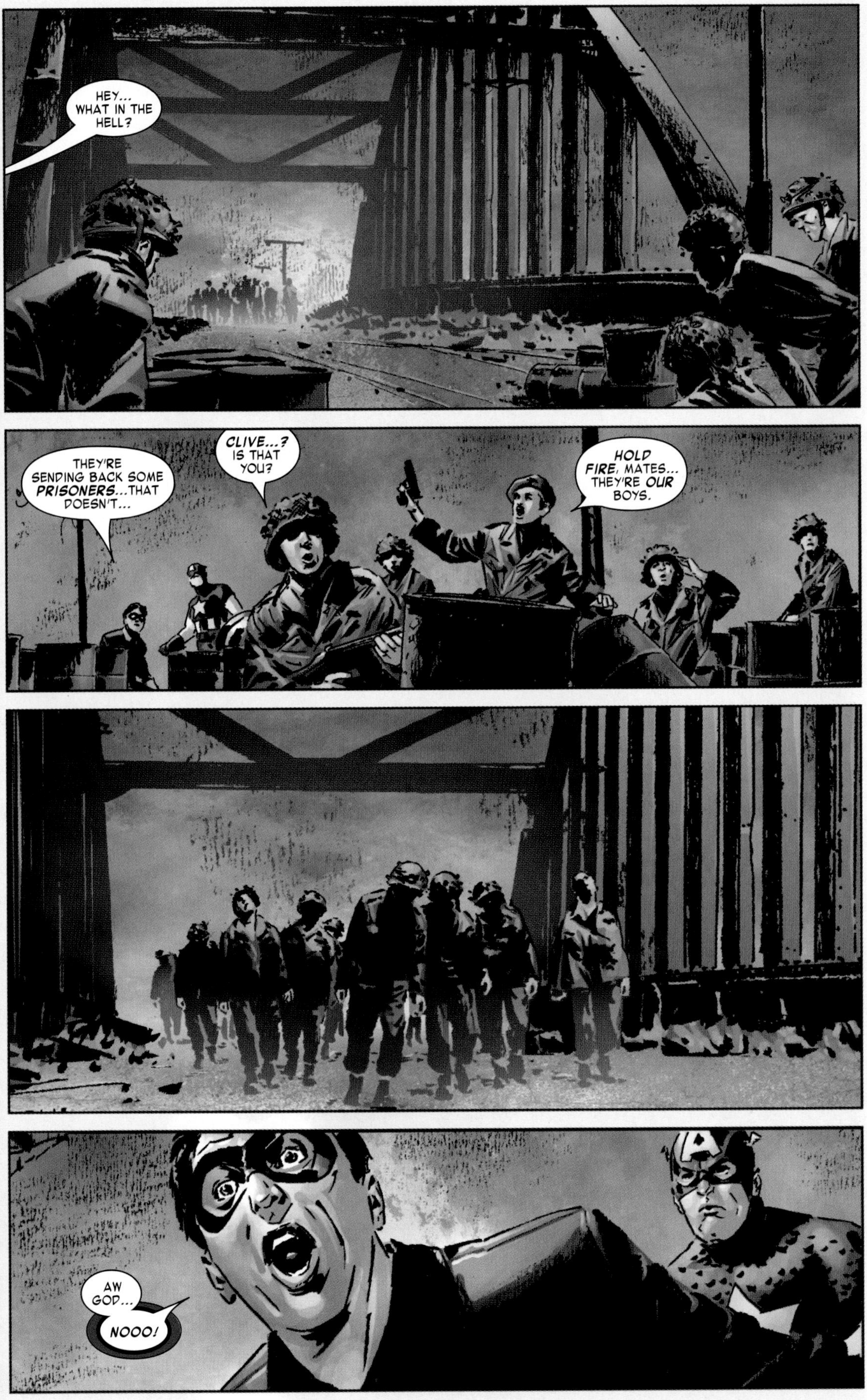
HEY... WHAT IN THE HELL?
THEY'RE SENDING BACK SOME PRISONERS...THAT DOESN'T...
CLIVE...? IS THAT YOU?
HOLD FIRE, MATES... THEY'RE OUR BOYS.
AW GOD...
NOOO!

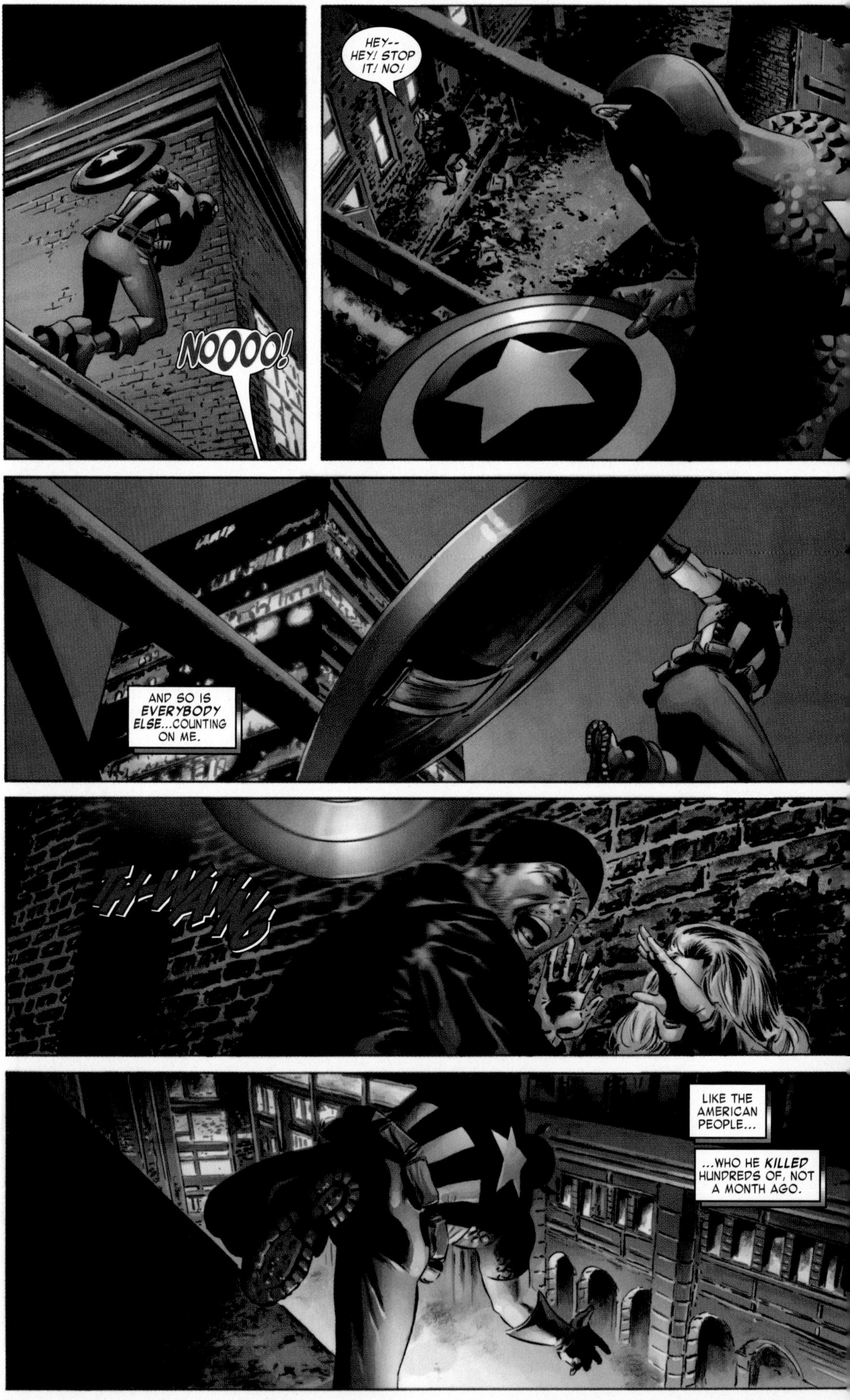
NOOOO!
HEY-- HEY! STOP IT! NO!
AND SO IS EVERYBODY ELSE...COUNTING ON ME.
TH-WANG
LIKE THE AMERICAN PEOPLE...
...WHO HE KILLED HUNDREDS OF, NOT A MONTH AGO.

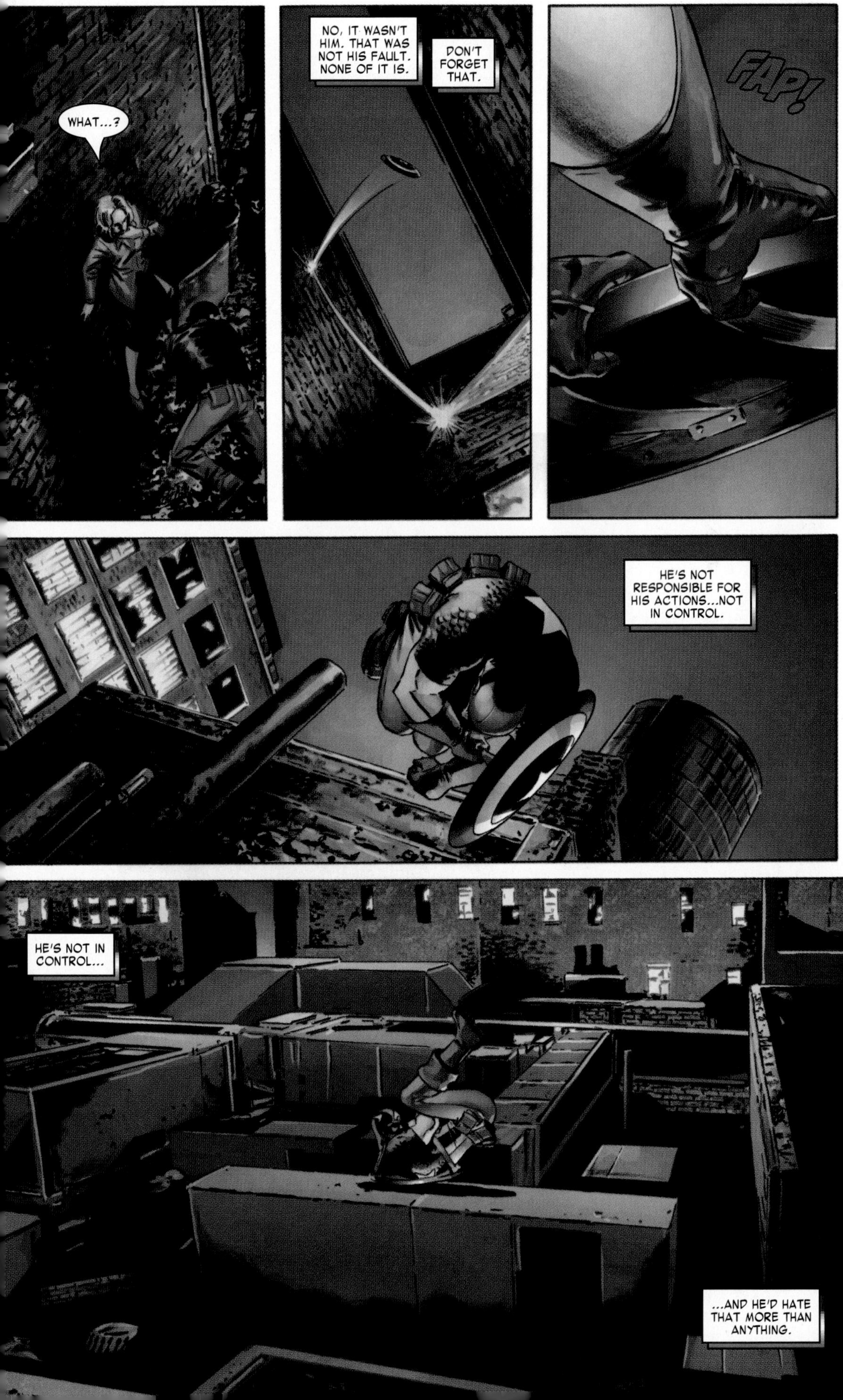
WHAT...?
NO, IT WASN'T HIM. THAT WAS NOT HIS FAULT. NONE OF IT IS.
DON'T FORGET THAT.
FAP!
HE'S NOT RESPONSIBLE FOR HIS ACTIONS...NOT IN CONTROL.
HE'S NOT IN CONTROL...
...AND HE'D HATE THAT MORE THAN ANYTHING.

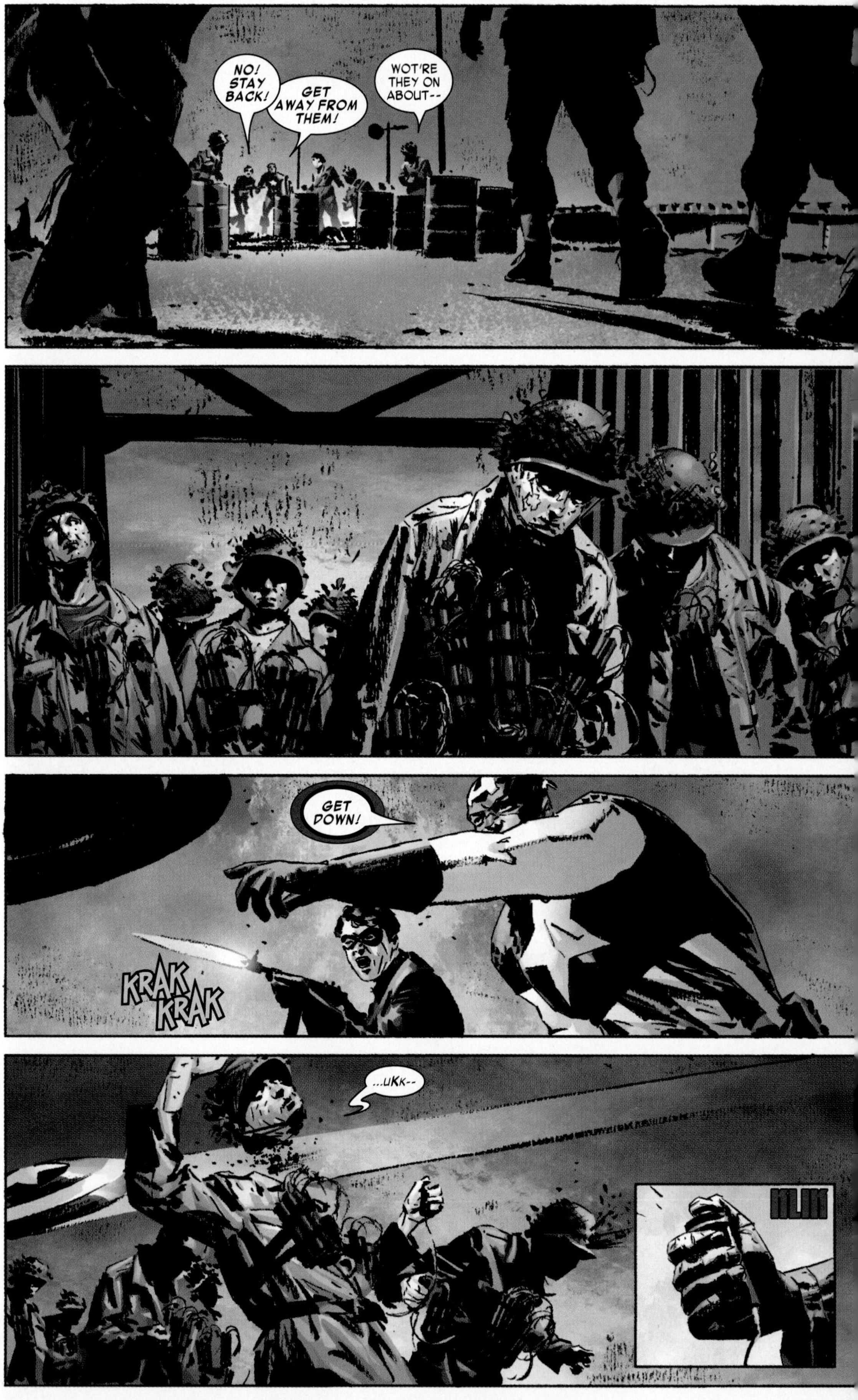
NO! STAY BACK!
GET AWAY FROM THEM!
WOT'RE THEY ON ABOUT--
GET DOWN!
KRAK KRAK
...UKK--
KLIK

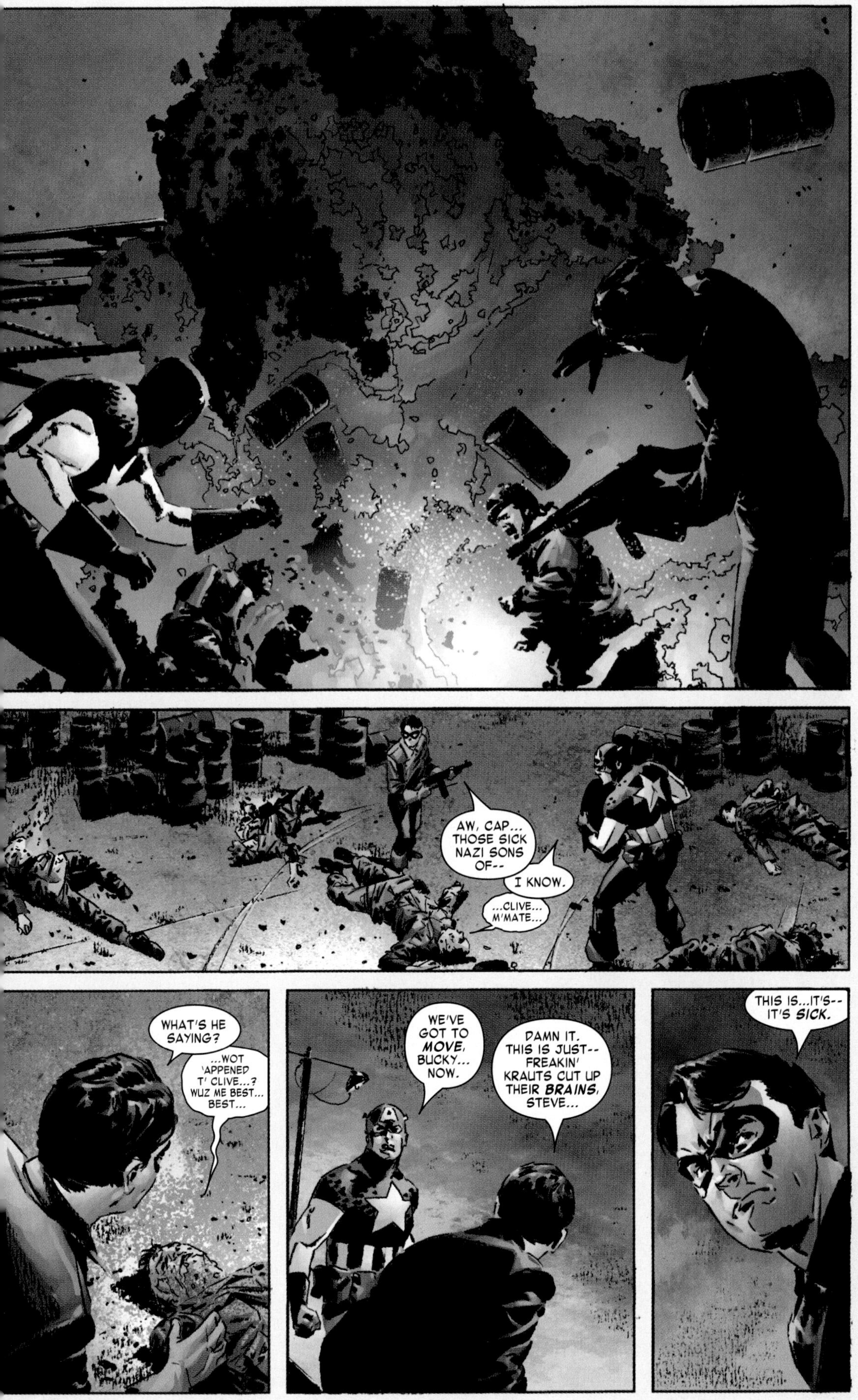
AW, CAP... THOSE SICK NAZI SONS OF--
I KNOW.
...CLIVE... M'MATE...
WHAT'S HE SAYING?
...WOT 'APPENED T' CLIVE...? WUZ ME BEST... BEST...
WE'VE GOT TO MOVE, BUCKY... NOW.
DAMN IT. THIS IS JUST-- FREAKIN' KRAUTS CUT UP THEIR BRAINS, STEVE...
THIS IS...IT'S-- IT'S SICK.

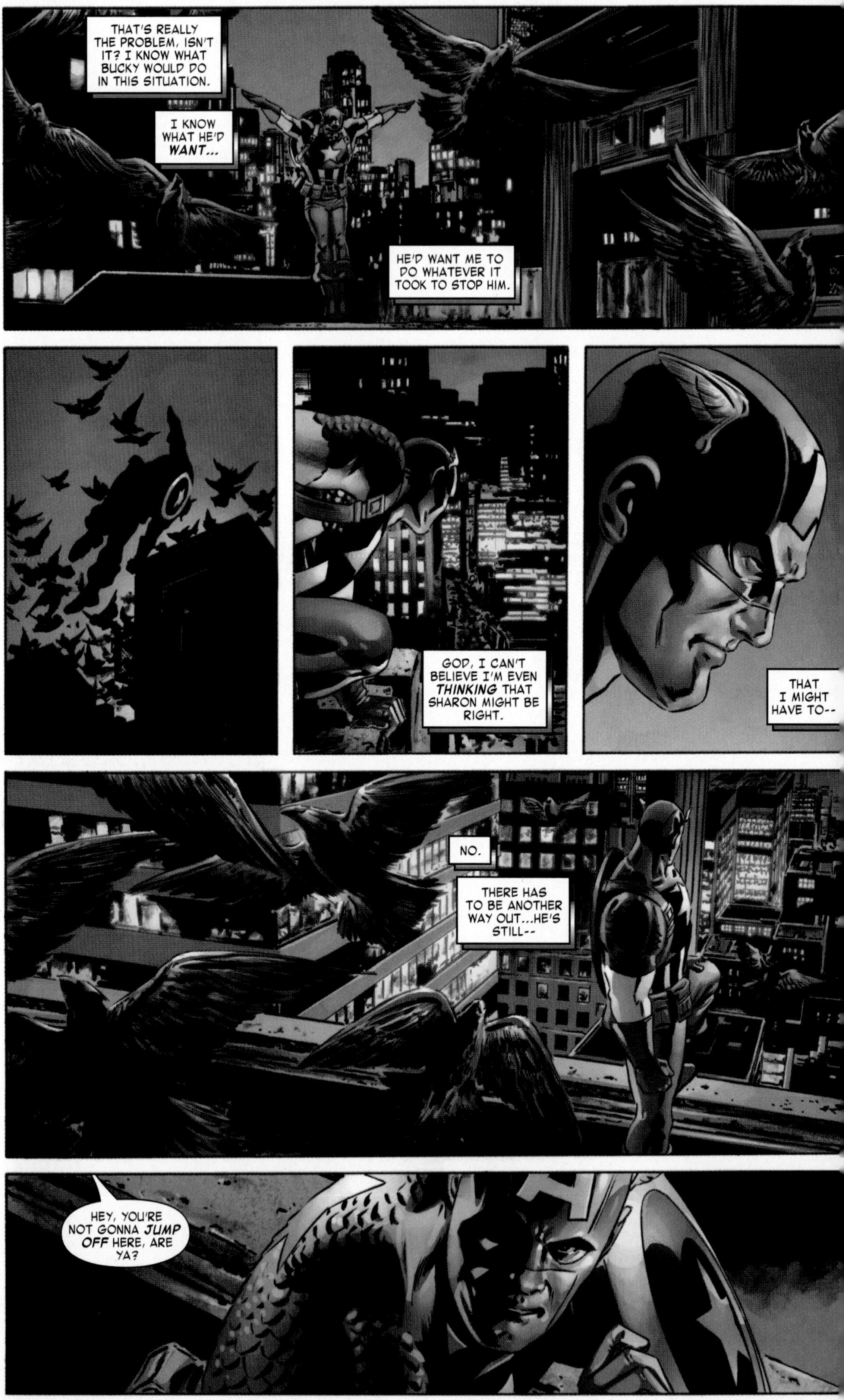
THAT'S REALLY THE PROBLEM, ISN'T IT? I KNOW WHAT BUCKY WOULD DO IN THIS SITUATION.
I KNOW WHAT HE'D *WANT...*
HE'D WANT ME TO DO WHATEVER IT TOOK TO STOP HIM.
GOD, I CAN'T BELIEVE I'M EVEN *THINKING* THAT SHARON MIGHT BE RIGHT.
THAT I MIGHT HAVE TO--
NO.
THERE HAS TO BE ANOTHER WAY OUT...HE'S STILL--
HEY, YOU'RE NOT GONNA *JUMP OFF* HERE, ARE YA?

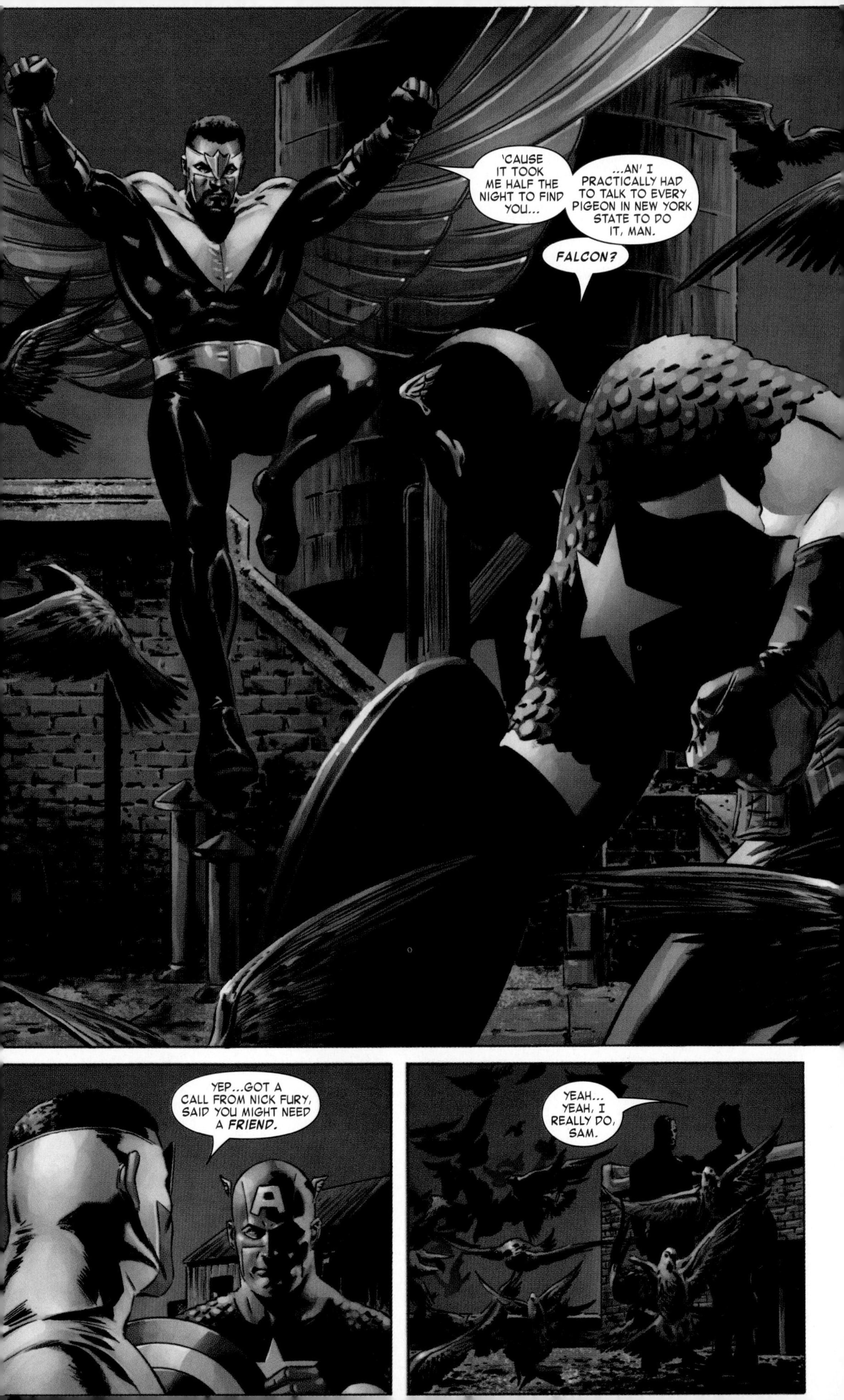
'CAUSE IT TOOK ME HALF THE NIGHT TO FIND YOU...
...AN' I PRACTICALLY HAD TO TALK TO EVERY PIGEON IN NEW YORK STATE TO DO IT, MAN.
FALCON?
YEP...GOT A CALL FROM NICK FURY, SAID YOU MIGHT NEED A FRIEND.
YEAH... YEAH, I REALLY DO, SAM.

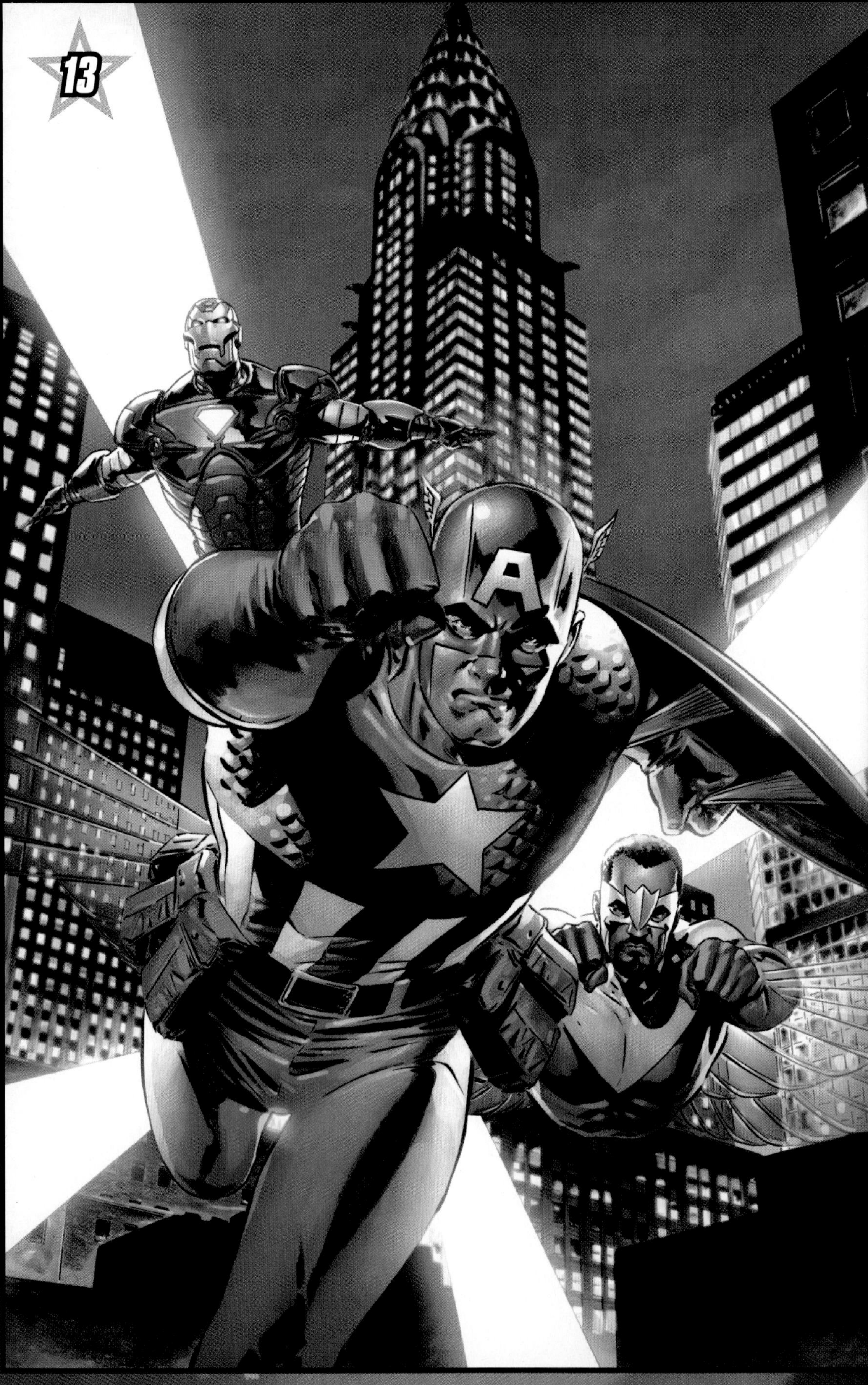
13

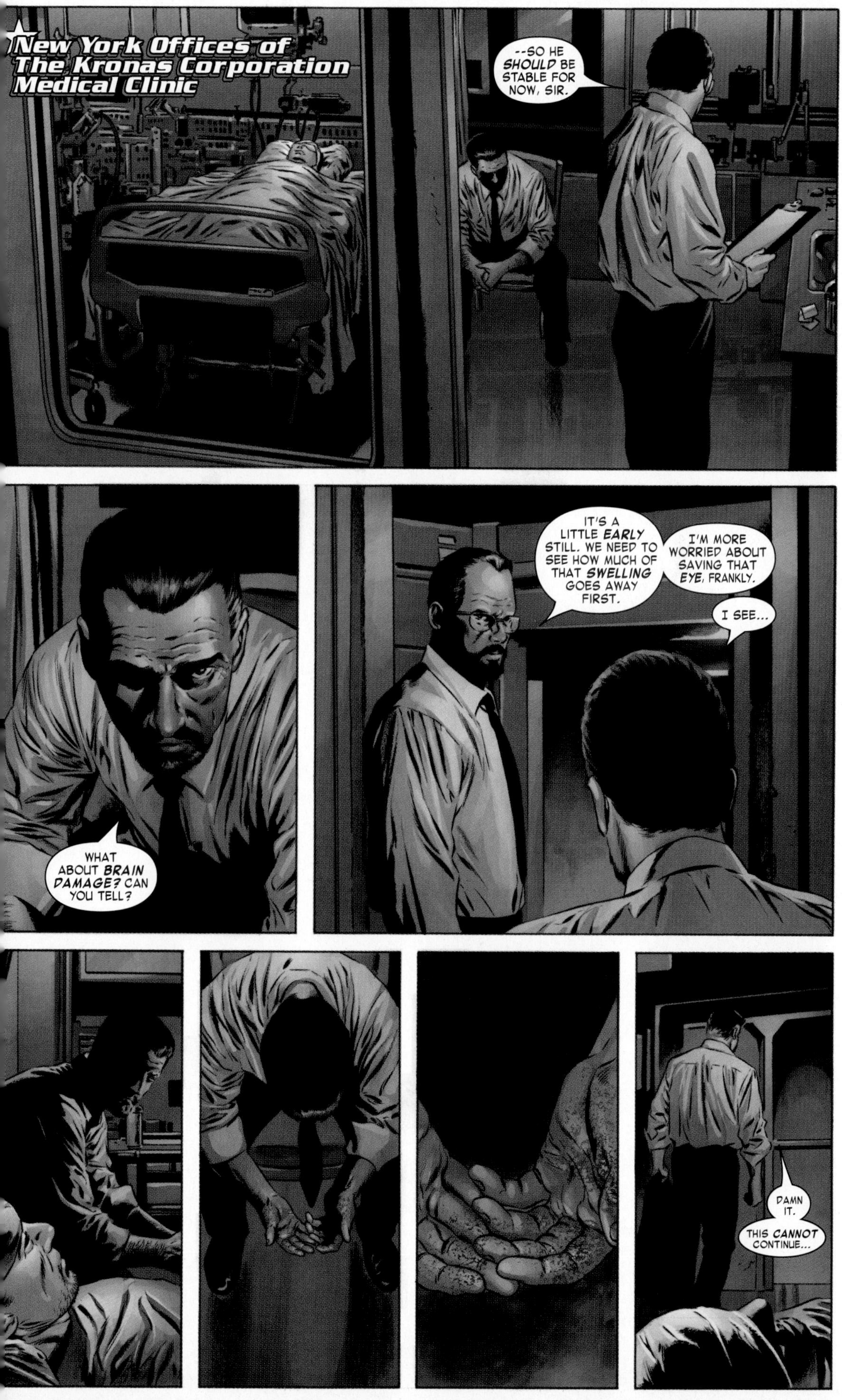
New York Offices of The Kronas Corporation Medical Clinic
--SO HE SHOULD BE STABLE FOR NOW, SIR.
WHAT ABOUT BRAIN DAMAGE? CAN YOU TELL?
IT'S A LITTLE EARLY STILL. WE NEED TO SEE HOW MUCH OF THAT SWELLING GOES AWAY FIRST.
I'M MORE WORRIED ABOUT SAVING THAT EYE, FRANKLY.
I SEE...
DAMN IT.
THIS CANNOT CONTINUE...

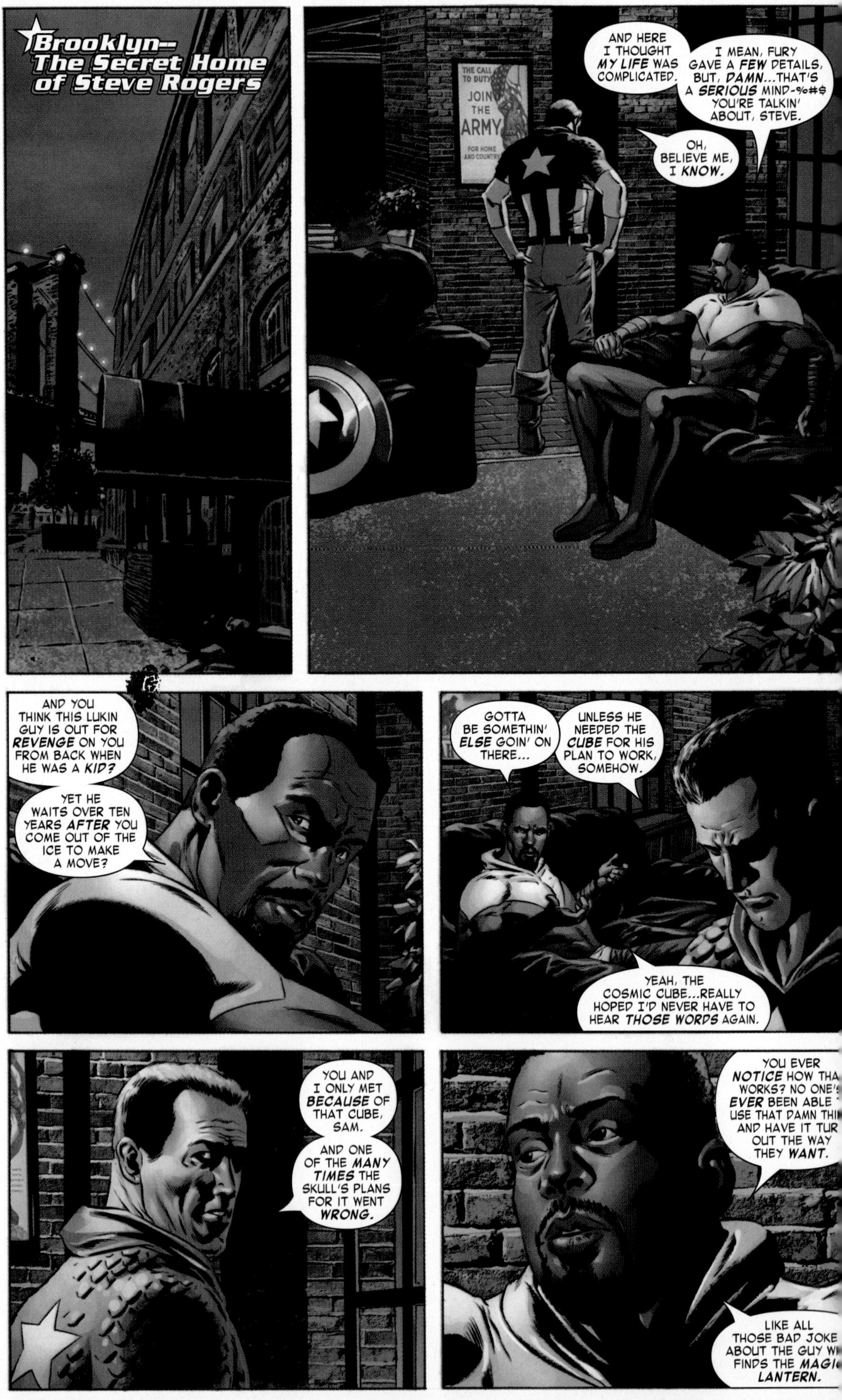

Brooklyn-- The Secret Home of Steve Rogers
THE CALL TO DUTY JOIN THE ARMY FOR HOME AND COUNTRY
AND HERE I THOUGHT MY LIFE WAS COMPLICATED.
I MEAN, FURY GAVE A FEW DETAILS, BUT, DAMN...THAT'S A SERIOUS MIND-%#$ YOU'RE TALKIN' ABOUT, STEVE.
OH, BELIEVE ME, I KNOW.
AND YOU THINK THIS LUKIN GUY IS OUT FOR REVENGE ON YOU FROM BACK WHEN HE WAS A KID?
YET HE WAITS OVER TEN YEARS AFTER YOU COME OUT OF THE ICE TO MAKE A MOVE?
GOTTA BE SOMETHIN' ELSE GOIN' ON THERE...
UNLESS HE NEEDED THE CUBE FOR HIS PLAN TO WORK, SOMEHOW.
YEAH, THE COSMIC CUBE...REALLY HOPED I'D NEVER HAVE TO HEAR THOSE WORDS AGAIN.
YOU AND I ONLY MET BECAUSE OF THAT CUBE, SAM.
AND ONE OF THE MANY TIMES THE SKULL'S PLANS FOR IT WENT WRONG.
YOU EVER NOTICE HOW THA WORKS? NO ONE'S EVER BEEN ABLE USE THAT DAMN THI AND HAVE IT TUR OUT THE WAY THEY WANT.
LIKE ALL THOSE BAD JOKE ABOUT THE GUY W FINDS THE MAGI LANTERN.

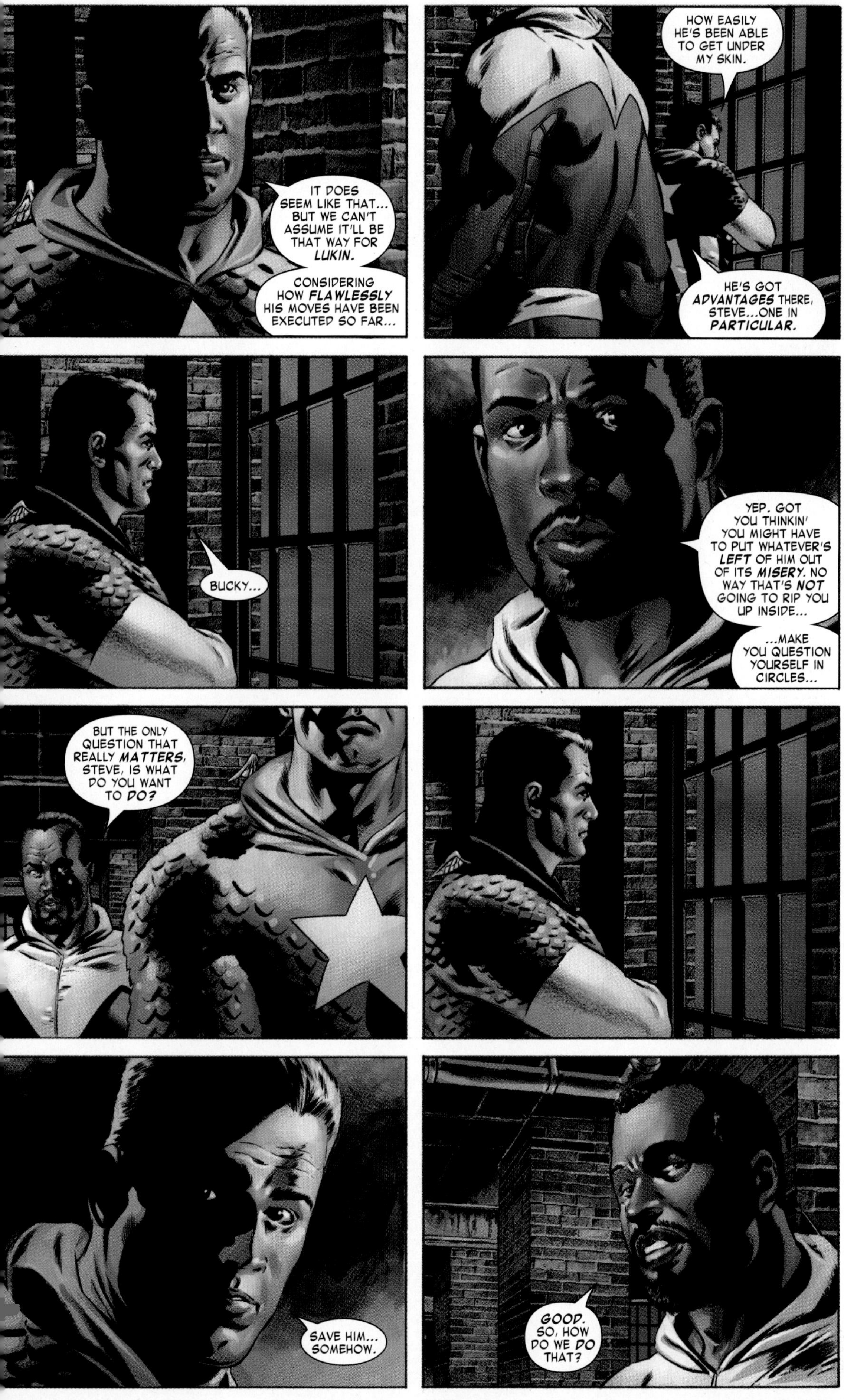
IT DOES SEEM LIKE THAT... BUT WE CAN'T ASSUME IT'LL BE THAT WAY FOR LUKIN.
CONSIDERING HOW FLAWLESSLY HIS MOVES HAVE BEEN EXECUTED SO FAR...
HOW EASILY HE'S BEEN ABLE TO GET UNDER MY SKIN.
HE'S GOT ADVANTAGES THERE, STEVE...ONE IN PARTICULAR.
BUCKY...
YEP. GOT YOU THINKIN' YOU MIGHT HAVE TO PUT WHATEVER'S LEFT OF HIM OUT OF ITS MISERY. NO WAY THAT'S NOT GOING TO RIP YOU UP INSIDE...
...MAKE YOU QUESTION YOURSELF IN CIRCLES...
BUT THE ONLY QUESTION THAT REALLY MATTERS, STEVE, IS WHAT DO YOU WANT TO DO?
SAVE HIM... SOMEHOW.
GOOD. SO, HOW DO WE DO THAT?

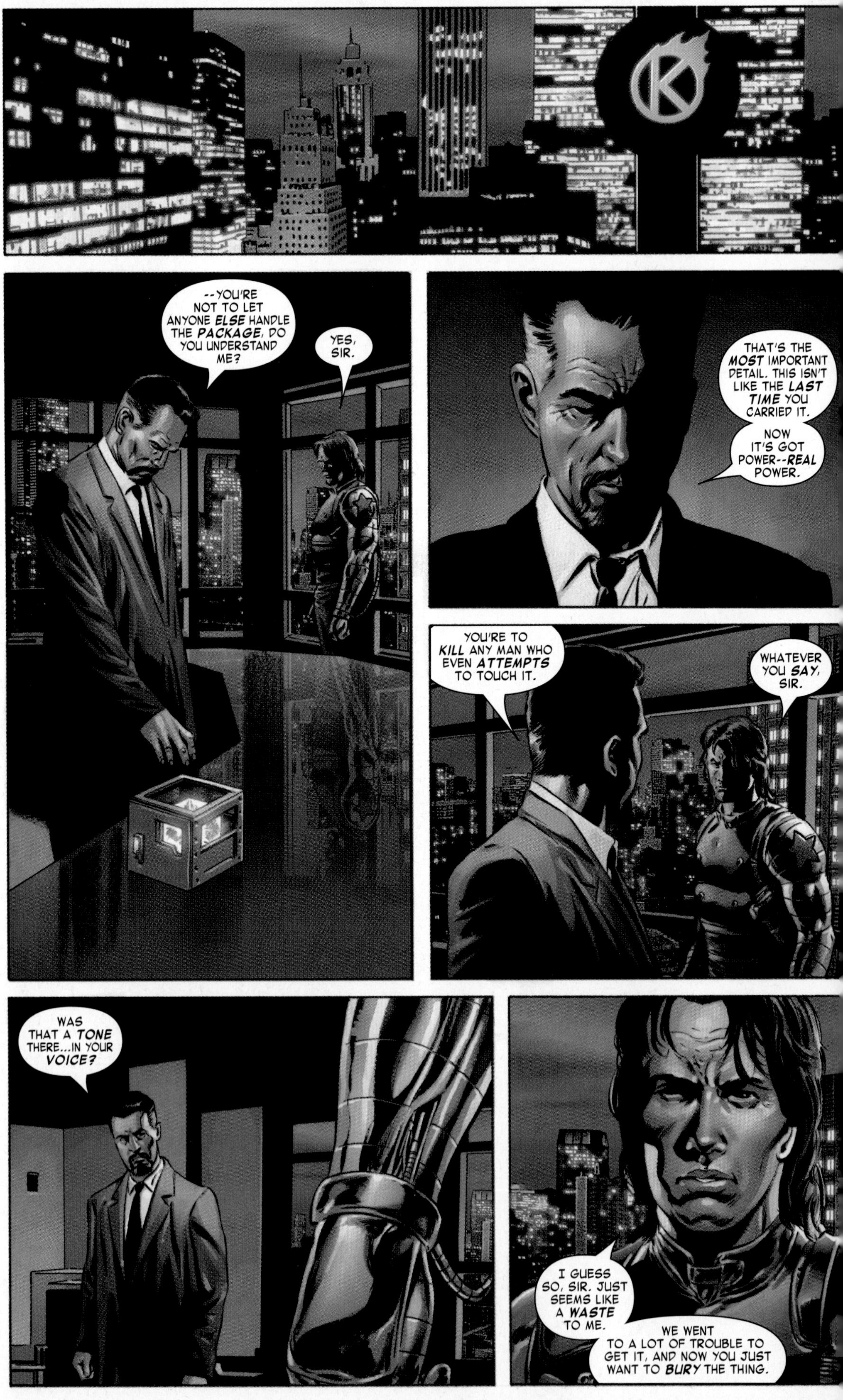
--YOU'RE NOT TO LET ANYONE ELSE HANDLE THE PACKAGE, DO YOU UNDERSTAND ME?
YES, SIR.
THAT'S THE MOST IMPORTANT DETAIL. THIS ISN'T LIKE THE LAST TIME YOU CARRIED IT.
NOW IT'S GOT POWER--REAL POWER.
YOU'RE TO KILL ANY MAN WHO EVEN ATTEMPTS TO TOUCH IT.
WHATEVER YOU SAY, SIR.
WAS THAT A TONE THERE...IN YOUR VOICE?
I GUESS SO, SIR. JUST SEEMS LIKE A WASTE TO ME.
WE WENT TO A LOT OF TROUBLE TO GET IT, AND NOW YOU JUST WANT TO BURY THE THING.

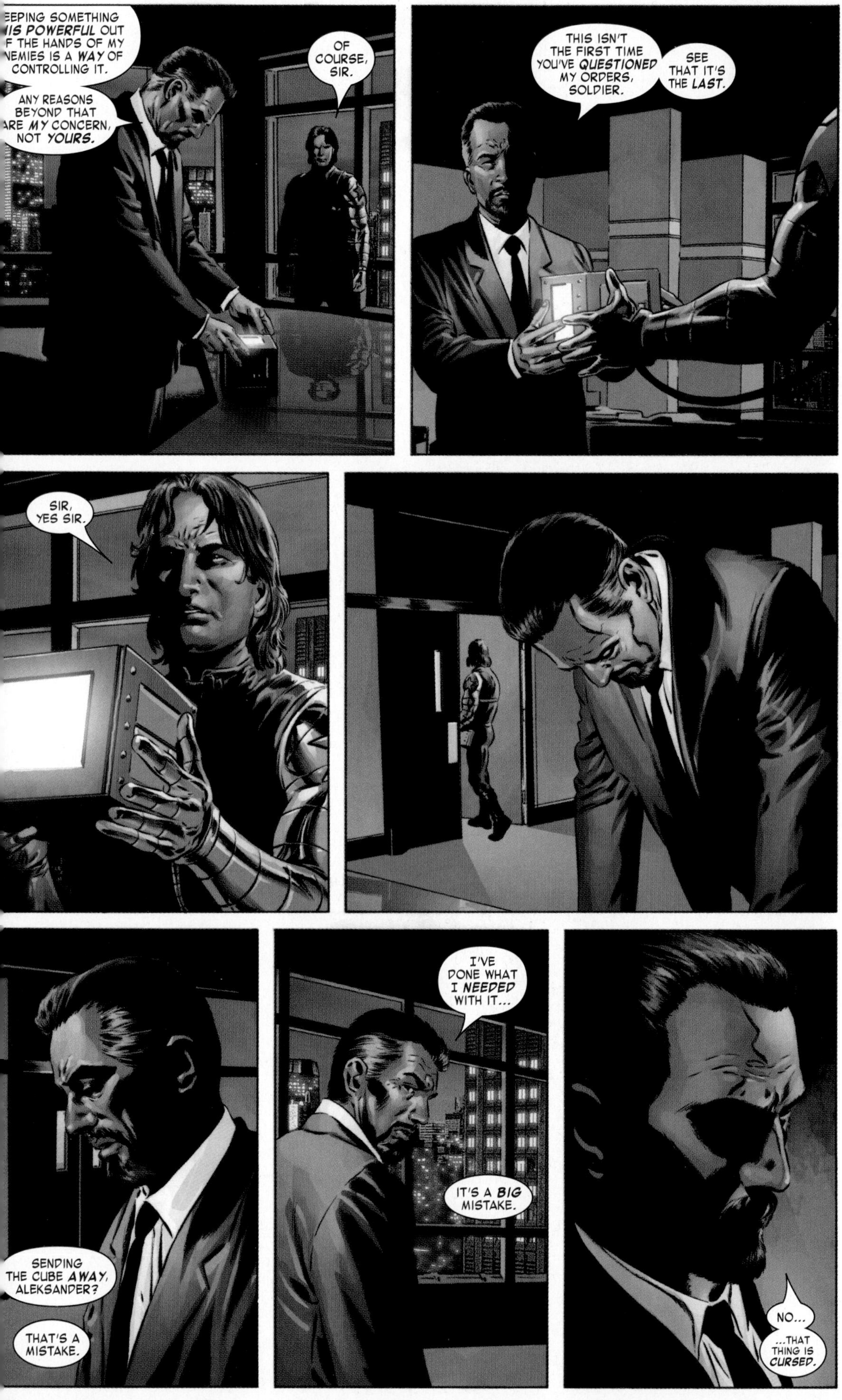

EEPING SOMETHING HIS POWERFUL OUT F THE HANDS OF MY NEMIES IS A WAY OF CONTROLLING IT.
ANY REASONS BEYOND THAT ARE MY CONCERN, NOT YOURS.
OF COURSE, SIR.
THIS ISN'T THE FIRST TIME YOU'VE QUESTIONED MY ORDERS, SOLDIER.
SEE THAT IT'S THE LAST.
SIR, YES SIR.
SENDING THE CUBE AWAY, ALEKSANDER?
THAT'S A MISTAKE.
I'VE DONE WHAT I NEEDED WITH IT...
IT'S A BIG MISTAKE.
NO...
...THAT THING IS CURSED.

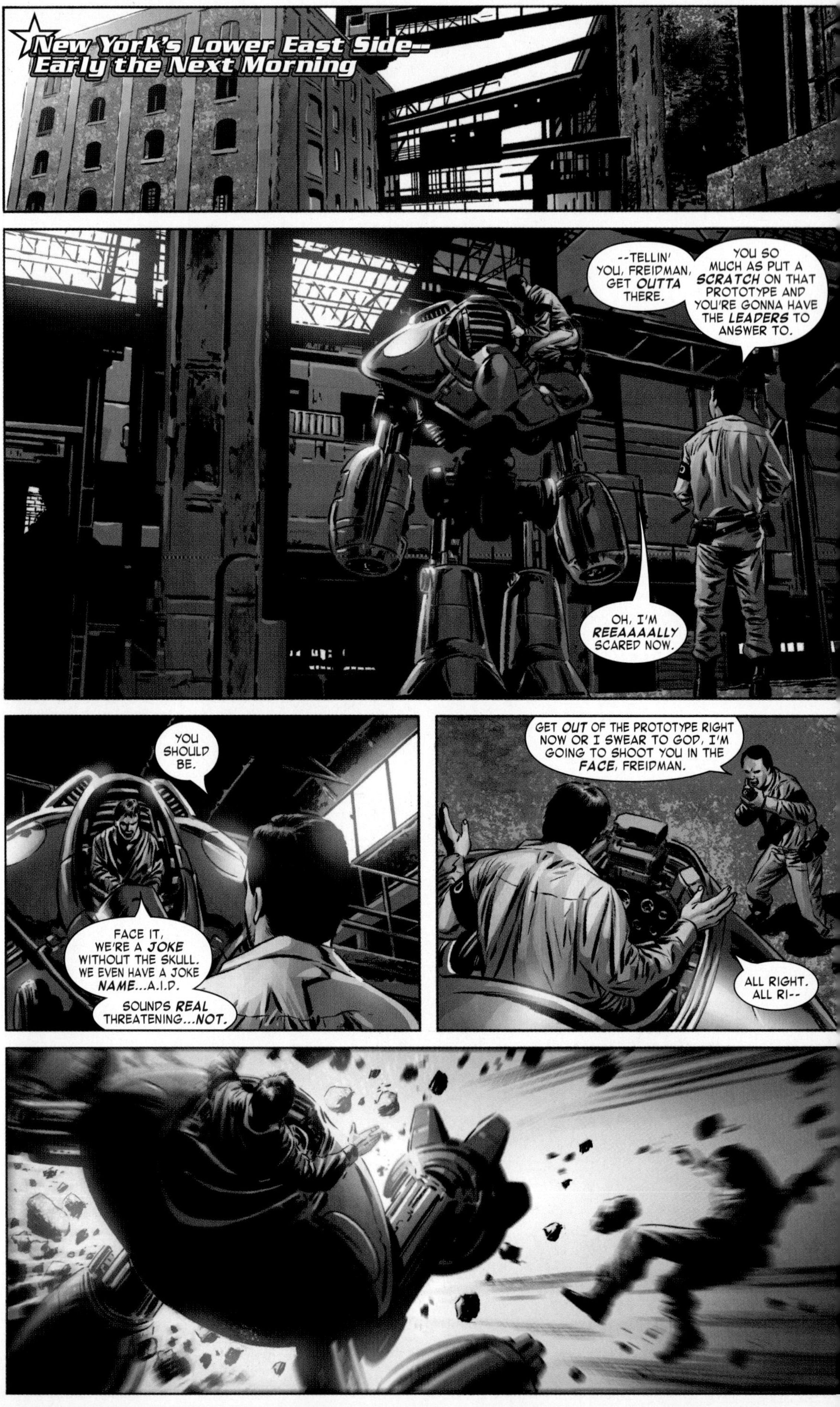
New York's Lower East Side--
Early the Next Morning
--TELLIN' YOU, FREIDMAN, GET OUTTA THERE.
YOU SO MUCH AS PUT A SCRATCH ON THAT PROTOTYPE AND YOU'RE GONNA HAVE THE LEADERS TO ANSWER TO.
OH, I'M REEAAAALLY SCARED NOW.
YOU SHOULD BE.
FACE IT, WE'RE A JOKE WITHOUT THE SKULL. WE EVEN HAVE A JOKE NAME...A.I.D.
SOUNDS REAL THREATENING...NOT.
GET OUT OF THE PROTOTYPE RIGHT NOW OR I SWEAR TO GOD, I'M GOING TO SHOOT YOU IN THE FACE, FREIDMAN.
ALL RIGHT. ALL RI--

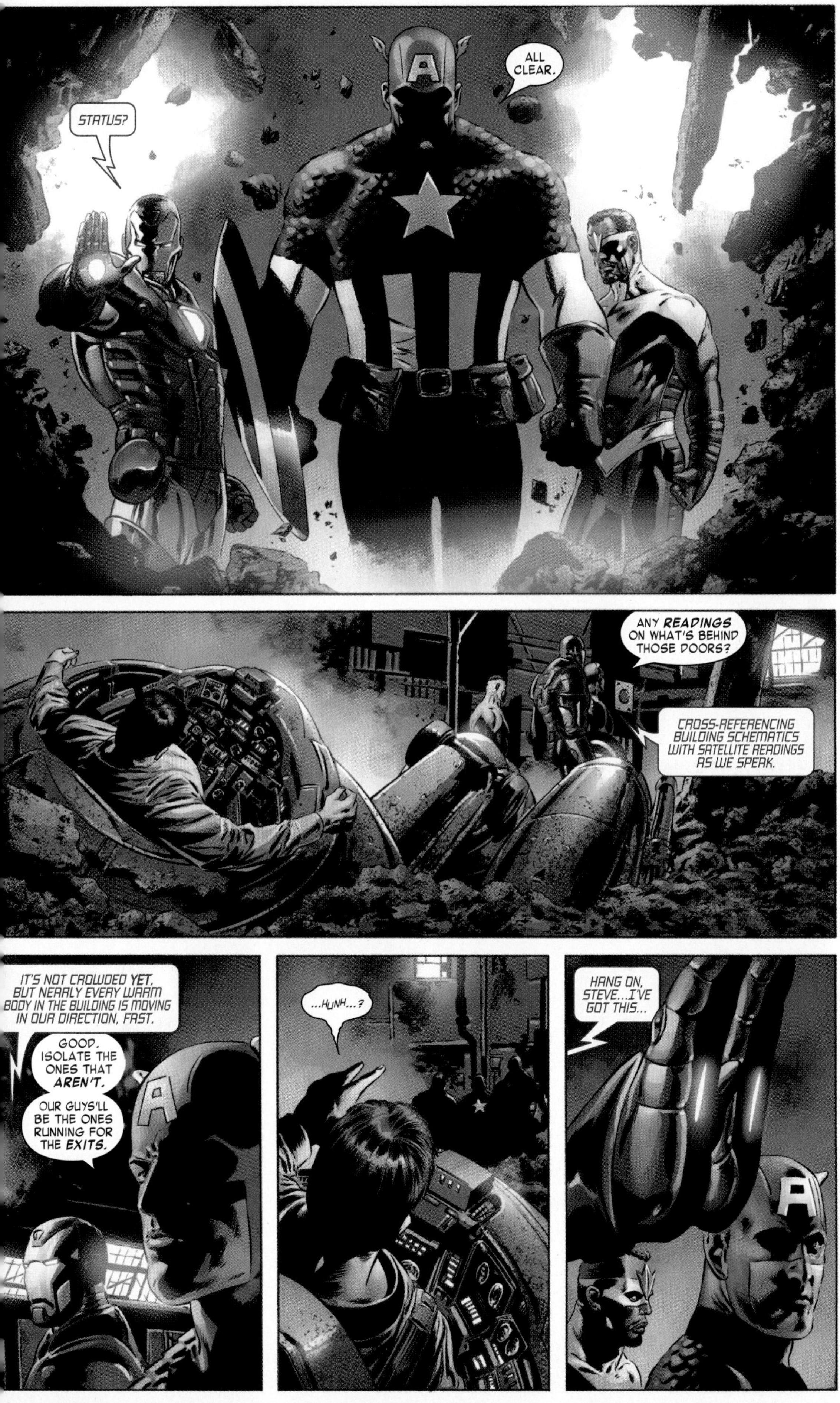
STATUS?
ALL CLEAR.
ANY READINGS ON WHAT'S BEHIND THOSE DOORS?
CROSS-REFERENCING BUILDING SCHEMATICS WITH SATELLITE READINGS AS WE SPEAK.
IT'S NOT CROWDED YET, BUT NEARLY EVERY WARM BODY IN THE BUILDING IS MOVING IN OUR DIRECTION, FAST.
GOOD. ISOLATE THE ONES THAT AREN'T.
OUR GUYS'LL BE THE ONES RUNNING FOR THE EXITS.
...HUNH...?
HANG ON, STEVE...I'VE GOT THIS...

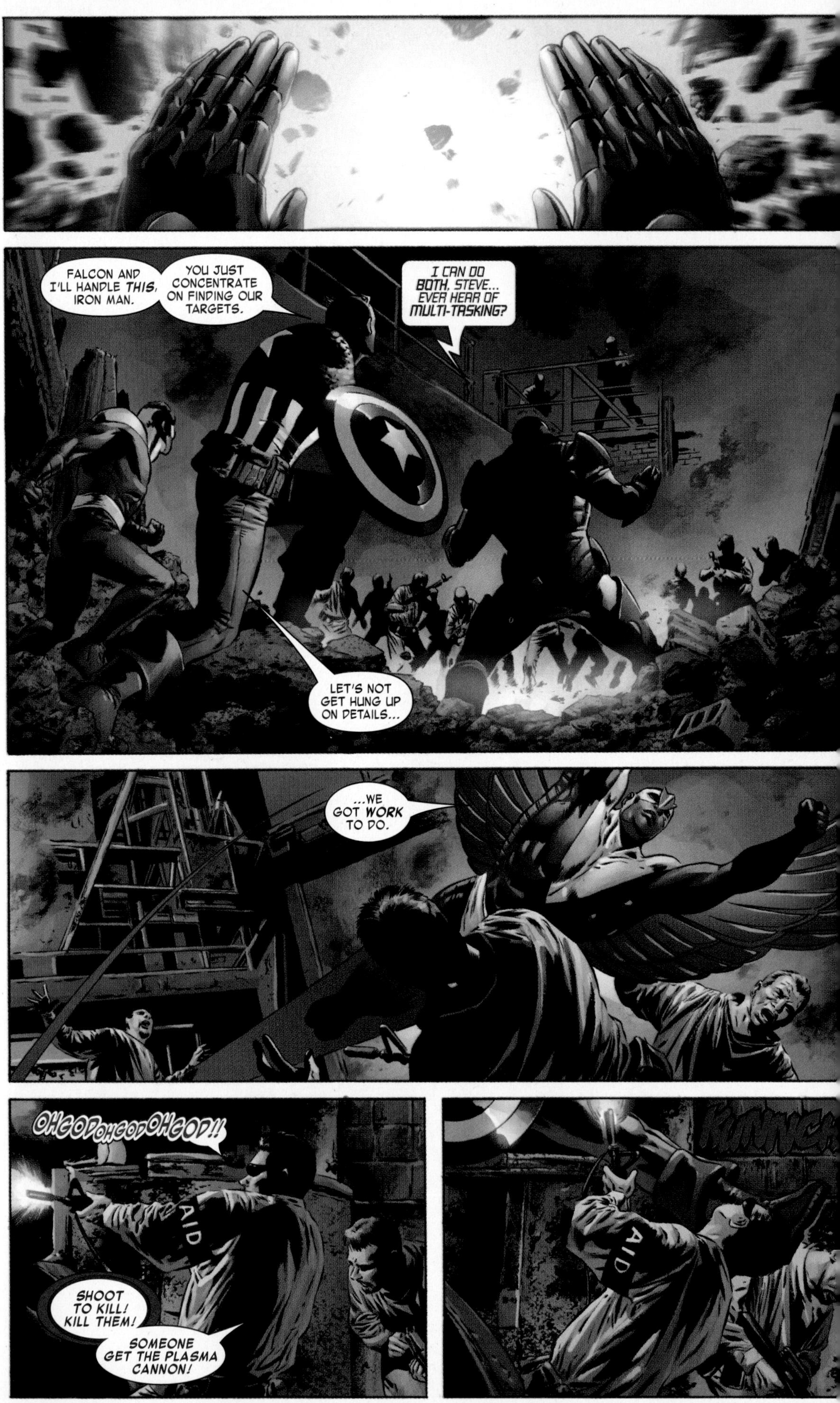
FALCON AND I'LL HANDLE THIS, IRON MAN.
YOU JUST CONCENTRATE ON FINDING OUR TARGETS.
I CAN DO BOTH, STEVE... EVER HEAR OF MULTI-TASKING?
LET'S NOT GET HUNG UP ON DETAILS...
...WE GOT WORK TO DO.
OHGODOHGODOHGOD!!
AID
SHOOT TO KILL! KILL THEM!
SOMEONE GET THE PLASMA CANNON!
AID

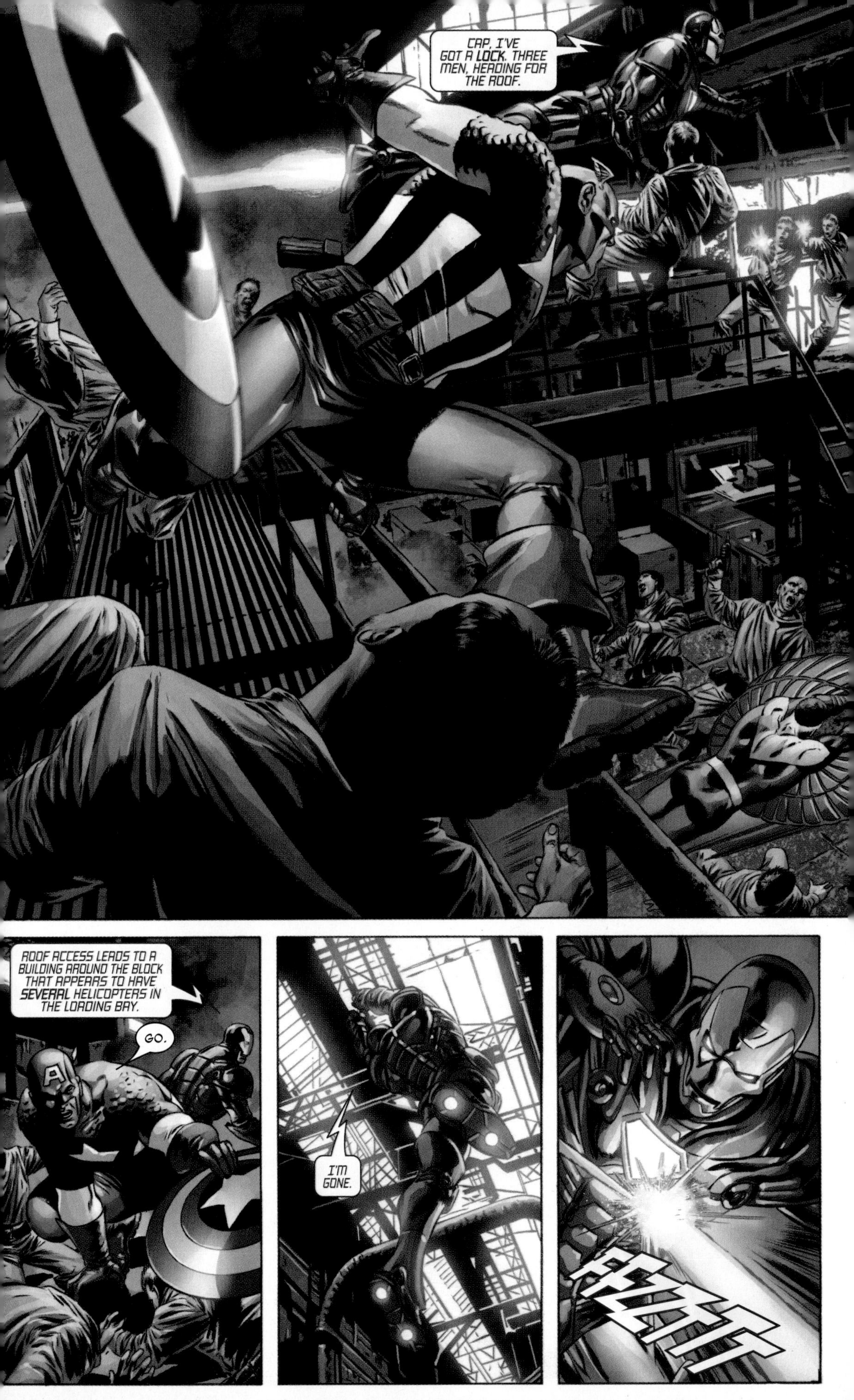
CAP, I'VE GOT A LOCK. THREE MEN, HEADING FOR THE ROOF.
ROOF ACCESS LEADS TO A BUILDING AROUND THE BLOCK THAT APPEARS TO HAVE SEVERAL HELICOPTERS IN THE LOADING BAY.
GO.
I'M GONE.

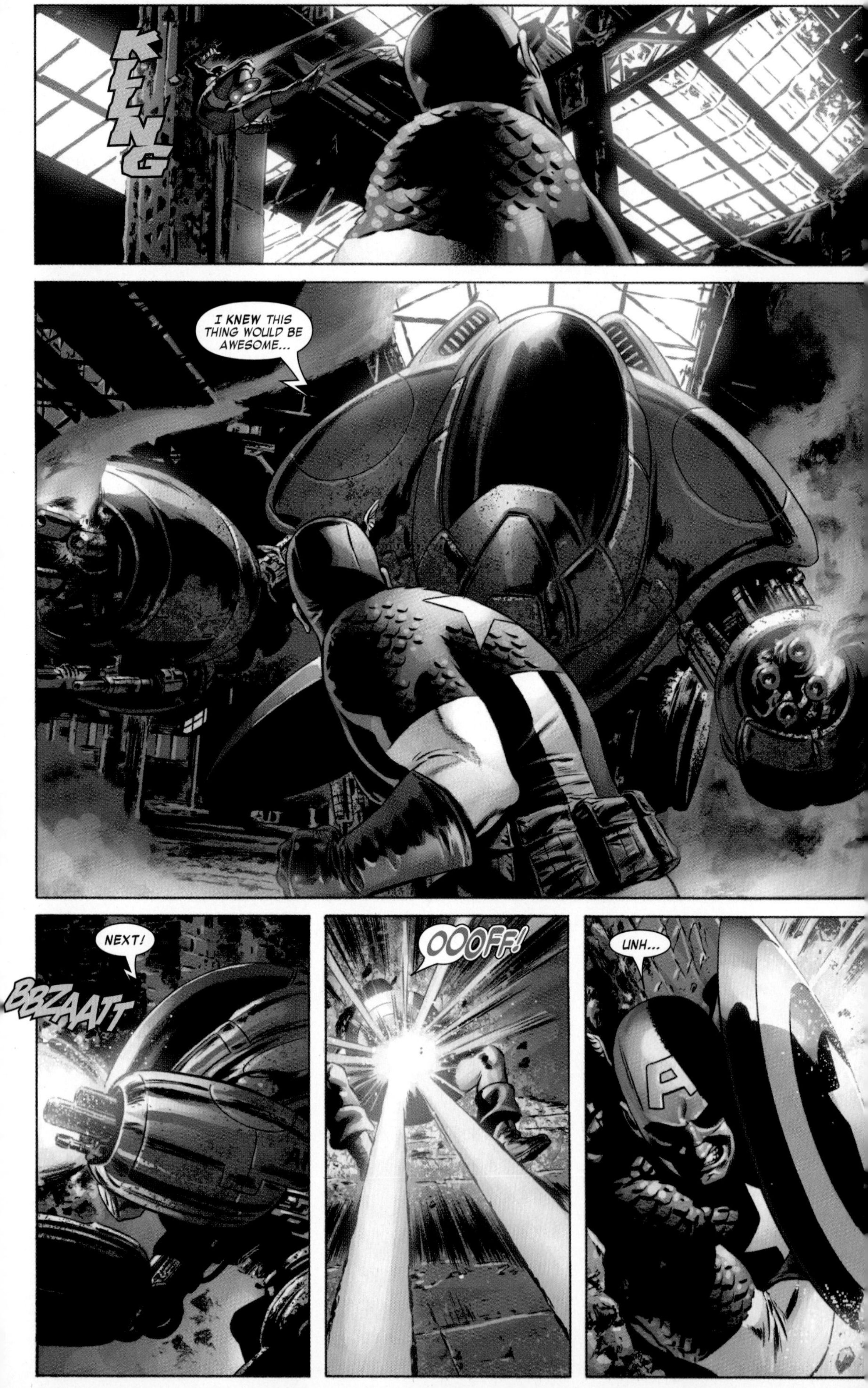
KLANG
I KNEW THIS THING WOULD BE AWESOME...
NEXT!
BBZAATT
OOOFF!
UNH...

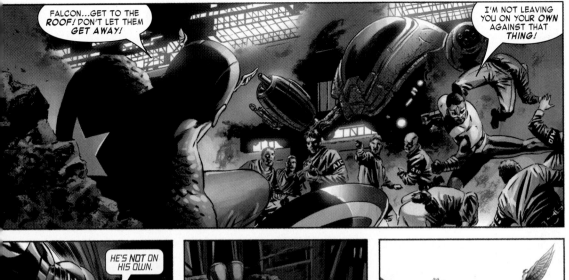

FALCON...GET TO THE ROOF! DON'T LET THEM GET AWAY!

I'M NOT LEAVING YOU ON YOUR OWN AGAINST THAT THING!

HEY--

HE'S NOT ON HIS OWN.

ALL RIGHT, THEN... I'M OUT.

KKRSSHH

KKKRAANG

AID

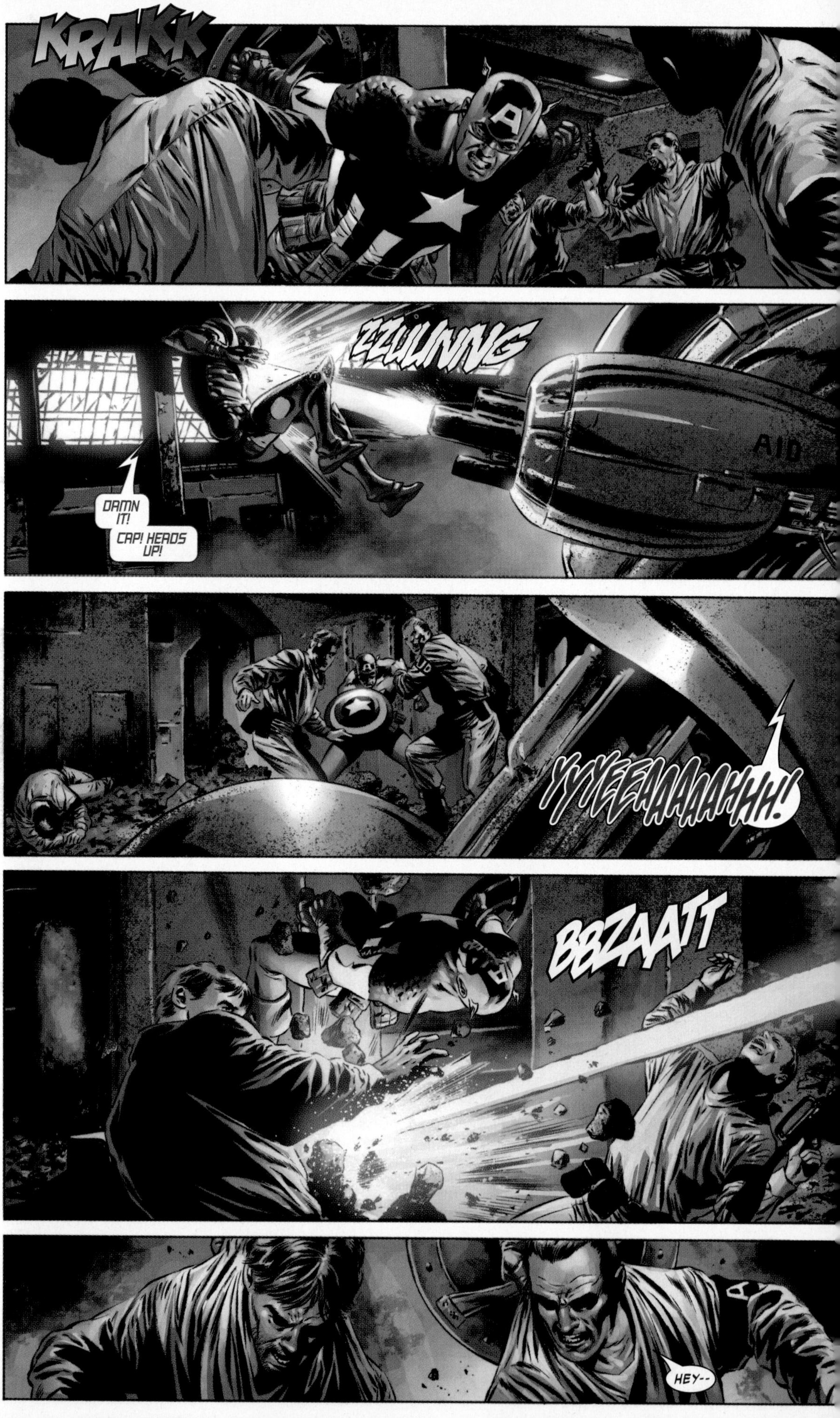
KRAKK
ZZUUNNG
DAMN IT!
CAP! HEADS UP!
AID
YYYEEAAAAAAHHH!
BBZAATT
HEY--

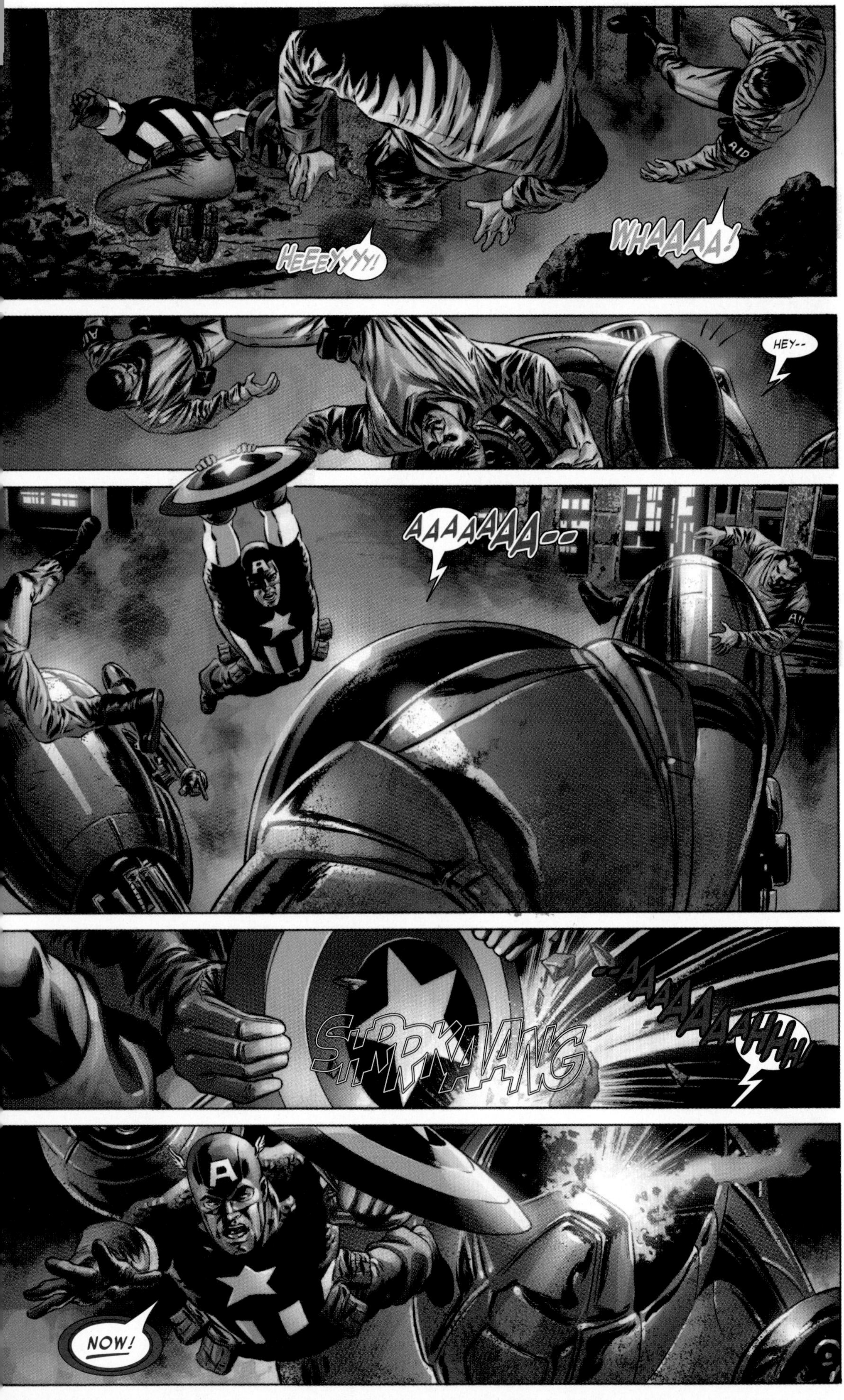
HEEEYYYY!
WHAAAA!
HEY--
AAAAAAA--
SHRKAANG
--AAAAAAAHHH!
NOW!

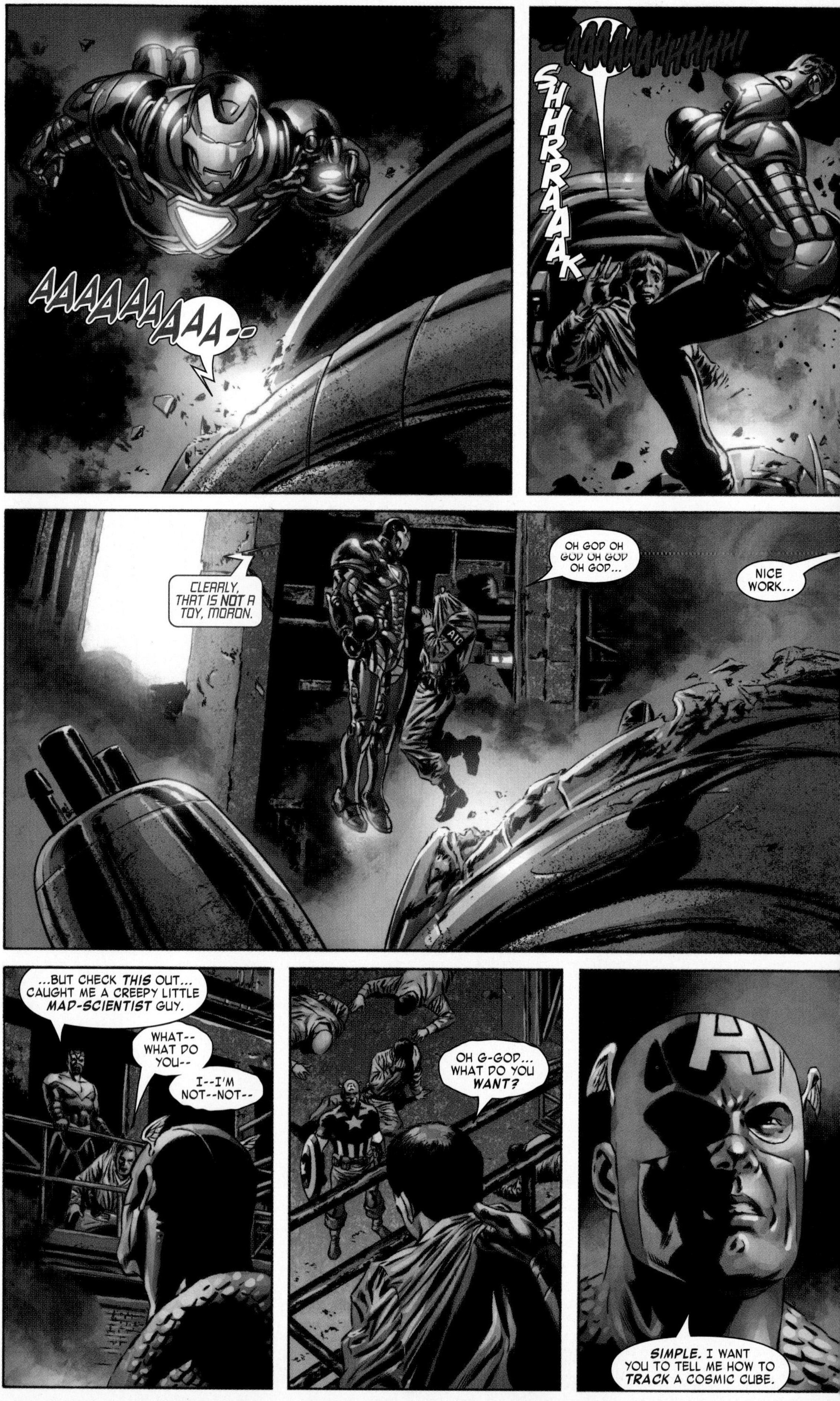
AAAAAAAAAA--
--AAAAAAAHHHHHH!
SHHRAAAK
CLEARLY, THAT IS NOT A TOY, MORON.
OH GOD OH GOD OH GOD OH GOD...
NICE WORK...
...BUT CHECK THIS OUT... CAUGHT ME A CREEPY LITTLE MAD-SCIENTIST GUY.
WHAT-- WHAT DO YOU--
I--I'M NOT--NOT--
OH G-GOD... WHAT DO YOU WANT?
SIMPLE. I WANT YOU TO TELL ME HOW TO TRACK A COSMIC CUBE.

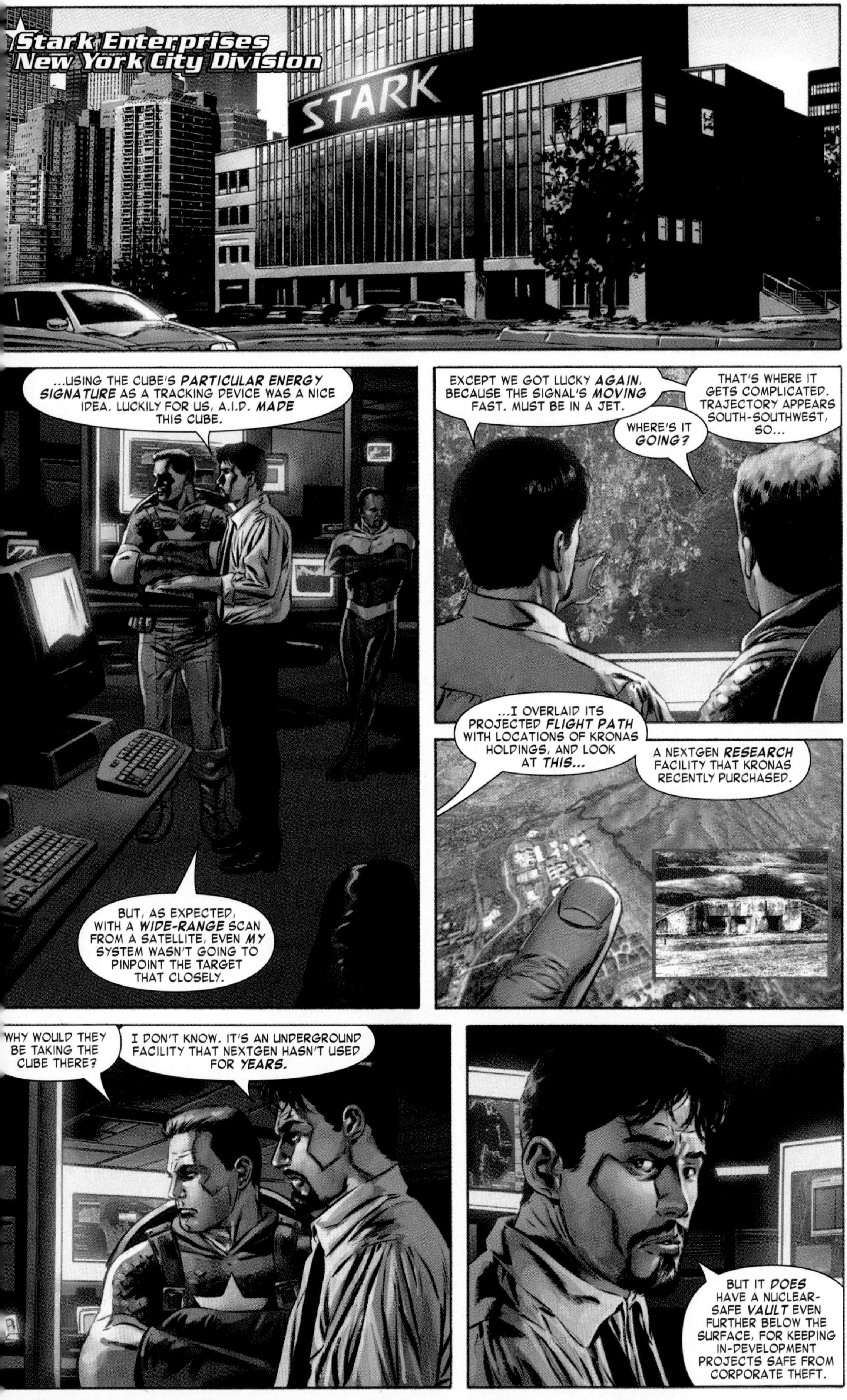
Stark Enterprises New York City Division
STARK
...USING THE CUBE'S PARTICULAR ENERGY SIGNATURE AS A TRACKING DEVICE WAS A NICE IDEA. LUCKILY FOR US, A.I.D. MADE THIS CUBE.
BUT, AS EXPECTED, WITH A WIDE-RANGE SCAN FROM A SATELLITE, EVEN MY SYSTEM WASN'T GOING TO PINPOINT THE TARGET THAT CLOSELY.
EXCEPT WE GOT LUCKY AGAIN, BECAUSE THE SIGNAL'S MOVING FAST. MUST BE IN A JET.
WHERE'S IT GOING?
THAT'S WHERE IT GETS COMPLICATED. TRAJECTORY APPEARS SOUTH-SOUTHWEST, SO...
...I OVERLAID ITS PROJECTED FLIGHT PATH WITH LOCATIONS OF KRONAS HOLDINGS, AND LOOK AT THIS...
A NEXTGEN RESEARCH FACILITY THAT KRONAS RECENTLY PURCHASED.
WHY WOULD THEY BE TAKING THE CUBE THERE?
I DON'T KNOW. IT'S AN UNDERGROUND FACILITY THAT NEXTGEN HASN'T USED FOR YEARS.
BUT IT DOES HAVE A NUCLEAR-SAFE VAULT EVEN FURTHER BELOW THE SURFACE, FOR KEEPING IN-DEVELOPMENT PROJECTS SAFE FROM CORPORATE THEFT.

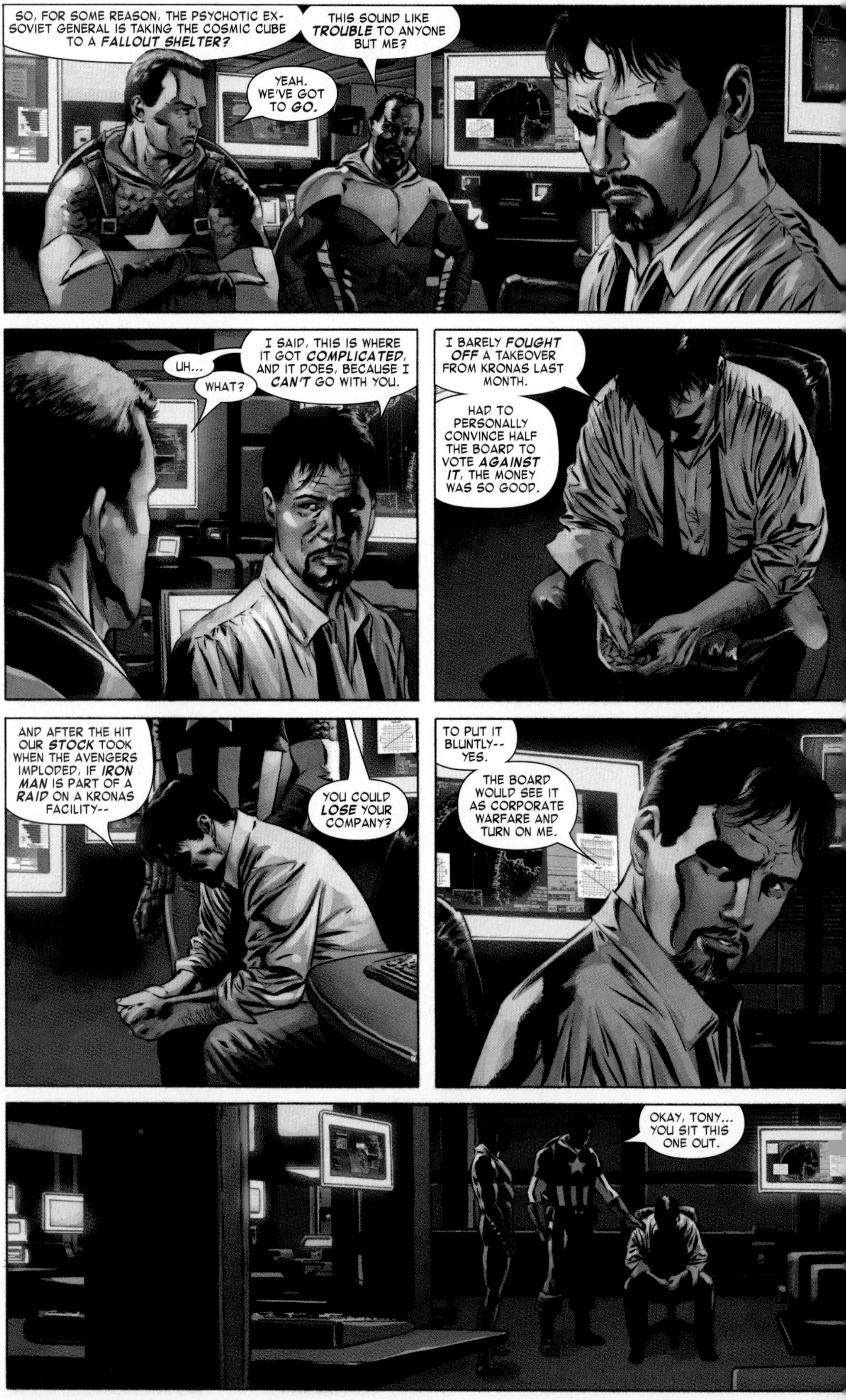
SO, FOR SOME REASON, THE PSYCHOTIC EX-SOVIET GENERAL IS TAKING THE COSMIC CUBE TO A FALLOUT SHELTER?
THIS SOUND LIKE TROUBLE TO ANYONE BUT ME?
YEAH. WE'VE GOT TO GO.
UH...
WHAT?
I SAID, THIS IS WHERE IT GOT COMPLICATED, AND IT DOES, BECAUSE I CAN'T GO WITH YOU.
I BARELY FOUGHT OFF A TAKEOVER FROM KRONAS LAST MONTH.
HAD TO PERSONALLY CONVINCE HALF THE BOARD TO VOTE AGAINST IT, THE MONEY WAS SO GOOD.
AND AFTER THE HIT OUR STOCK TOOK WHEN THE AVENGERS IMPLODED, IF IRON MAN IS PART OF A RAID ON A KRONAS FACILITY--
YOU COULD LOSE YOUR COMPANY?
TO PUT IT BLUNTLY-- YES.
THE BOARD WOULD SEE IT AS CORPORATE WARFARE AND TURN ON ME.
OKAY, TONY... YOU SIT THIS ONE OUT.

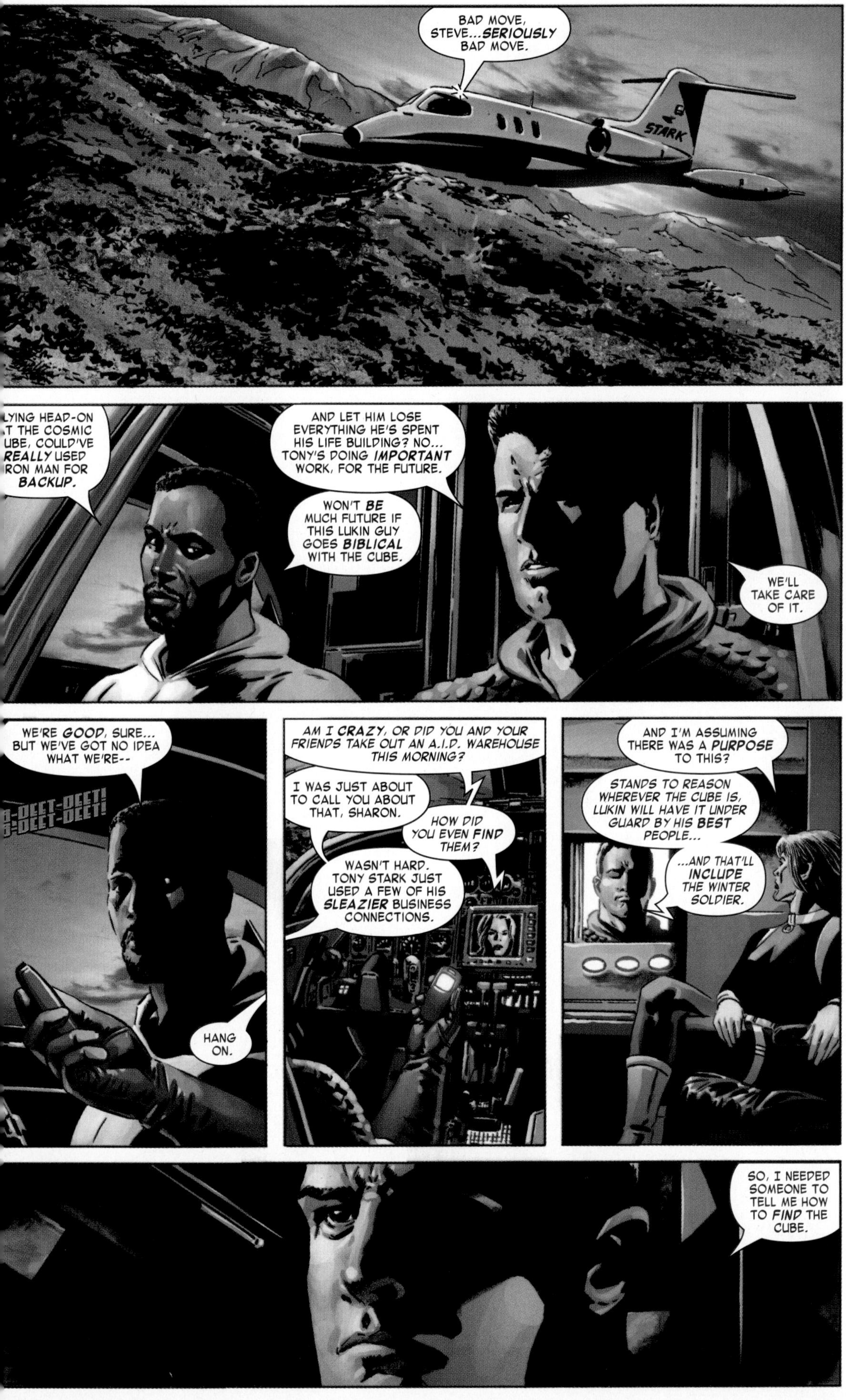
BAD MOVE, STEVE...SERIOUSLY BAD MOVE.
LYING HEAD-ON T THE COSMIC UBE, COULD'VE REALLY USED RON MAN FOR BACKUP.
AND LET HIM LOSE EVERYTHING HE'S SPENT HIS LIFE BUILDING? NO... TONY'S DOING IMPORTANT WORK, FOR THE FUTURE.
WON'T BE MUCH FUTURE IF THIS LUKIN GUY GOES BIBLICAL WITH THE CUBE.
WE'LL TAKE CARE OF IT.
WE'RE GOOD, SURE... BUT WE'VE GOT NO IDEA WHAT WE'RE--
HANG ON.
AM I CRAZY, OR DID YOU AND YOUR FRIENDS TAKE OUT AN A.I.D. WAREHOUSE THIS MORNING?
I WAS JUST ABOUT TO CALL YOU ABOUT THAT, SHARON.
HOW DID YOU EVEN FIND THEM?
WASN'T HARD. TONY STARK JUST USED A FEW OF HIS SLEAZIER BUSINESS CONNECTIONS.
AND I'M ASSUMING THERE WAS A PURPOSE TO THIS?
STANDS TO REASON WHEREVER THE CUBE IS, LUKIN WILL HAVE IT UNDER GUARD BY HIS BEST PEOPLE...
...AND THAT'LL INCLUDE THE WINTER SOLDIER.
SO, I NEEDED SOMEONE TO TELL ME HOW TO FIND THE CUBE.

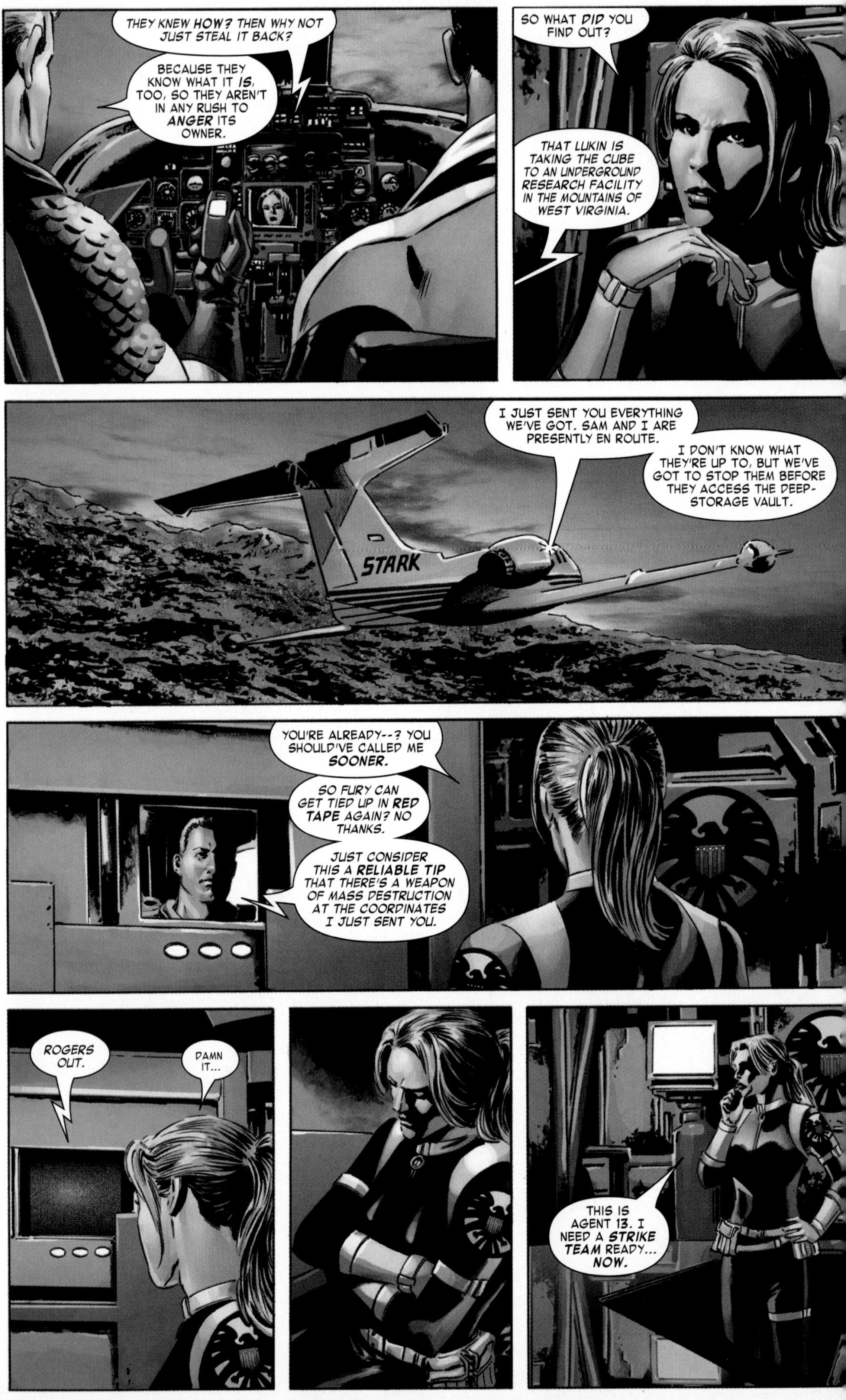

THEY KNEW HOW? THEN WHY NOT JUST STEAL IT BACK?
BECAUSE THEY KNOW WHAT IT IS, TOO, SO THEY AREN'T IN ANY RUSH TO ANGER ITS OWNER.
SO WHAT DID YOU FIND OUT?
THAT LUKIN IS TAKING THE CUBE TO AN UNDERGROUND RESEARCH FACILITY IN THE MOUNTAINS OF WEST VIRGINIA.
I JUST SENT YOU EVERYTHING WE'VE GOT. SAM AND I ARE PRESENTLY EN ROUTE.
I DON'T KNOW WHAT THEY'RE UP TO, BUT WE'VE GOT TO STOP THEM BEFORE THEY ACCESS THE DEEP-STORAGE VAULT.
STARK
YOU'RE ALREADY--? YOU SHOULD'VE CALLED ME SOONER.
SO FURY CAN GET TIED UP IN RED TAPE AGAIN? NO THANKS.
JUST CONSIDER THIS A RELIABLE TIP THAT THERE'S A WEAPON OF MASS DESTRUCTION AT THE COORDINATES I JUST SENT YOU.
ROGERS OUT.
DAMN IT...
THIS IS AGENT 13. I NEED A STRIKE TEAM READY... NOW.

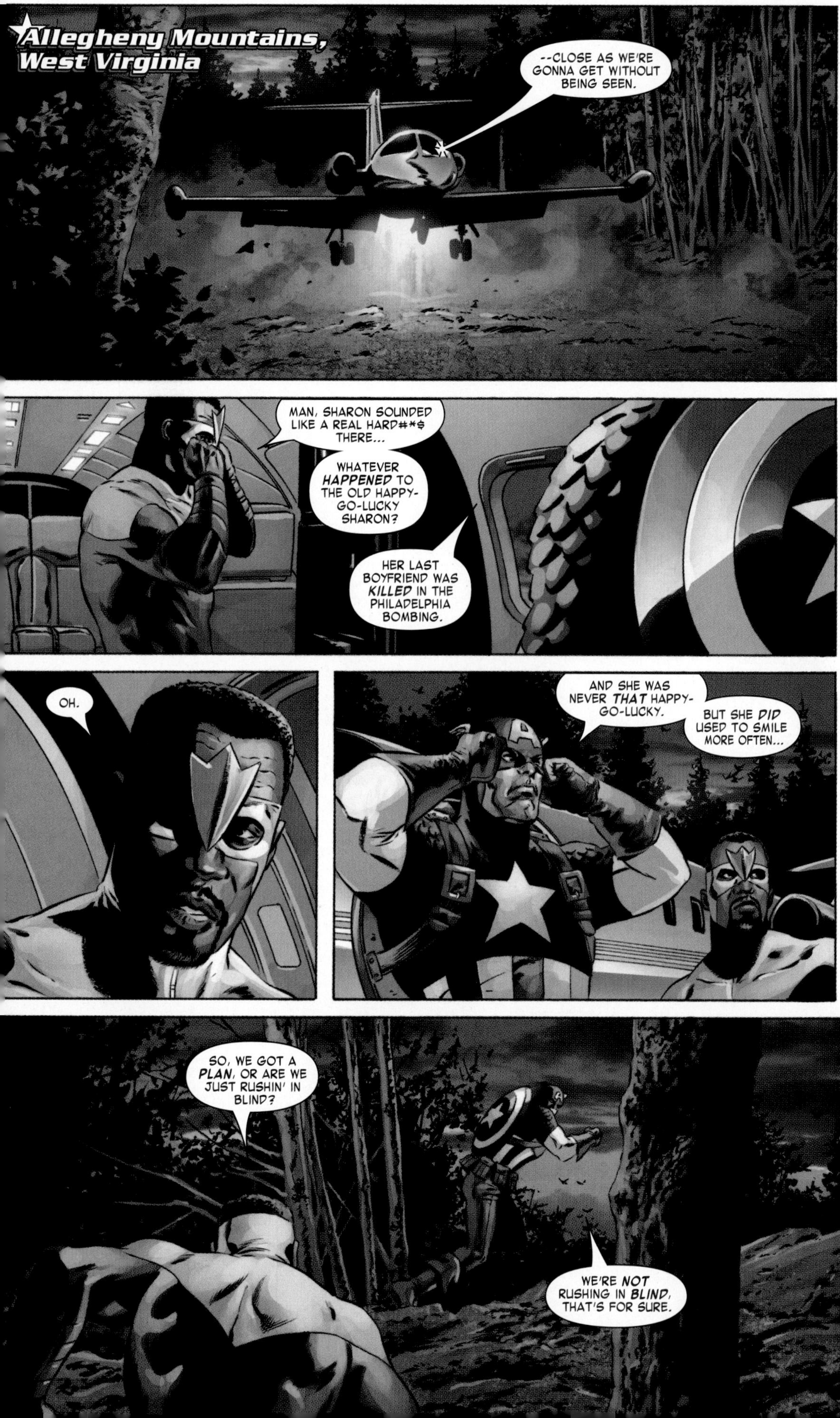
Allegheny Mountains, West Virginia
--CLOSE AS WE'RE GONNA GET WITHOUT BEING SEEN.
MAN, SHARON SOUNDED LIKE A REAL HARD#*$ THERE...
WHATEVER HAPPENED TO THE OLD HAPPY-GO-LUCKY SHARON?
HER LAST BOYFRIEND WAS KILLED IN THE PHILADELPHIA BOMBING.
OH.
AND SHE WAS NEVER THAT HAPPY-GO-LUCKY.
BUT SHE DID USED TO SMILE MORE OFTEN...
SO, WE GOT A PLAN, OR ARE WE JUST RUSHIN' IN BLIND?
WE'RE NOT RUSHING IN BLIND, THAT'S FOR SURE.

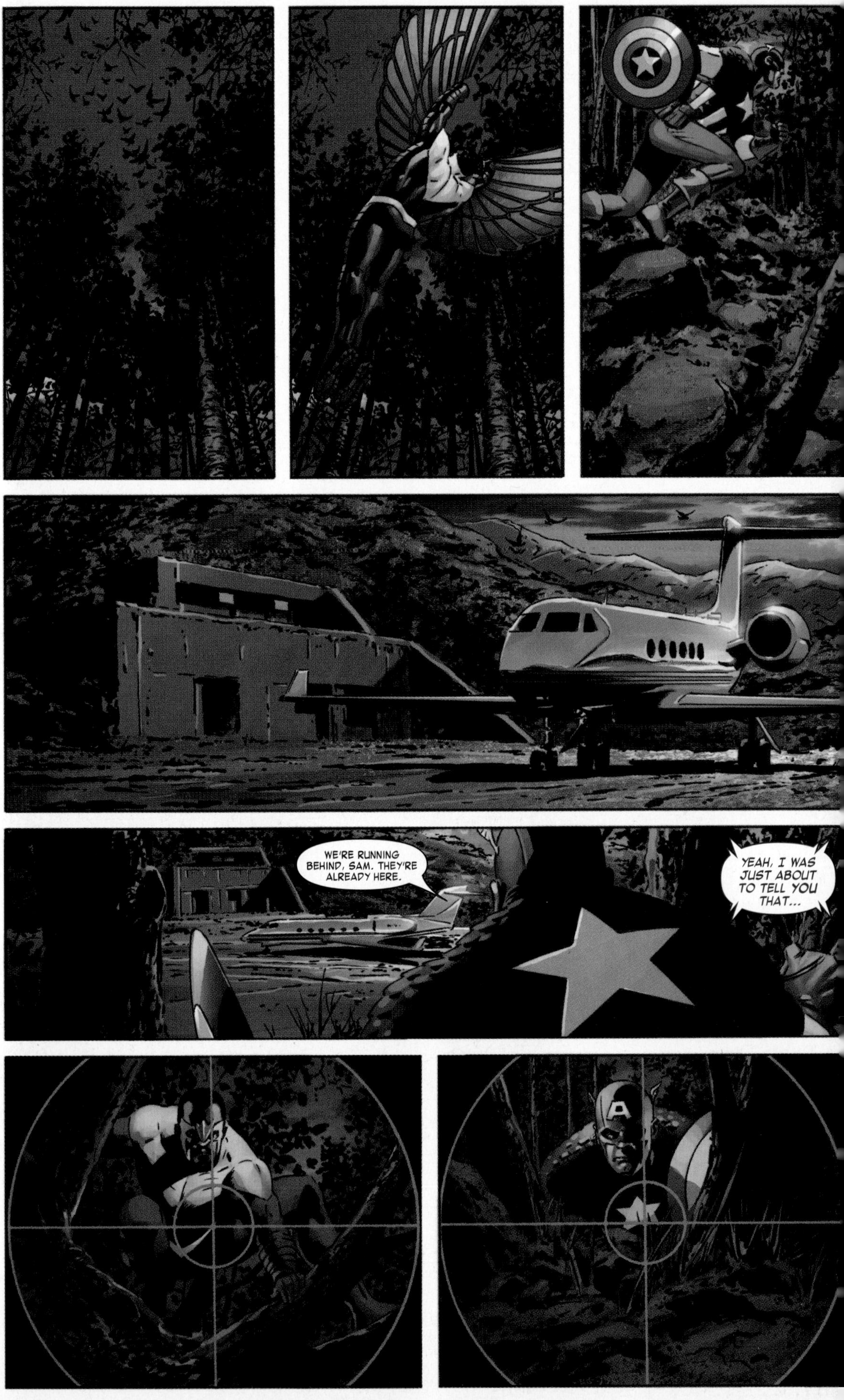
WE'RE RUNNING BEHIND, SAM. THEY'RE ALREADY HERE.
YEAH, I WAS JUST ABOUT TO TELL YOU THAT...

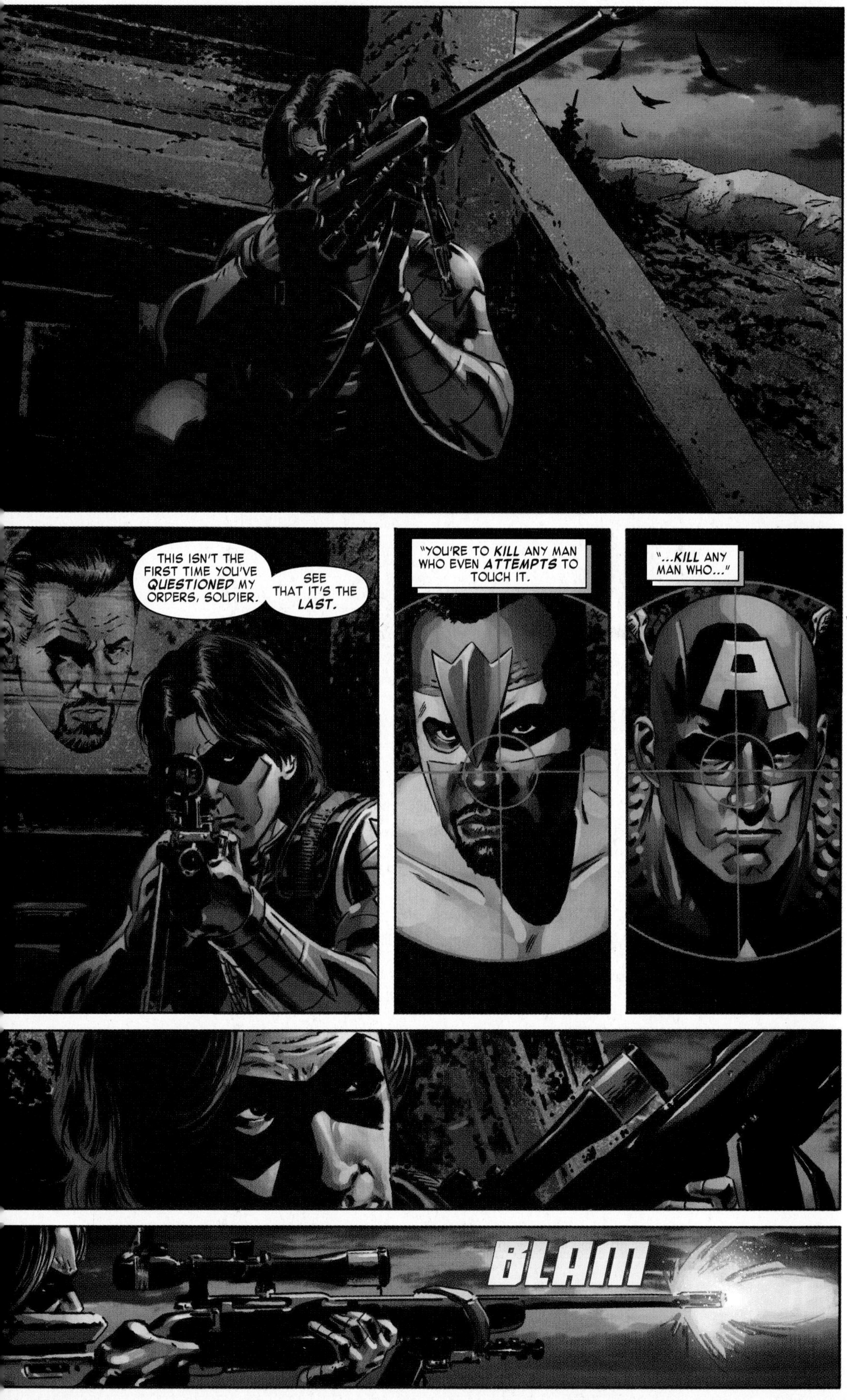
THIS ISN'T THE FIRST TIME YOU'VE *QUESTIONED* MY ORDERS, SOLDIER.
SEE THAT IT'S THE *LAST.*
"YOU'RE TO *KILL* ANY MAN WHO EVEN *ATTEMPTS* TO TOUCH IT.
"...*KILL* ANY MAN WHO..."
BLAM

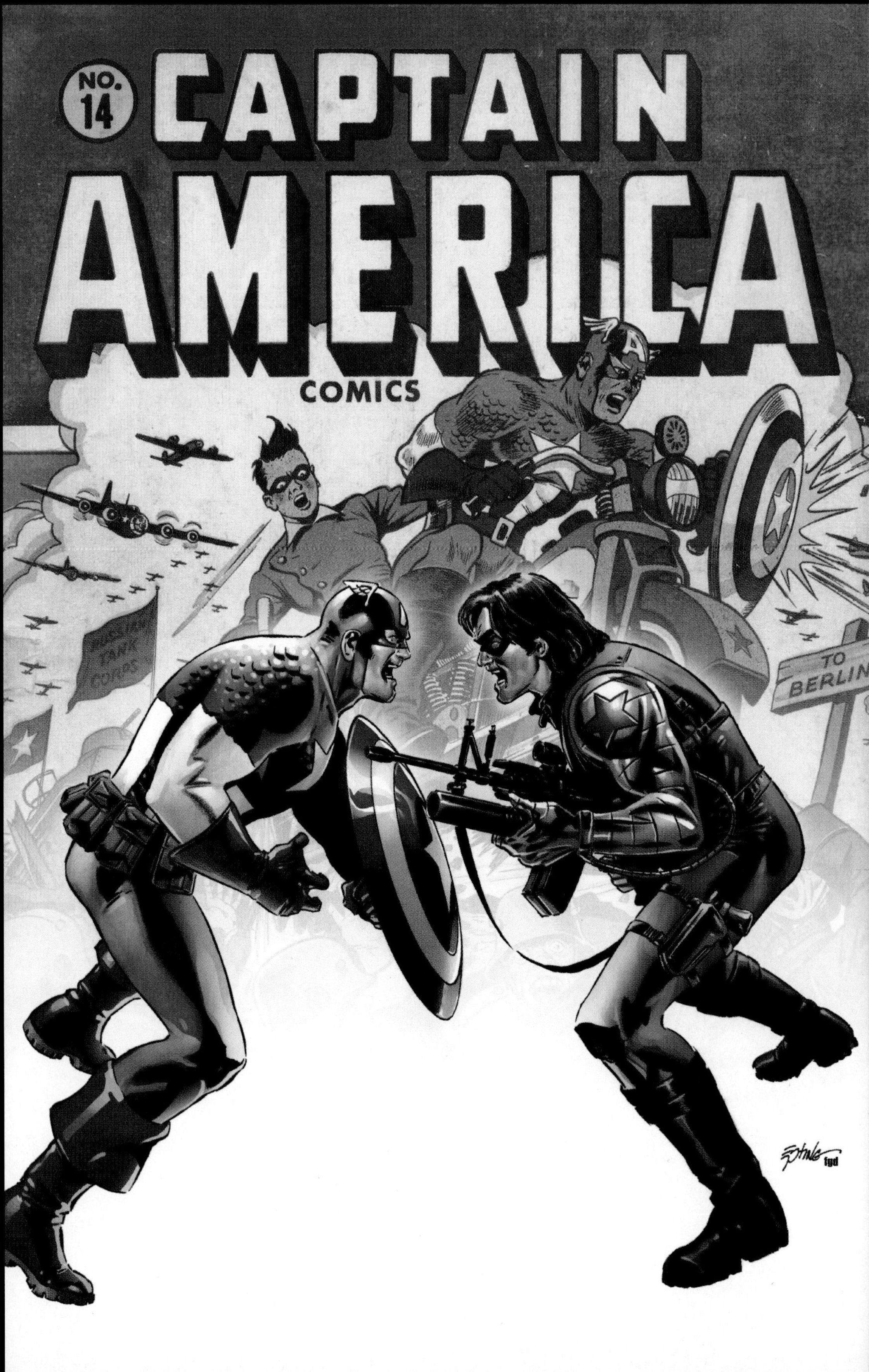
NO. 14
CAPTAIN AMERICA
COMICS
RUSSIAN TANK CORPS
TO BERLIN

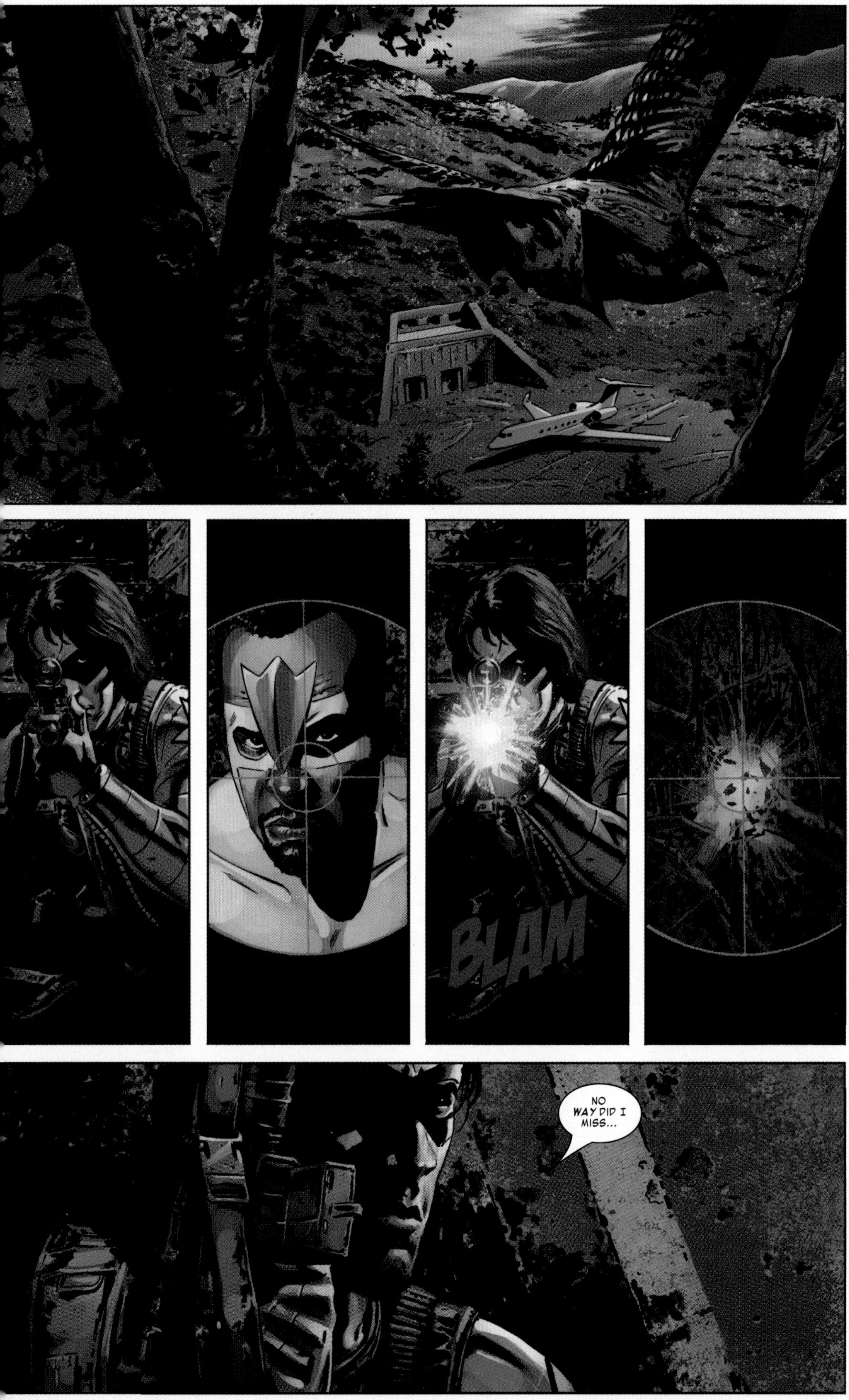
BLAM
NO WAY DID I MISS...

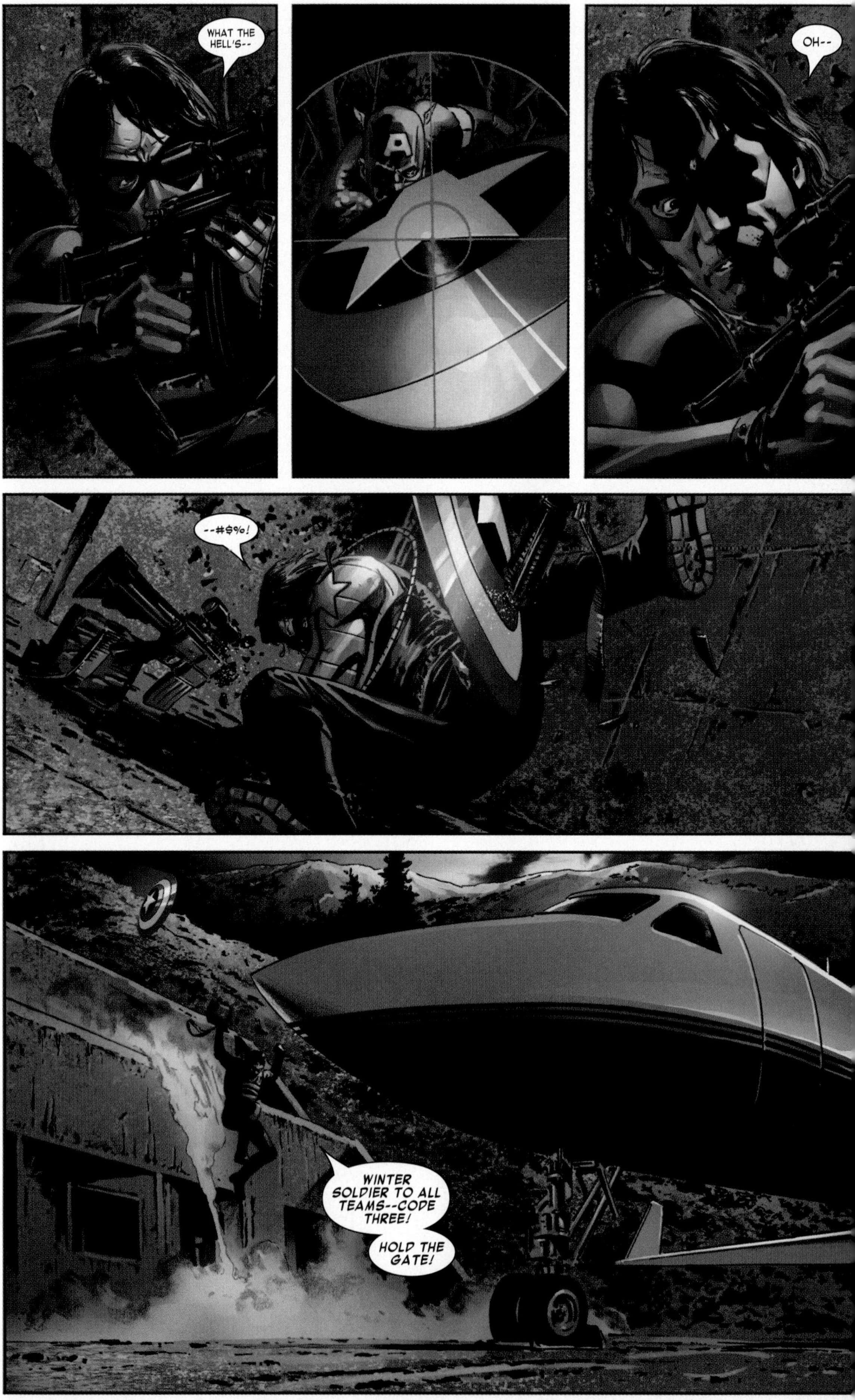
WHAT THE HELL'S--
OH--
--#$%!
WINTER SOLDIER TO ALL TEAMS--CODE THREE!
HOLD THE GATE!

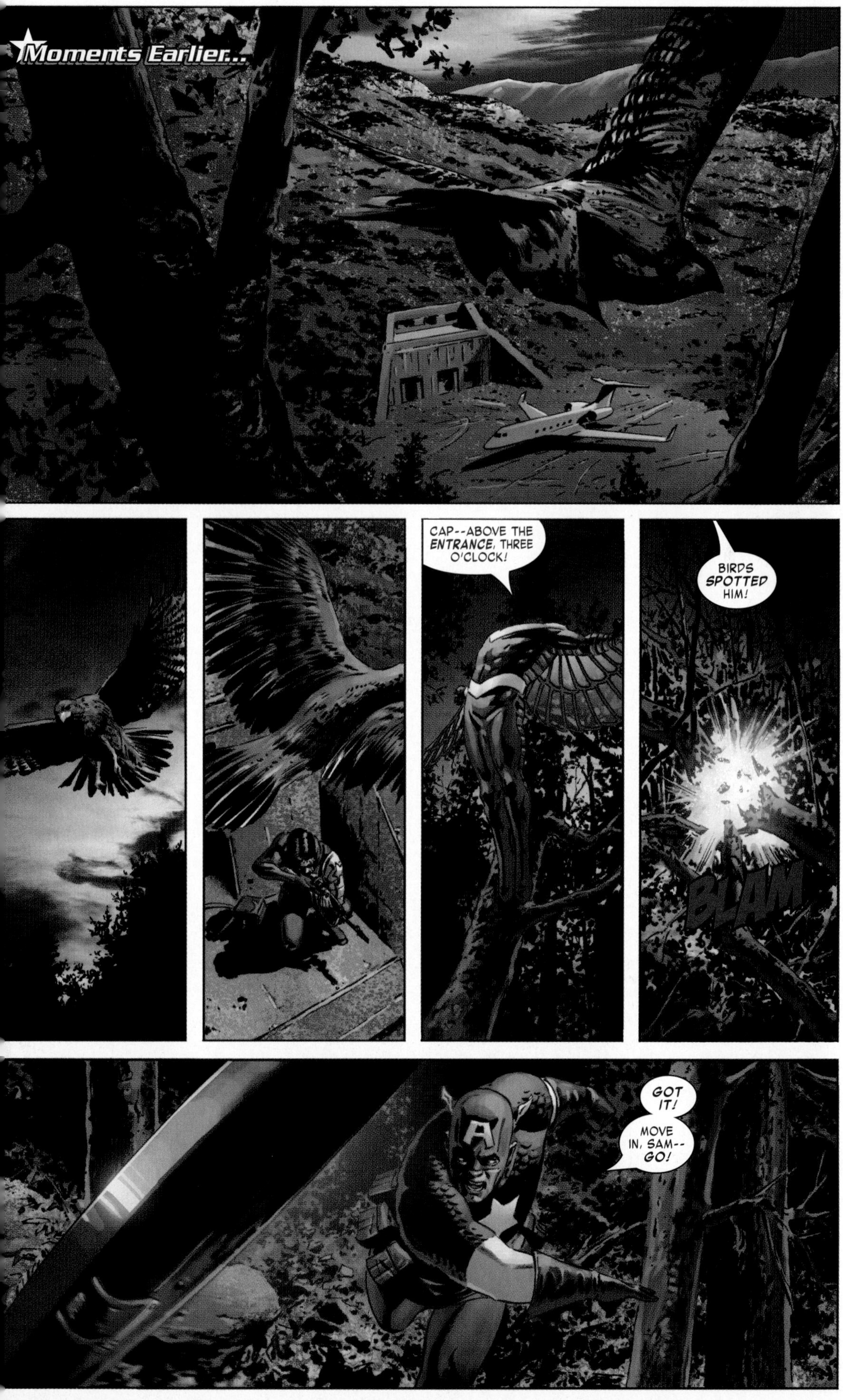
Moments Earlier...
CAP--ABOVE THE ENTRANCE, THREE O'CLOCK!
BIRDS SPOTTED HIM!
BLAM
GOT IT!
MOVE IN, SAM-- GO!

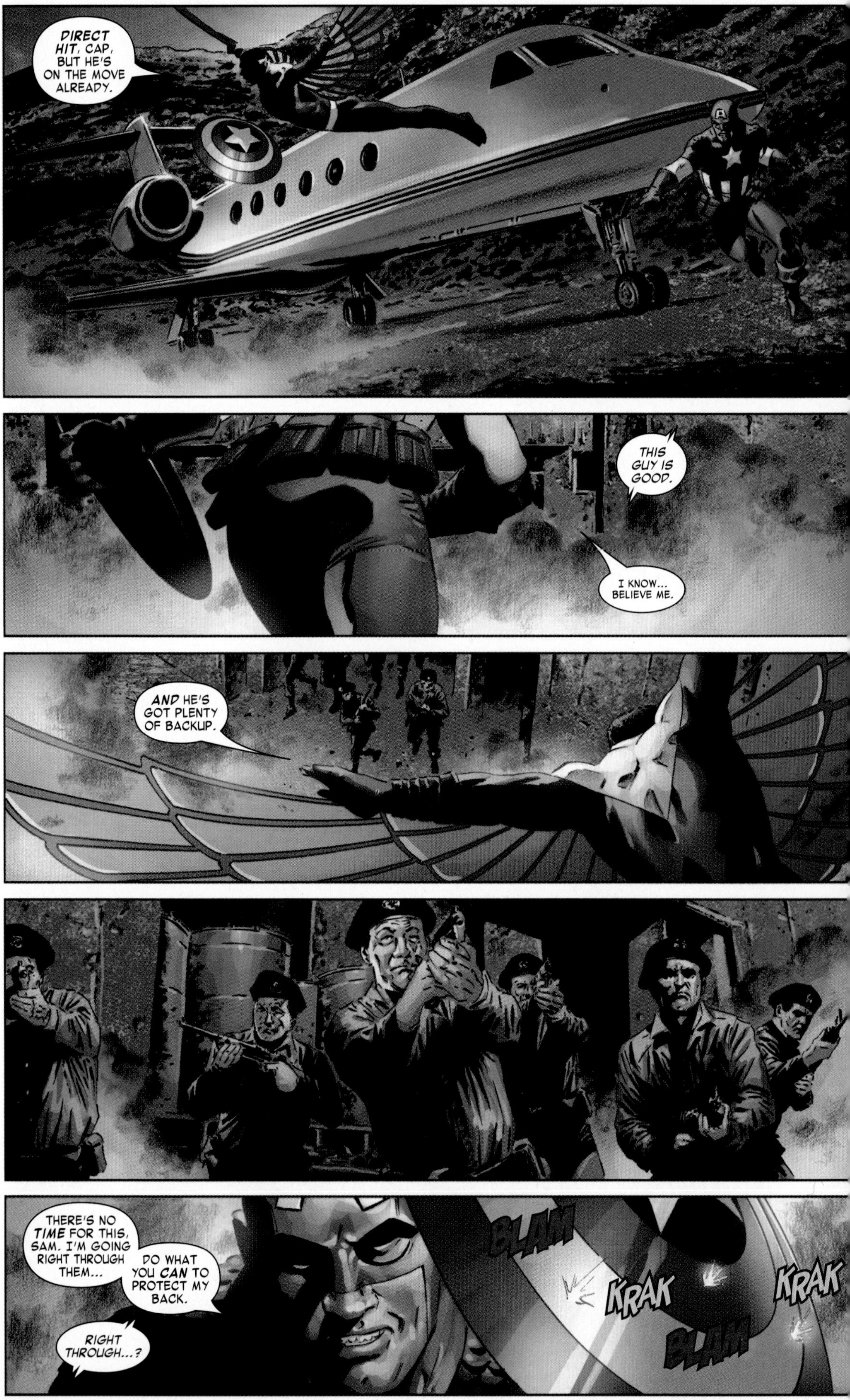
DIRECT HIT, CAP, BUT HE'S ON THE MOVE ALREADY.
THIS GUY IS GOOD.
I KNOW... BELIEVE ME.
AND HE'S GOT PLENTY OF BACKUP.
THERE'S NO TIME FOR THIS, SAM. I'M GOING RIGHT THROUGH THEM...
DO WHAT YOU CAN TO PROTECT MY BACK.
BLAM
KRAK
KRAK
BLAM
RIGHT THROUGH...?

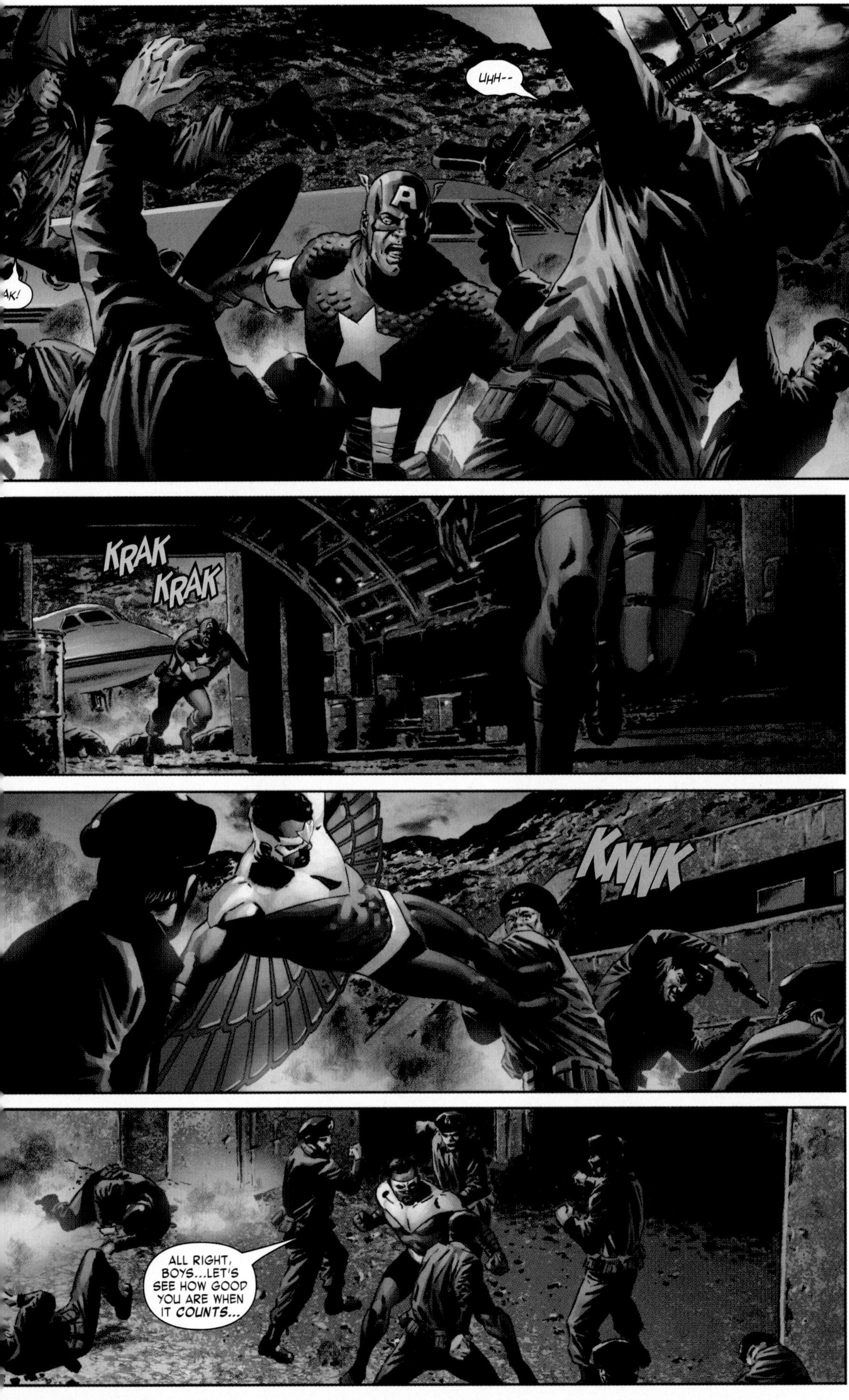
UHH--
AK!
KRAK
KRAK
KNNK
ALL RIGHT, BOYS...LET'S SEE HOW GOOD YOU ARE WHEN IT COUNTS...

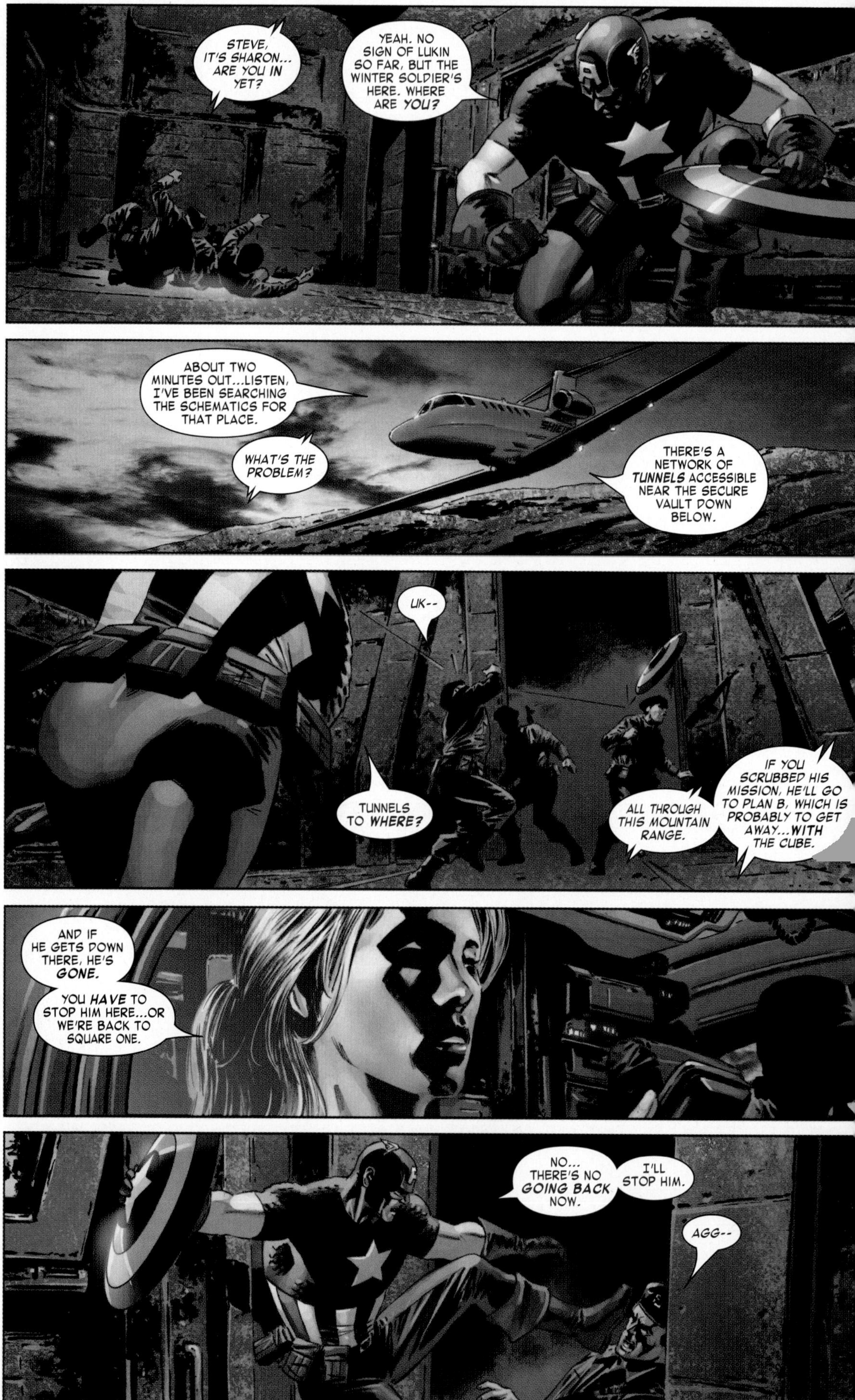
STEVE, IT'S SHARON... ARE YOU IN YET?
YEAH. NO SIGN OF LUKIN SO FAR, BUT THE WINTER SOLDIER'S HERE. WHERE ARE YOU?
ABOUT TWO MINUTES OUT...LISTEN, I'VE BEEN SEARCHING THE SCHEMATICS FOR THAT PLACE.
WHAT'S THE PROBLEM?
THERE'S A NETWORK OF TUNNELS ACCESSIBLE NEAR THE SECURE VAULT DOWN BELOW.
UK--
TUNNELS TO WHERE?
ALL THROUGH THIS MOUNTAIN RANGE.
IF YOU SCRUBBED HIS MISSION, HE'LL GO TO PLAN B, WHICH IS PROBABLY TO GET AWAY...WITH THE CUBE.
AND IF HE GETS DOWN THERE, HE'S GONE.
YOU HAVE TO STOP HIM HERE...OR WE'RE BACK TO SQUARE ONE.
NO... THERE'S NO GOING BACK NOW.
I'LL STOP HIM.
AGG--

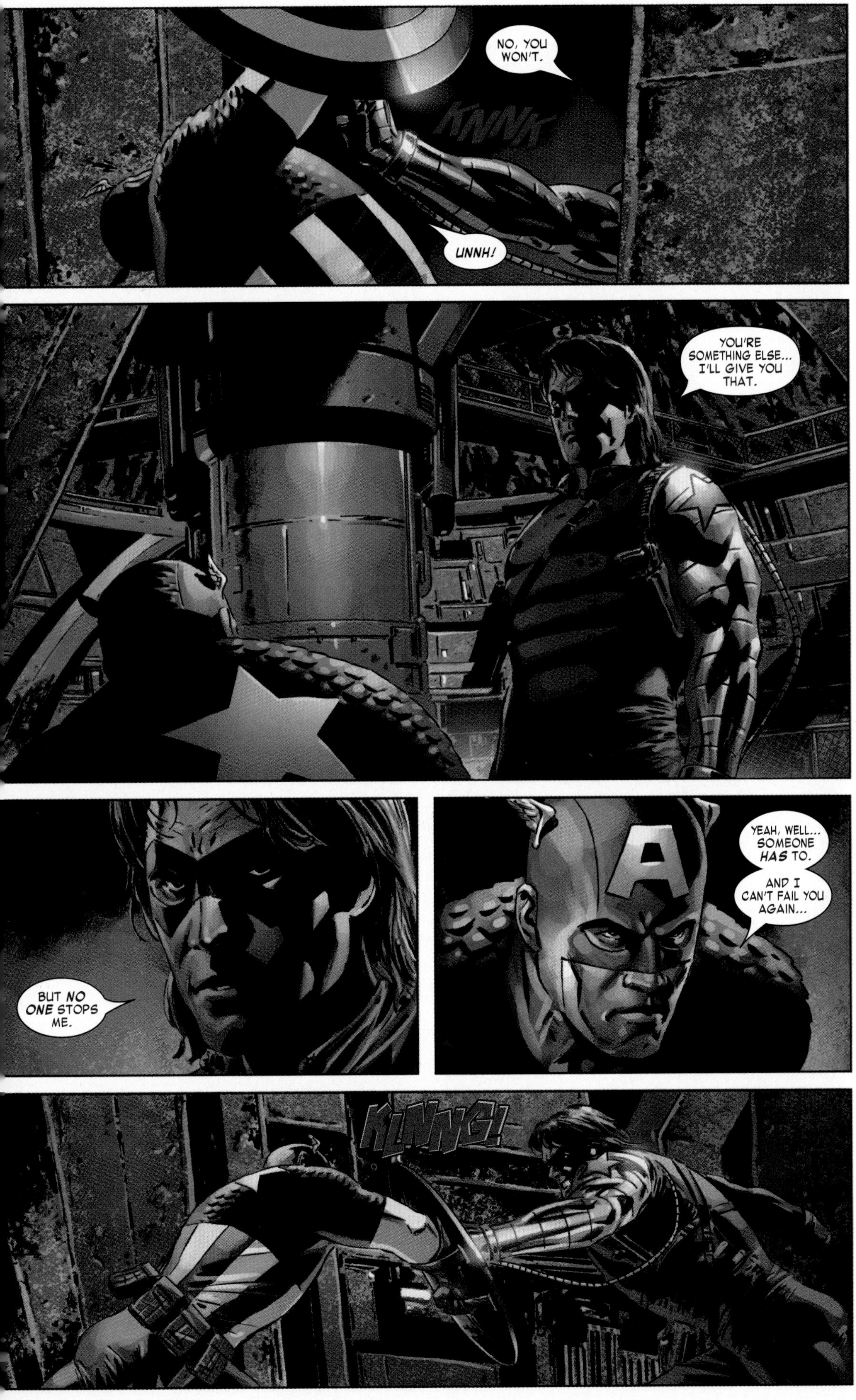
NO, YOU WON'T.
KNNK
UNNH!
YOU'RE SOMETHING ELSE... I'LL GIVE YOU THAT.
BUT NO ONE STOPS ME.
YEAH, WELL... SOMEONE HAS TO.
AND I CAN'T FAIL YOU AGAIN...
KLNNG!

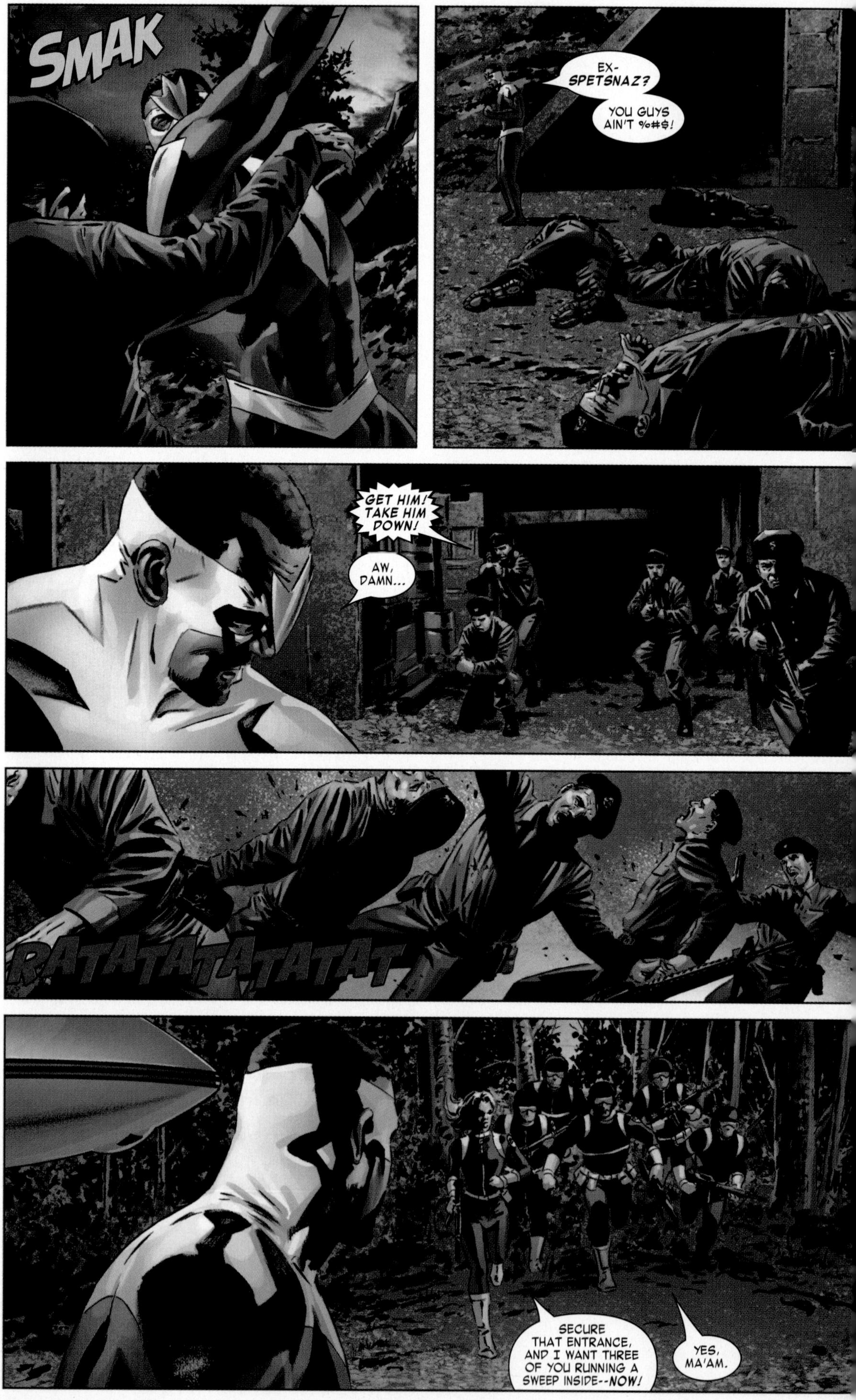
SMAK
EX-SPETSNAZ?
YOU GUYS AIN'T %#$!
GET HIM! TAKE HIM DOWN!
AW, DAMN...
RATATATATATATAT
SECURE THAT ENTRANCE, AND I WANT THREE OF YOU RUNNING A SWEEP INSIDE--NOW!
YES, MA'AM.

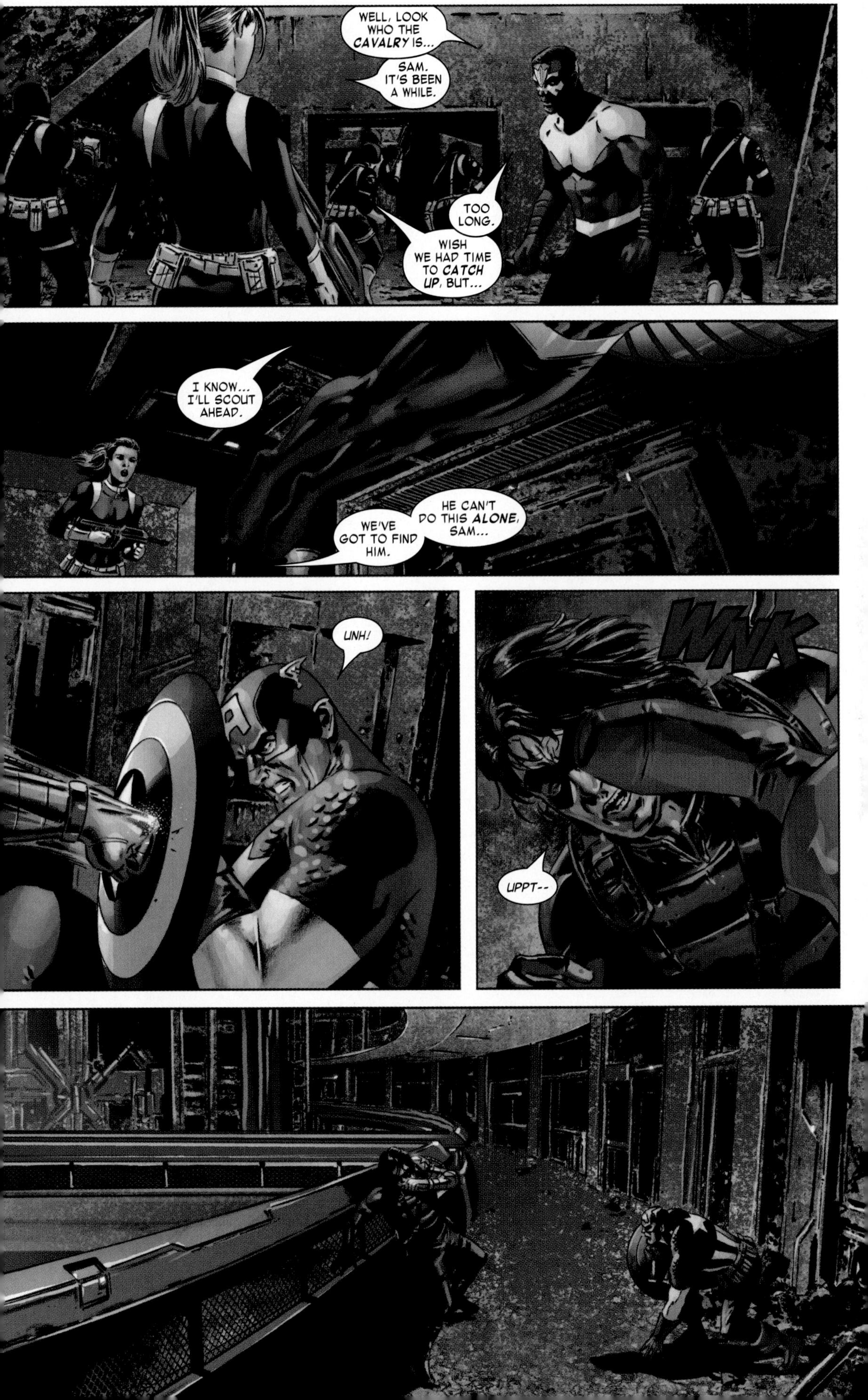
WELL, LOOK WHO THE CAVALRY IS...
SAM. IT'S BEEN A WHILE.
TOO LONG.
WISH WE HAD TIME TO CATCH UP, BUT...
I KNOW... I'LL SCOUT AHEAD.
HE CAN'T DO THIS ALONE, SAM...
WE'VE GOT TO FIND HIM.
UNH!
WNK
UPPT--

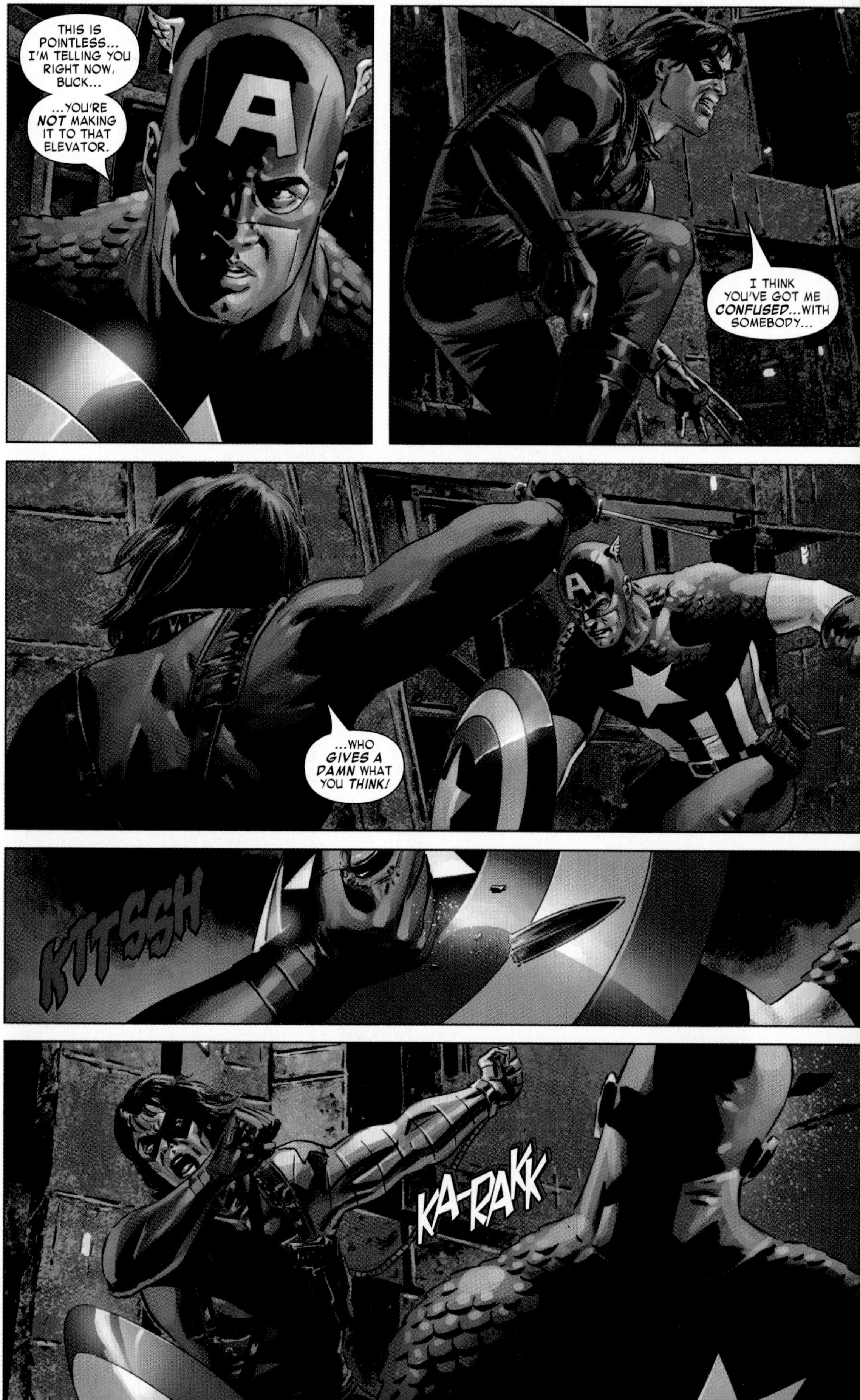
THIS IS POINTLESS... I'M TELLING YOU RIGHT NOW, BUCK...
...YOU'RE NOT MAKING IT TO THAT ELEVATOR.
I THINK YOU'VE GOT ME CONFUSED...WITH SOMEBODY...
...WHO GIVES A DAMN WHAT YOU THINK!
KTTSSH
KA-RAKK

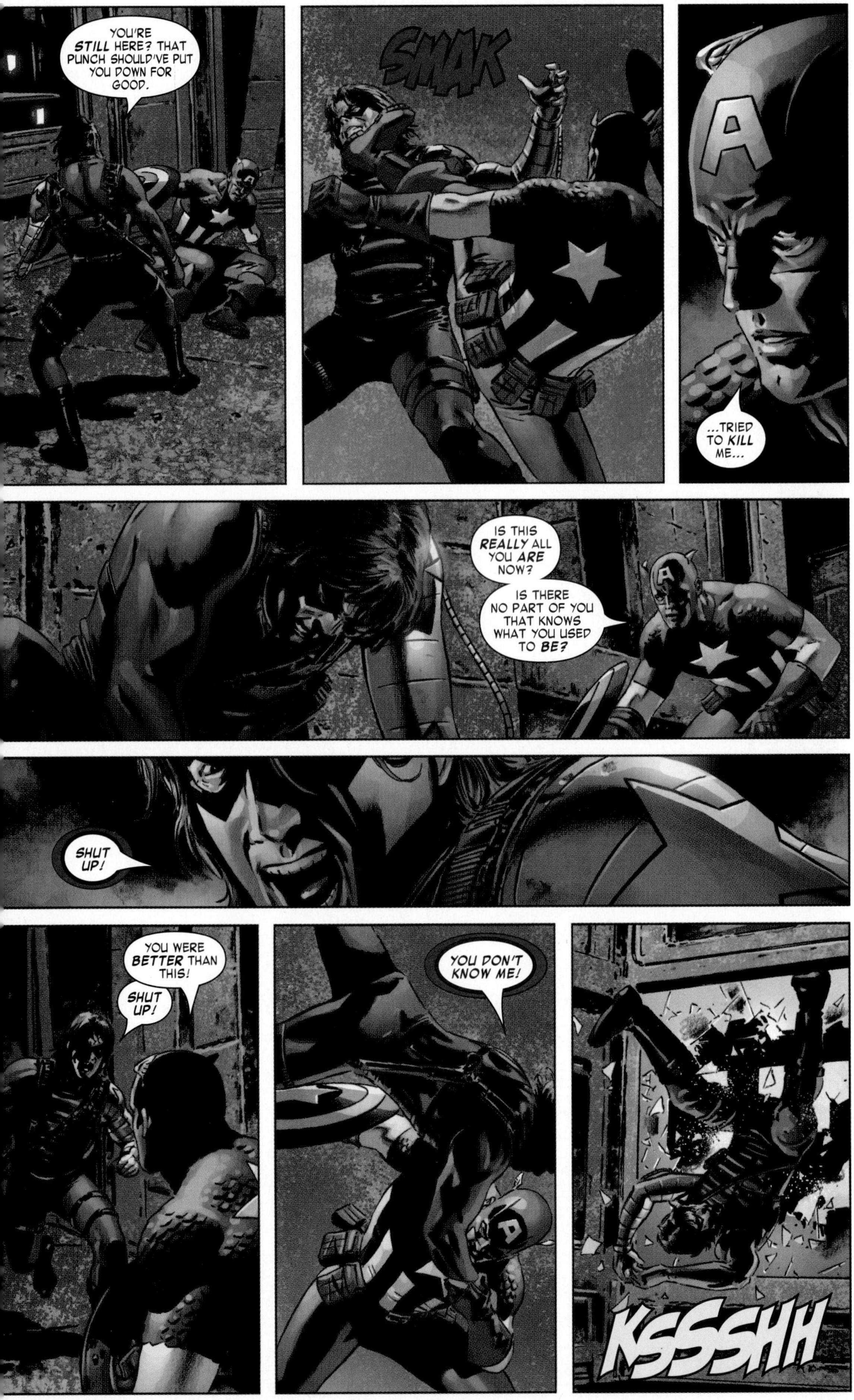
YOU'RE STILL HERE? THAT PUNCH SHOULD'VE PUT YOU DOWN FOR GOOD.
SMAK
...TRIED TO KILL ME...
IS THIS REALLY ALL YOU ARE NOW?
IS THERE NO PART OF YOU THAT KNOWS WHAT YOU USED TO BE?
SHUT UP!
YOU WERE BETTER THAN THIS!
SHUT UP!
YOU DON'T KNOW ME!
KSSSHH

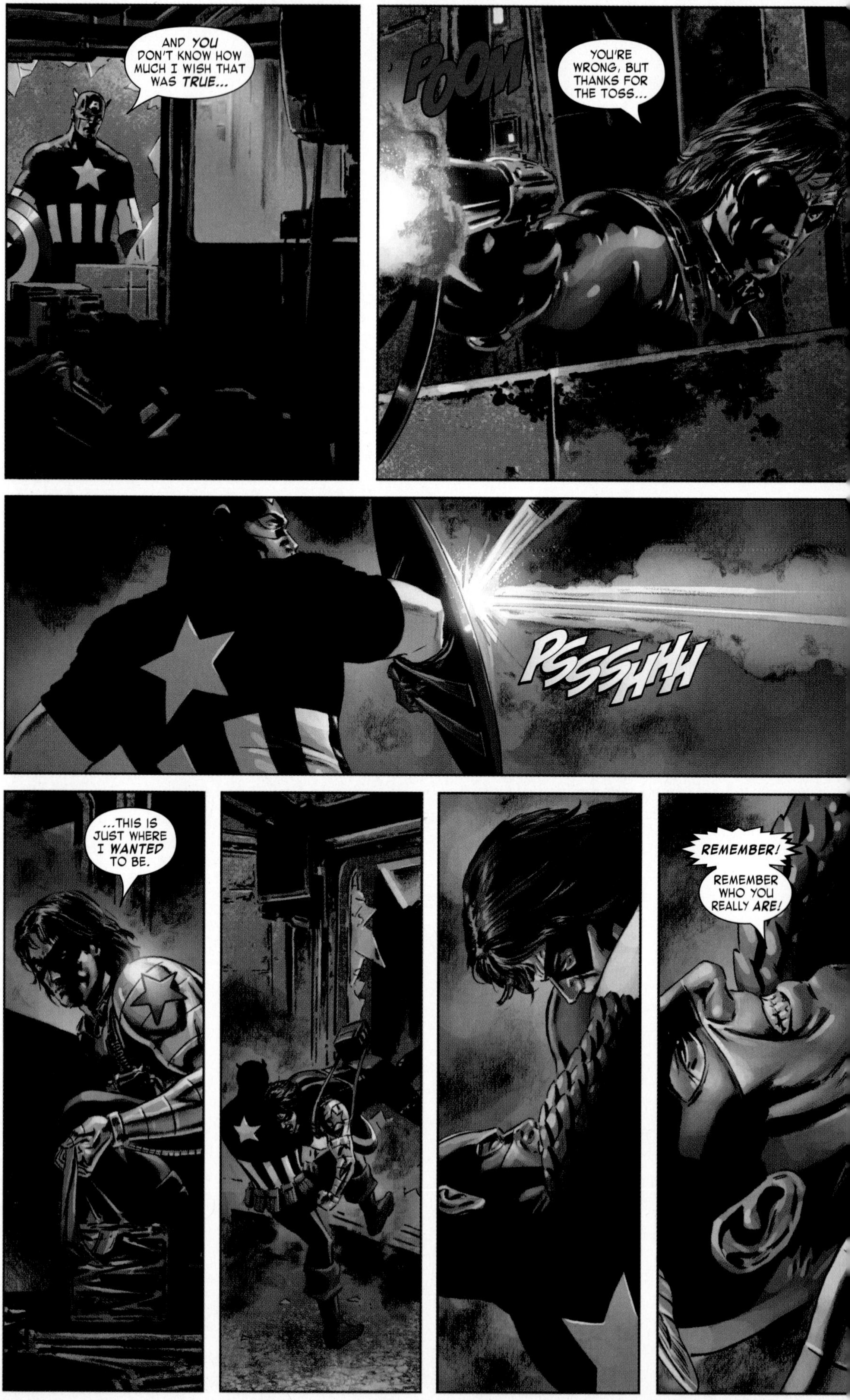
AND YOU DON'T KNOW HOW MUCH I WISH THAT WAS TRUE...
POOM
YOU'RE WRONG, BUT THANKS FOR THE TOSS...
PSSSHHH
...THIS IS JUST WHERE I WANTED TO BE.
REMEMBER!
REMEMBER WHO YOU REALLY ARE!

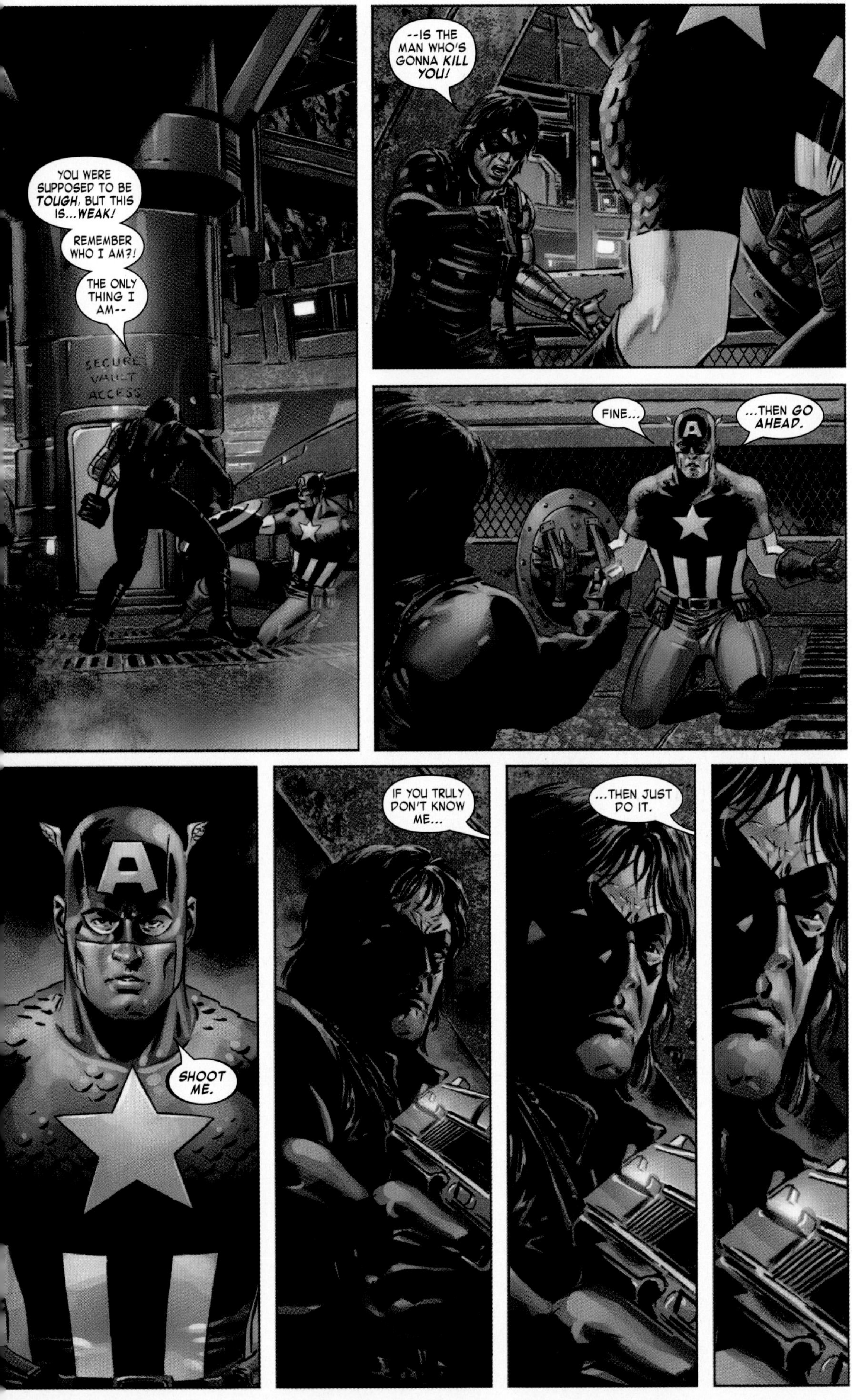
YOU WERE SUPPOSED TO BE TOUGH, BUT THIS IS...WEAK!
REMEMBER WHO I AM?!
THE ONLY THING I AM--
SECURE VAULT ACCESS
--IS THE MAN WHO'S GONNA KILL YOU!
FINE...
...THEN GO AHEAD.
SHOOT ME.
IF YOU TRULY DON'T KNOW ME...
...THEN JUST DO IT.

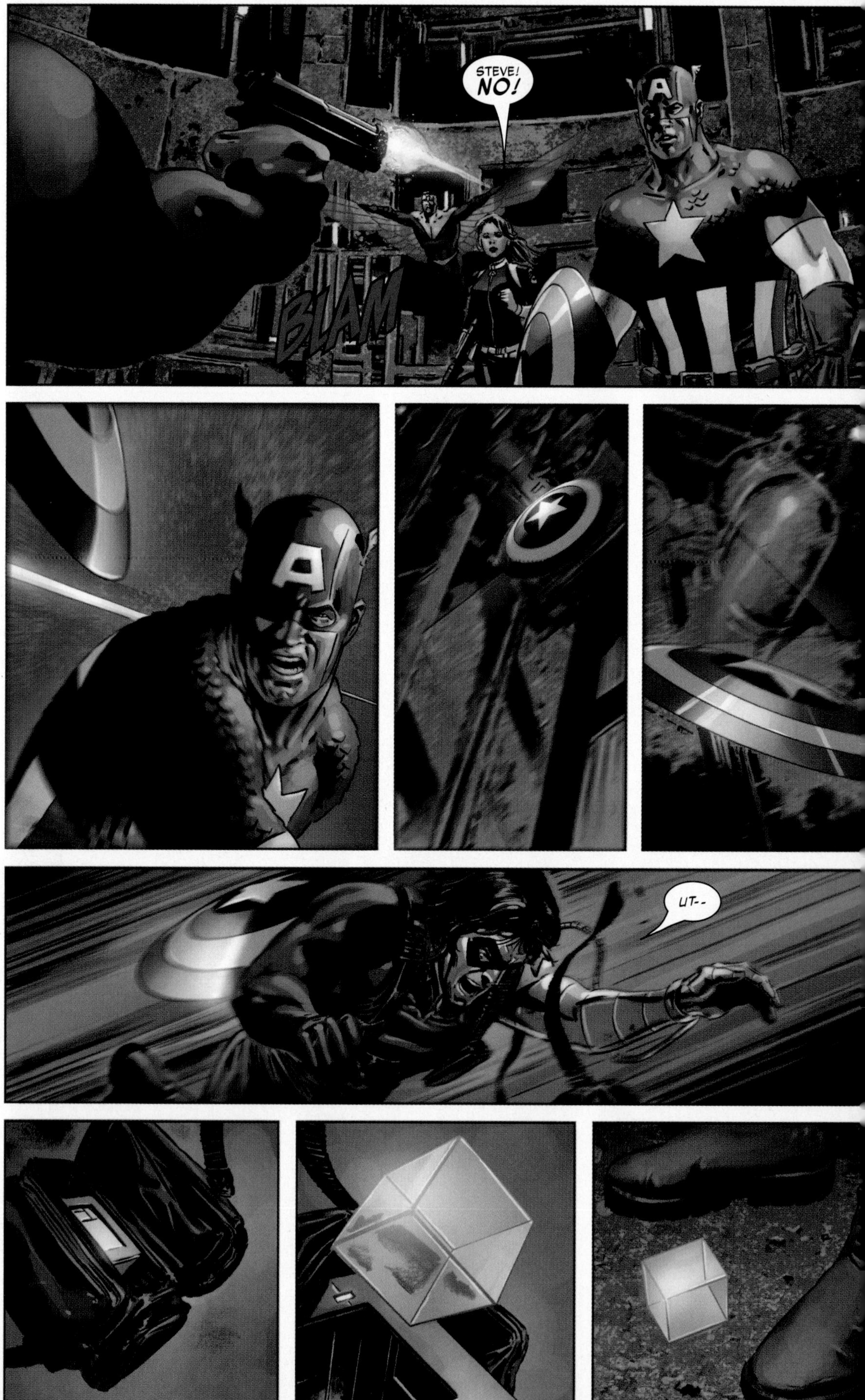
STEVE! NO!
BLAM
UT--

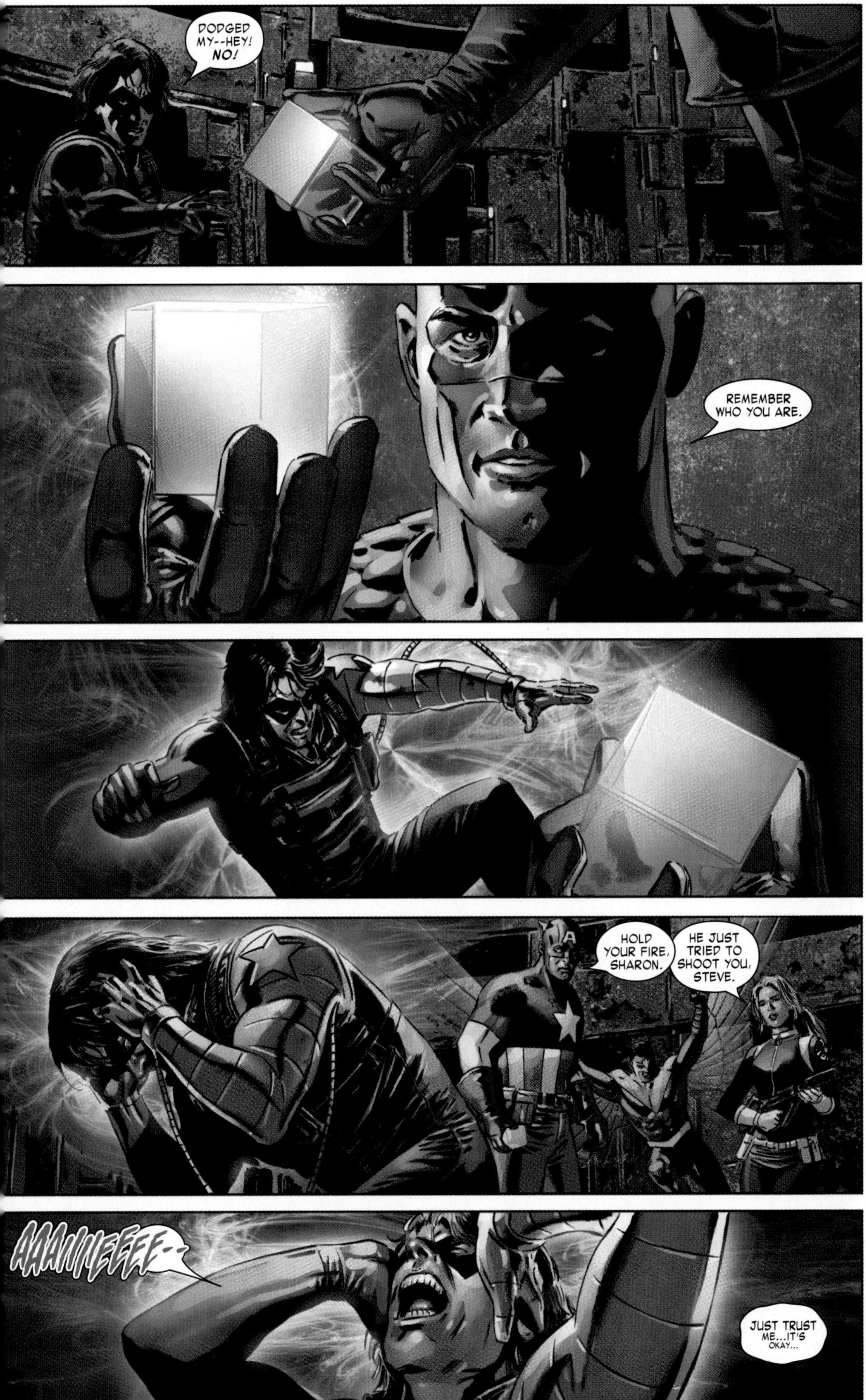
DODGED MY--HEY! NO!
REMEMBER WHO YOU ARE.
HOLD YOUR FIRE, SHARON.
HE JUST TRIED TO SHOOT YOU, STEVE.
AAAIIIIEEEE--
JUST TRUST ME...IT'S OKAY...

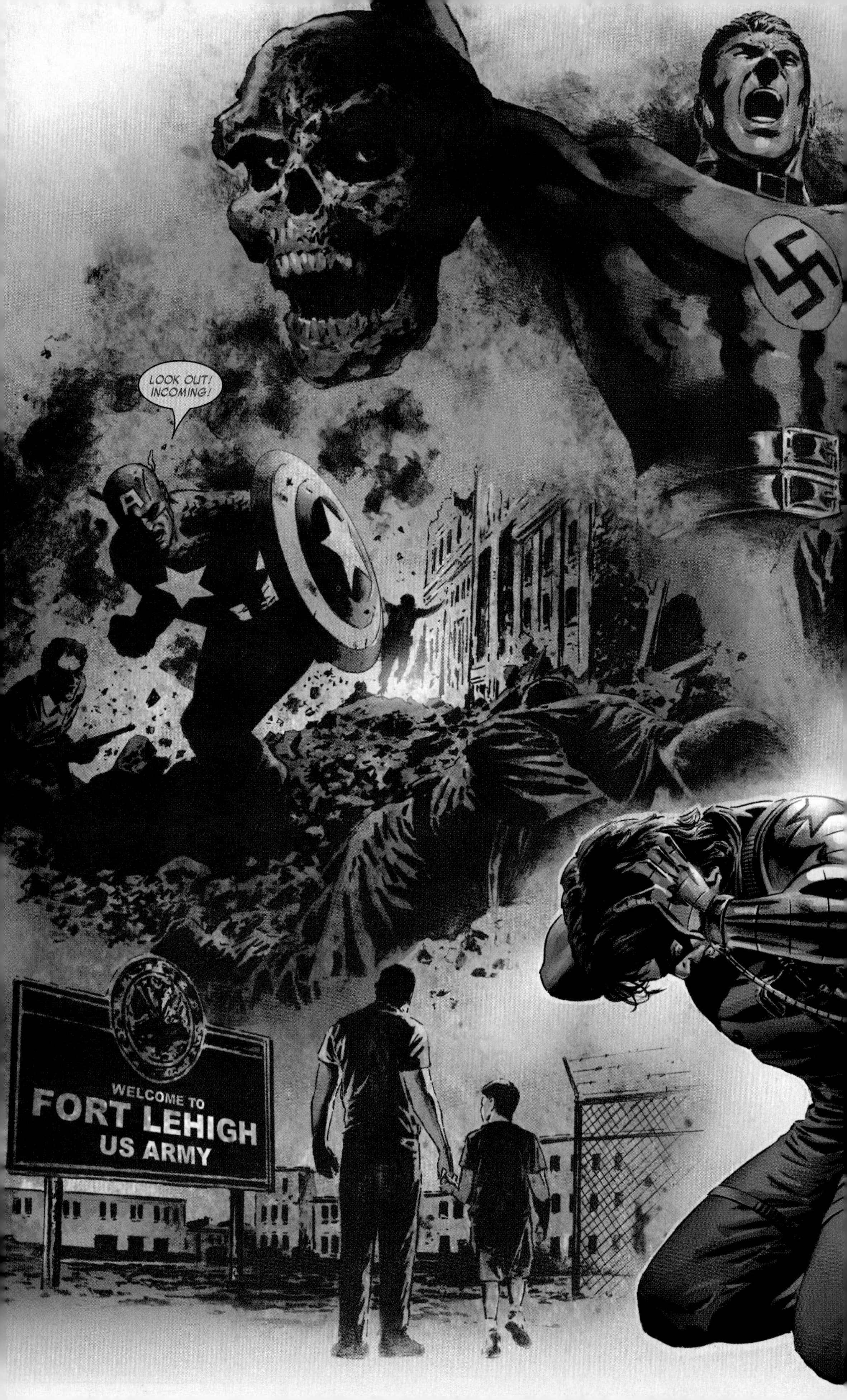
LOOK OUT! INCOMING!
WELCOME TO
FORT LEHIGH
US ARMY

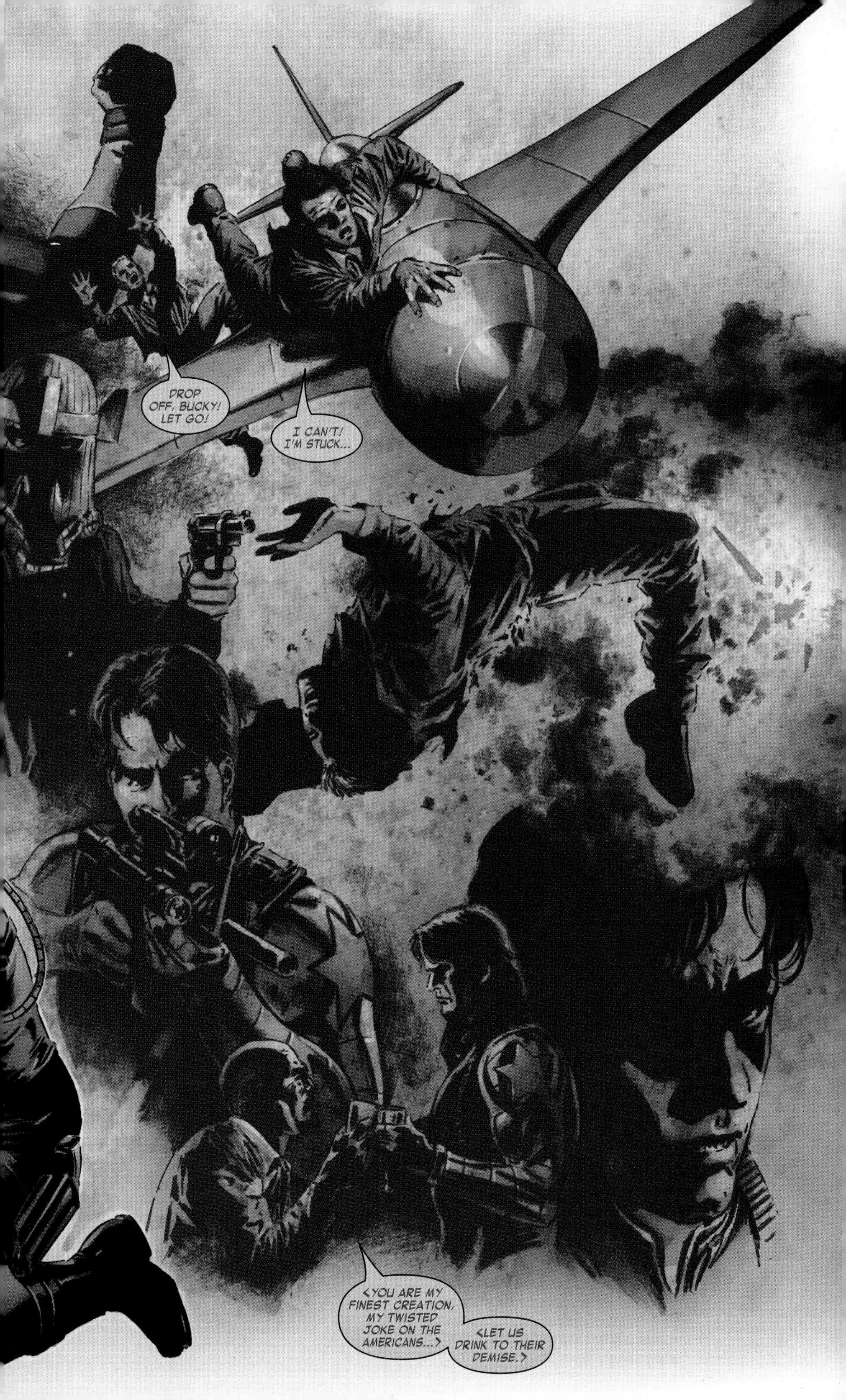
DROP OFF, BUCKY! LET GO!
I CAN'T! I'M STUCK...
<YOU ARE MY FINEST CREATION, MY TWISTED JOKE ON THE AMERICANS...>
<LET US DRINK TO THEIR DEMISE.>

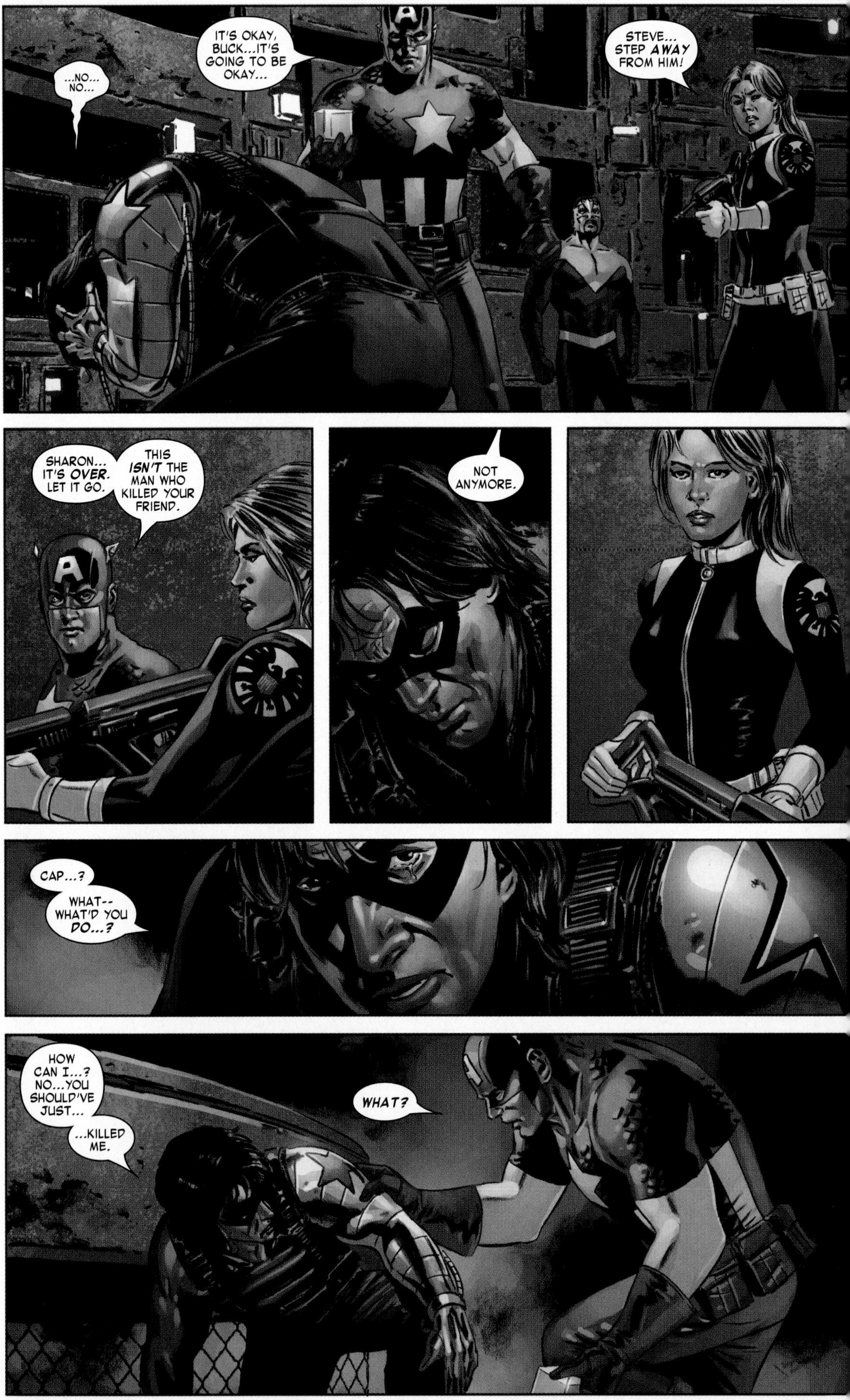
...NO... NO...
IT'S OKAY, BUCK...IT'S GOING TO BE OKAY...
STEVE... STEP AWAY FROM HIM!
SHARON... IT'S OVER. LET IT GO.
THIS ISN'T THE MAN WHO KILLED YOUR FRIEND.
NOT ANYMORE.
CAP...?
WHAT-- WHAT'D YOU DO...?
HOW CAN I...? NO...YOU SHOULD'VE JUST...
...KILLED ME.
WHAT?

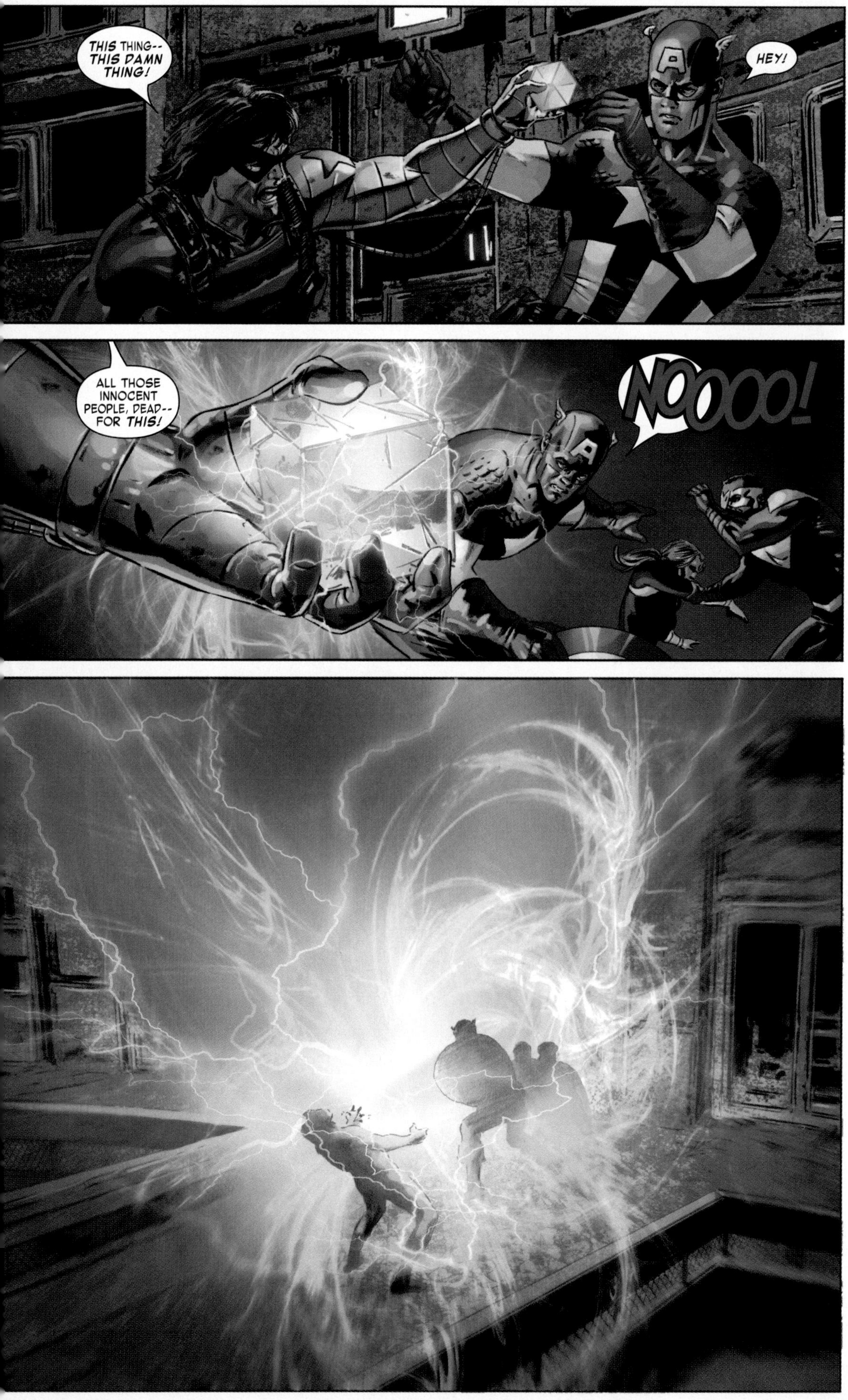
THIS THING-- THIS DAMN THING!
HEY!
ALL THOSE INNOCENT PEOPLE, DEAD-- FOR THIS!
NOOOO!

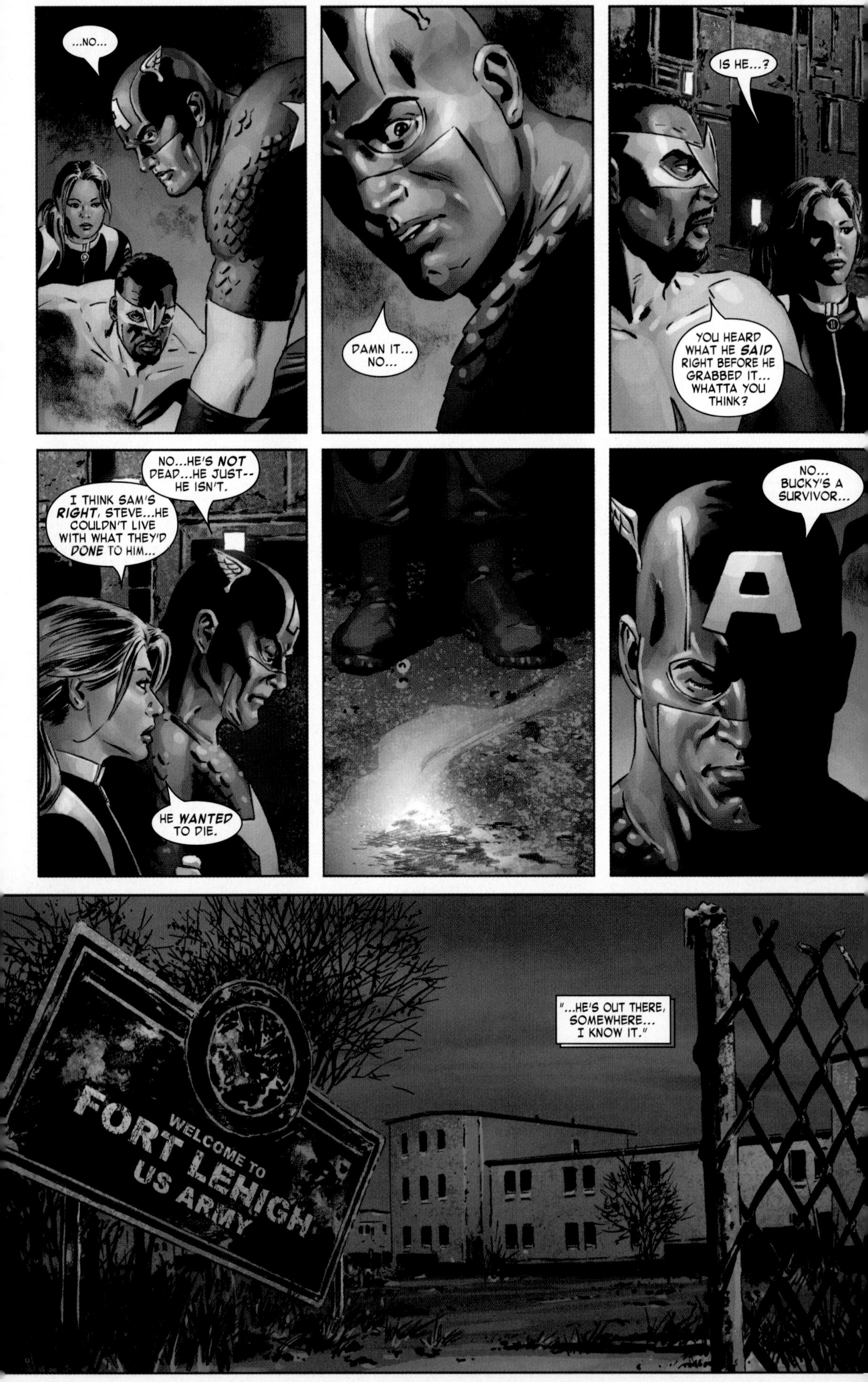
...NO...
DAMN IT... NO...
IS HE...?
YOU HEARD WHAT HE SAID RIGHT BEFORE HE GRABBED IT... WHATTA YOU THINK?
I THINK SAM'S RIGHT, STEVE...HE COULDN'T LIVE WITH WHAT THEY'D DONE TO HIM...
NO...HE'S NOT DEAD...HE JUST-- HE ISN'T.
HE WANTED TO DIE.
NO... BUCKY'S A SURVIVOR...
"...HE'S OUT THERE, SOMEWHERE... I KNOW IT."
WELCOME TO
FORT LEHIGH
US ARMY

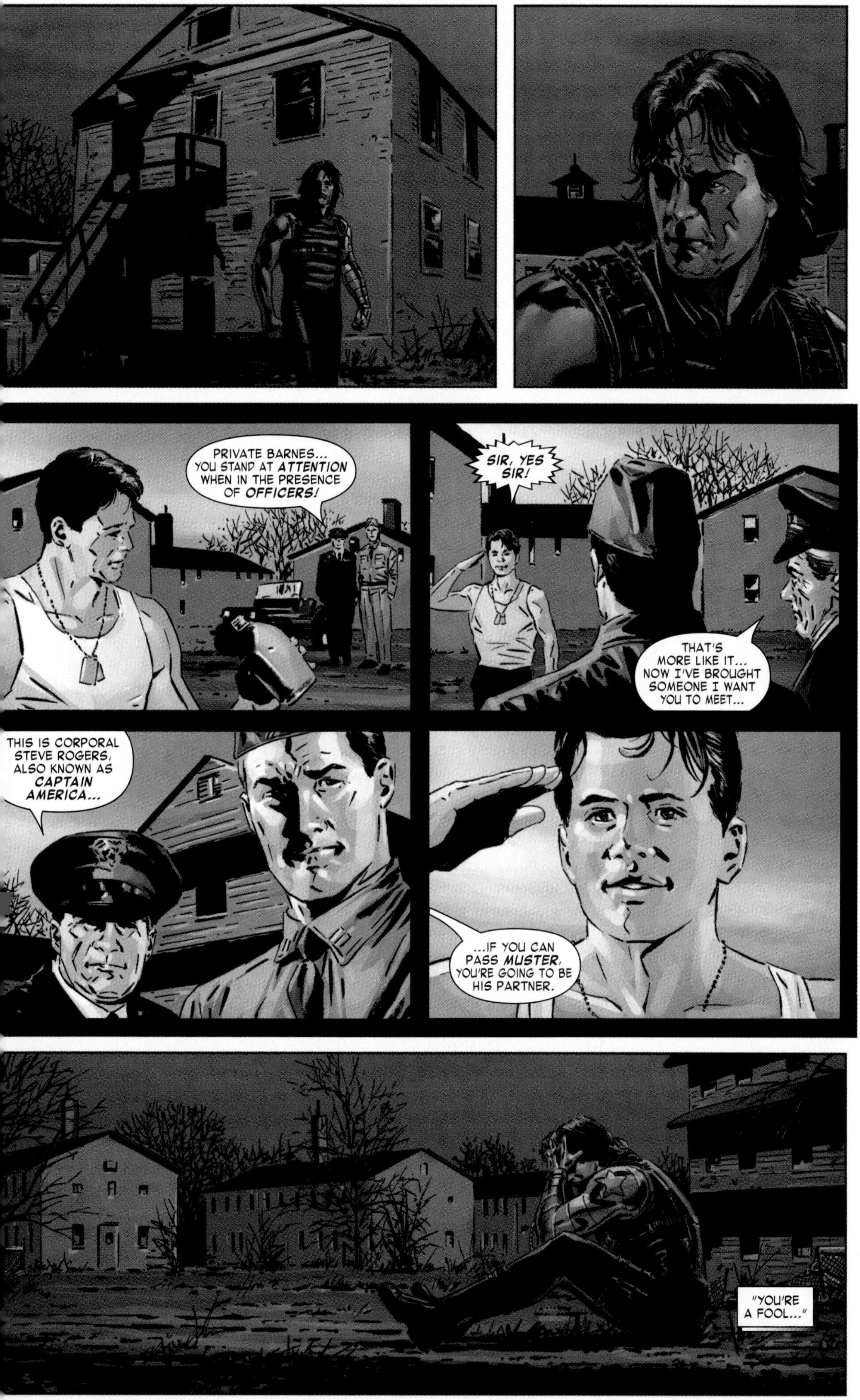
PRIVATE BARNES... YOU STAND AT ATTENTION WHEN IN THE PRESENCE OF OFFICERS!
SIR, YES SIR!
THAT'S MORE LIKE IT... NOW I'VE BROUGHT SOMEONE I WANT YOU TO MEET...
THIS IS CORPORAL STEVE ROGERS, ALSO KNOWN AS CAPTAIN AMERICA...
...IF YOU CAN PASS MUSTER, YOU'RE GOING TO BE HIS PARTNER.
"YOU'RE A FOOL..."

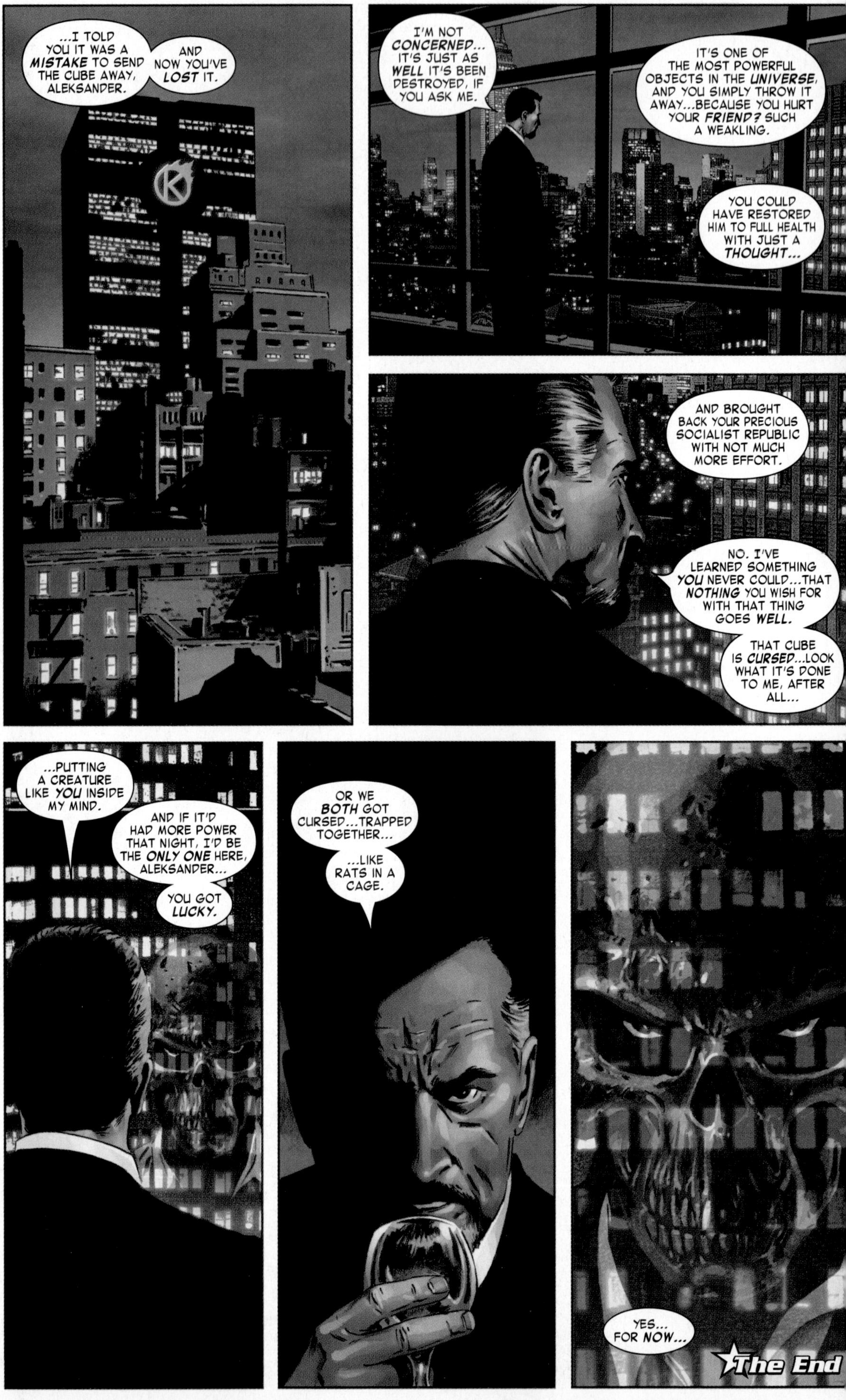
...I TOLD YOU IT WAS A MISTAKE TO SEND THE CUBE AWAY, ALEKSANDER.
AND NOW YOU'VE LOST IT.
I'M NOT CONCERNED... IT'S JUST AS WELL IT'S BEEN DESTROYED, IF YOU ASK ME.
IT'S ONE OF THE MOST POWERFUL OBJECTS IN THE UNIVERSE, AND YOU SIMPLY THROW IT AWAY...BECAUSE YOU HURT YOUR FRIEND? SUCH A WEAKLING.
YOU COULD HAVE RESTORED HIM TO FULL HEALTH WITH JUST A THOUGHT...
AND BROUGHT BACK YOUR PRECIOUS SOCIALIST REPUBLIC WITH NOT MUCH MORE EFFORT.
NO. I'VE LEARNED SOMETHING YOU NEVER COULD...THAT NOTHING YOU WISH FOR WITH THAT THING GOES WELL.
THAT CUBE IS CURSED...LOOK WHAT IT'S DONE TO ME, AFTER ALL...
...PUTTING A CREATURE LIKE YOU INSIDE MY MIND.
AND IF IT'D HAD MORE POWER THAT NIGHT, I'D BE THE ONLY ONE HERE, ALEKSANDER...
YOU GOT LUCKY.
OR WE BOTH GOT CURSED...TRAPPED TOGETHER...
...LIKE RATS IN A CAGE.
YES... FOR NOW...
The End